BASICS OF INTERNATIONAL BANKING

BASICS OF INTERNATIONAL BANKING

Emmanuel N. Roussakis
Florida International University

Printed in the United States of America.

ISBN 13: 978-1-50669-761-1

Fourth Printing January 2020.

Library of Congress Control Number: 2017900118

4750 Venture Drive,
Suite 400
Ann Arbor, MI 48108
800-562-2147
www.xanedu.com

Contents

PREFACE

The unprecedented expansion in international trade and investment that the world economy has experienced since the 1990s has contributed to a phenomenal growth in the internationalization of banking activity. New types of services have been introduced; strategies and processes have evolved; the volume of international services has expanded; and the number of banks offering these services has increased. Technology and globalization have been a major force in the transformation of international banking. These important developments have occurred so rapidly that the existing literature has yet to match the significance of this change. This book has been undertaken in an effort to narrow the gap in the literature.

Basics of International Banking is designed for both students and professionals, as well as for anyone interested in the fundamentals of international banking from a management perspective. It has been written with the objective of providing a description and an analysis of some of the more important challenges confronting international bankers today. Although, in principle, the issues bank managers face can be easily identified and rationally considered, in practice solutions are anything but watertight. In the real world in which the banker operates, applications of the principles discussed in this book becomes an exercise in informed judgment. The principles presented therefore must be viewed as guidelines that will assist the banker in the systematic evaluation of the relevant facts. This book does not provide the final answers, which vary among banks, and even for the same bank, over a period of time.

The book's organizational structure is made up of two parts. Part I provides an overview of the international financial environment in which banks operate and some of the traditional services they extend to their clients. Part II focuses on the principles and procedures in international lending. Some of the chapters in this part represent modified versions of material contributed by authors in my earlier publication, *International Banking: Principles and Practices.* These include Laurel A. Nichols (Chapter 8: Legal Considerations for International Lending), Andrew M. MacLaren (Chapter 11: Syndication), and Robert S. Damerjian (Chapter 12: Loans and Placements to Foreign Banks). Roger A. Coe, and Bob Kurau, were my co-authors on Chapter 9: Credit Analysis of Foreign Loans, and Chapter 10: Import Financing, respectively.

Special debt is due to Richard Schwartz, Emeritus Professor of English at Florida International University, Miami, for his valuable editorial assistance. Thanks are also due to my grandson Emanuel Papageorgiou for redesigning many of the Exhibits in Chapters 1 and 2.

Finally, my deep appreciation to my wife, Sophie, for her unfailing love, and understanding, and our daughter Marina and son Nicholas, and their families, for their support and encouragement.

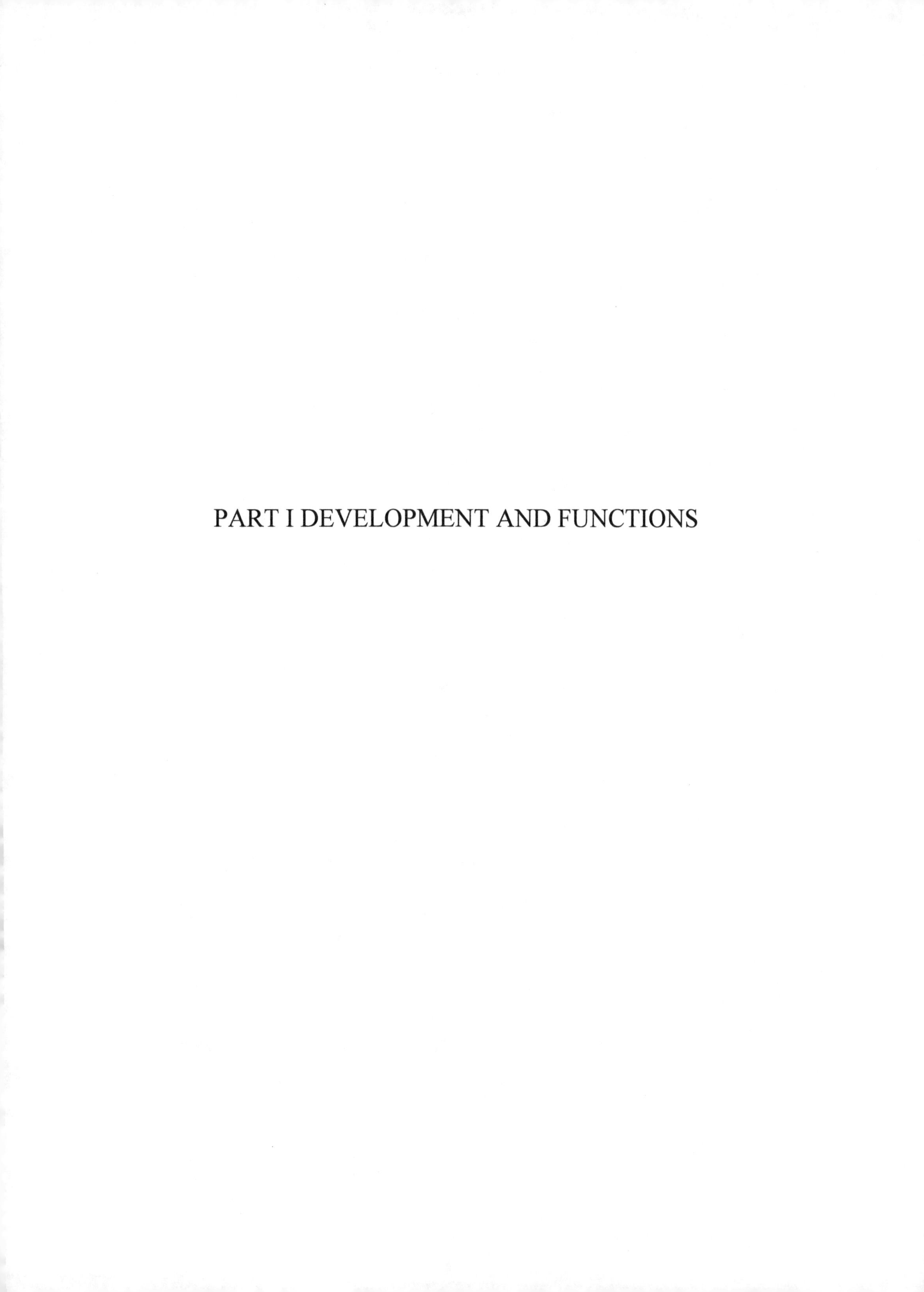

PART I DEVELOPMENT AND FUNCTIONS

1 INTERNATIONAL BANKING: ORIGINS AND EVOLUTION

Perhaps the most remarkable development that the banking industry has experienced since the end of World War II has been the internationalization of its services. The banks that took the lead and embarked on multinational banking were major commercial 'banking institutions, located principally in Western Europe and the western hemisphere. Unhampered by geographical restrictions, these banks embarked upon the creation of worldwide networks of outlets and became actively engaged in foreign markets. The international expansion of these banks has brought about the effective linkage of national financial markets and the increasing integration of worldwide banking systems. Despite apparent differences in the patterns of their international expansion, these banks have become a truly multinational set of competing financial institutions.

Banking is becoming an increasingly international business. Although the nationality of the leading international banks has changed from time to time, the overall trend of international banking has been the same--rapid expansion in the type and volume of services offered and in the number of banks providing these services. This chapter reviews the development of international banking, the vehicles used, and the services offered in building a multinational banking network.

DEVELOPMENT OF INTERNATIONAL BANKING

For several centuries the financing of interregional or international trade was controlled by European institutions. From the twelfth to the fifteenth century, Italian, banks were supreme in the area of international finance. This development was outcome of the maritime ties of coastal Italian cities with the Byzantine Empire and the growing Islamic countries. Of equal importance was the regional emergence of agricultural and manufacturing centers that grew to become hubs of commercial and financial network covering every major European city. The combined effect of these developments contributed to the emergence of the Italian coastal cities into important conduits for trade with the European interior. The Italian family-owned and managed merchant banking houses are generally viewed as the direct ancestors of modern commercial banks. They accepted deposits, made a market in foreign exchange; financed foreign trade; met the credit needs of their clients; and invested in industrial and commercial ventures.

The discovery by the Portuguese of the trading routes to the Indies shifted trading patterns from the Mediterranean to the Atlantic seaboard. This change contributed to the growth of Antwerp and the rise of German merchant banks to dominate banking and finance throughout the sixteenth century. As the Dutch gained control over the maritime trade with southern Asia, the winds of economic prosperity moved further north in Europe and Amsterdam emerged as a major financial center and the Dutch merchant bankers dominant of international banking and finance.

Rise of British Banking Houses

The end of the Napoleonic Wars ushered in a period of political stability and created an environment conducive to the growth of international trade and investment. Large-scale industry and capitalistic enterprise, which had begun to flourish in Great Britain in the early eighteenth century, grew very rapidly and contributed to the expansion of commerce with European, North American, and Asian markets. A number of merchant-banking houses rose to prominence by specializing in the financing of particular branches of trade. Export-led growth provided the momentum for the development of the British economy and the rise of London to be the leading financial center of the world.

Since Great Britain enjoyed significant savings and balance of payment surpluses, a large number of foreign borrowers--both private and government--floated debt and equity securities in London to finance a wide variety of industrial and infrastructural projects (e.g., railways, canals, factories, mines). British banks rose to a position of leadership in international finance that they maintained until World War I.

Internationalization of U.S. Banks

The United States entered World War I as a debtor nation and emerged as a creditor. The growing needs of the Allies and neutral nations generated the necessary momentum for the growth of exports. At the same time this war stimulated the influx of flight capital from Europe and thus contributed to the rise of New York as an international financial center.

In the postwar period, the United States experienced greater demand for its manufactured products, increased its investments abroad, and generally was transformed into an industrial and financial power. In fact, by 1929 it was the world's outstanding manufacturing power and its largest creditor. Foreign government bond issues in the United States outstripped those in London, and New York replaced Loudon as the most important financial center.

The banking collapses during the Great Depression, along with the huge foreign loan defaults, triggered a wave of protectionism and economic nationalism that affected the world economy until World War II. The period immediately following this war laid the foundations for the development of modern international banking. The establishment of new international organizations--such as the World Bank (formally known as the International Bank for Reconstruction and Development or IBRD), the International Monetary Fund (IMF), and the General Agreement on Tariffs and Trade (GATT)--and a more favorable international economic and political environment were conducive to the emergence of international banking.

The United States resumed its prewar role of principal capital exporter in the world. It extended assistance to Europe to help the reconstruction efforts and provided foreign aid to developing countries to promote the development of agriculture and industry. More important, it opened its markets to foreign goods and simultaneously exported a great deal of long-term capital. Some of this capital was raised by foreign borrowers who were attracted to U.S. financial markets because they were a cheaper and more convenient source of funds. A more sizable portion, however, was raised by U.S.-based corporations seeking to expand their operations internationally. As these corporations began to establish networks and develop global operations during the 1950s and 1960s, they created a natural incentive for expanding the foreign activities of U.S. commercial banks. Thus, large money-center banks, following their corporate and commercial customers abroad, expanded their international operations and presence overseas. A key consideration in this move was the introduction in the mid-1960s of capital-control measures aimed at curbing foreign borrowing and at diverting multinationals to foreign markets to finance their growing investments abroad.[1]

The international expansion of U.S. banks is exemplified in the following data. In 1960, 9 U.S. banks had a physical presence overseas, consisting of 139 branches and subsidiaries. By 1970, 80 U.S. banks operated abroad through 540 branches and subsidiaries. And by 1982, almost every large and medium-sized bank in this country engaged in international banking; 162 banks had 900 branches and 758 subsidiaries operating abroad. Their combined assets amounted to close to $471 billion; about half of this amount was held in major European centers, with London accounting for the largest share. U.S. banks were in active competition not only among themselves but also with the major international commercial banks, and merchant/investment banks, in loan syndications and Eurobond underwriting.

The quadrupling of oil prices in the 1970s created a great need for the global financial intermediation of the surplus oil revenues of the Organization of Petroleum Exporting Countries (OPEC). U.S. banks were in the forefront of this intermediation, recycling petrodollars from oil-exporting to oil-importing nations. Their international eminence contributed to attracting a large share of petrodollars in the form of deposits that were then loaned to various borrowers, including less developed countries (LDCs). Bank lending to these countries grew rapidly until the early 1980s. Pursuit of a tight U.S. monetary policy to curb inflationary pressures led the country into a deep recession that reduced the demand for imports and adversely affected world commodity prices. Similar conditions in other industrialized countries accentuated these trends and contributed to the collapse of the export markets of debtor nations, with drastic consequences for their ability to service their debts to major banks around the world. In the summer of 1982, when Mexico announced its inability to meet scheduled debt

[1]These measures were the Interest Equalization Tax (IET) of 1963, the Foreign Direct Investment Program (FDIP) of 1964, and the Voluntary Foreign Credit Restraint (VFCR) Program of 1965.

payments, it set off the *international debt crisis*. This announcement produced a chain reaction, and within a year 30 countries including Poland and many Latin American countries-followed suit. With the onset of the debt crisis, new lending to LDCs dried up and many U.S. banks took large losses. Exhibit 1.1 depicts the sequence of developments that followed the 1970s oil price shock.

International Expansion of Japanese Banks

As American banks were retreating from international lending, Japanese banks were filling the gap they left. Following the lead of their corporate clients (manufacturing companies and trading firms), Japanese banks began to expand their international operations and presence overseas in the late 1970s. Flush with the proceeds of Japan's trading surpluses, they set out to penetrate foreign markets and build market share at the expense of profits. In 1980, Japanese banks had a foreign network of 139 branches and subsidiaries with assets of $189 billion; by 1989, this network had grown to 300 and $1.4 trillion, respectively. Lending at low profit margins enabled Japanese banks to capture a sizable market share worldwide; it reached 40 percent of total international lending by 1989.

The early 1990s saw the international retrenchment of Japanese banks because of adversity at home. Financial market deregulation, combined with higher interest rates, raised the cost of funds and put pressure on banks to increase earnings. This pressure prompted Japanese banks to abandon their low-cost lending practices abroad in favor of loans that generated higher returns, boosted profits, and added to bank capital.

The new focus on profit was consistent with the need for Japanese banks to improve their capital adequacy ratios, in accordance with the Basel agreement, by1993. The Basel capital requirements, though fair and consistent in their application to different countries, were significantly higher than the ones Japanese banks had had to comply with at home. Under the circumstances, during 1988 and 1989 Japanese banks had undertaken significant capital-raising activities through issuance of new equity and convertible bonds and realization of gains from the sale of their shareholdings in other Japanese companies. But some of the improvement in the

Exhibit 1.1 The 1970s Oil Price Shock and the Ensuing Crisis

1973 – 1974	1974	1979 – 1980	1980 – 1982	1983
First oil shock (price of oil increases).	U.S banks recycle petrodollars; loans to oil-importing countries.	Second oil shock	- As LDCs reach their borrowing capacity, they make use of short term lines of credit (available for int'l trade financing) to fund their balance of payments deficits. Pursuit by industrialized countries of a tight monetary policy to curb inflationary pressures results in higher interest rates (which increase cost of LDC debt servicing). Ensuing recession reduces demand for imports and affects world commodity prices. Collapse of export markets undermines ability of debtor nations to service their debts. - August 1982, Mexico declares inability to pay its debt. Within a year, 30 countries follow suit.	- Forced lending by IMF to finance balance of payments deficits. - Rescheduling of short term loans.

The 1970s Oil Price Shock and the Ensuing Crisis (cont.)

1984 - 1985

- Forced lending by IMF to finance balance of payments deficits.
- Multi-year reschedulings (5-8 year maturities rescheduled to 15 years).
- Baker Plan
  Debtor countries to undertake growth-oriented structural reforms that would be supported by increased financing from the World Bank, modest lending from commercial banks, and a pledge by industrial nations to open their markets for LDC exports.

1986 - 1988

- Forced lending by IMF to finance balance of payments deficits.
- Mechanisms developed to deal with nonperforming foreign loans.
  1. Interbank debt swaps to reduce (diversify) exposure to particular countries.
  2. Discounting debt in secondary market (initial size of market small because of suppliers' concern not to have to write down balance of debt held at going market prices).
  3. Increasing loan loss reserves to write down the debt of foreign, genuinely insolvent, countries (e.g. African countries).
  4. Debt swaps:
     a) Debt for equity swaps
        Debt swapped for shares in local businesses and government-owned firms (participant countries included Argentina, Chile, Ecuador, Guatemala, Mexico, Uruguay, and Venezuela).
     b) Debt for nature swaps
        Foster environmental conservation programs (Bolivia, Costa Rica, Madagascar)
     c) Debt for development program swaps (Ecuador)
     d) Debt for debt swaps
        Issuance of bonds by debtor countries to swap for loans held by banks (Mexico swapped in 1988 part of its debt for bonds backed by 20-year, zero coupon U.S. Treasury securities).

1989

- Brady Plan. Creditor banks and debtor countries to negotiate a comprehensive package of debt and debt service reduction as deemed appropriate in each case. Creditor banks can either make new loans or write off portions of existing loans in exchange for new collateralized government securities (Brady bonds) whose interest payments are backed with funds from the IMF.
- Negotiations with debtor countries.

capitalization of Japanese banks was undone by the ensuing sharp stock market decline of the 1990-92 period. This decline made it difficult for banks not only to raise additional equity but also to liquidate their shareholdings to bolster their capital positions. The depressed value of their shareholdings affected bank capital in another way. Japanese banks were allowed to count as part of their capital base (Tier II capital) 45 percent of the unrealized capital gains from their stock portfolios. With stock prices drastically reduced, the contribution of these shareholdings to bank capital suffered accordingly.

The worldwide recession and the collapse of Japan's speculative economy put further pressure on Japanese banks in the form of substantial losses from international and domestic operations. In the United States most of their losses were on real estate in the depressed Northeast and California markets. In the domestic market, the tripling of land and stock market prices during the prosperous 1980s gave way to an economic slump which turned into a deflation (hence the reference to the 1990s as the "lost decade"). Exhibit 1.2 portrays the plunge of the Nikkei stock index by more than 55 percent by 1992, only to drop further in the course of the decade. Exhibit 1.3 depicts the plummeting value of commercial property in major Japanese cities. The combined decline in equity and property prices left overly leveraged Japanese banks and insurance companies with a huge accumulation of non-performing loans which by some estimates exceeded $1.0 trillion by 1995. The impact of the crisis upon financial institutions elicited their bailout through capital infusions from the government, loans and cheap credit from the central bank, and the ability to postpone the recognition of losses. Japanese banks, in turn, continued to support many unprofitable and debt-ridden firms which led to their nickname, "Zombie companies."

Exhibit 1.4 shows two key indicators of Japan's short term interest rates in the 1990s--the call money rate (the rate that banks charge brokerage firms to finance investors' margin accounts) and the discount rate (the rate the central bank charges borrowing institutions). Of special interest is the latter as it portrays the monetary easing policy pursued by the Bank of Japan as economic conditions worsened. From a 6 percent high in (August) 1990, the Bank of Japan lowered its policy interest rate to the

Exhibit 1.2 Gloom Taking Hold of Japan's Stock Market, 1990-1998
(weekly close of the Nikkei 225-Stock-Average Index)

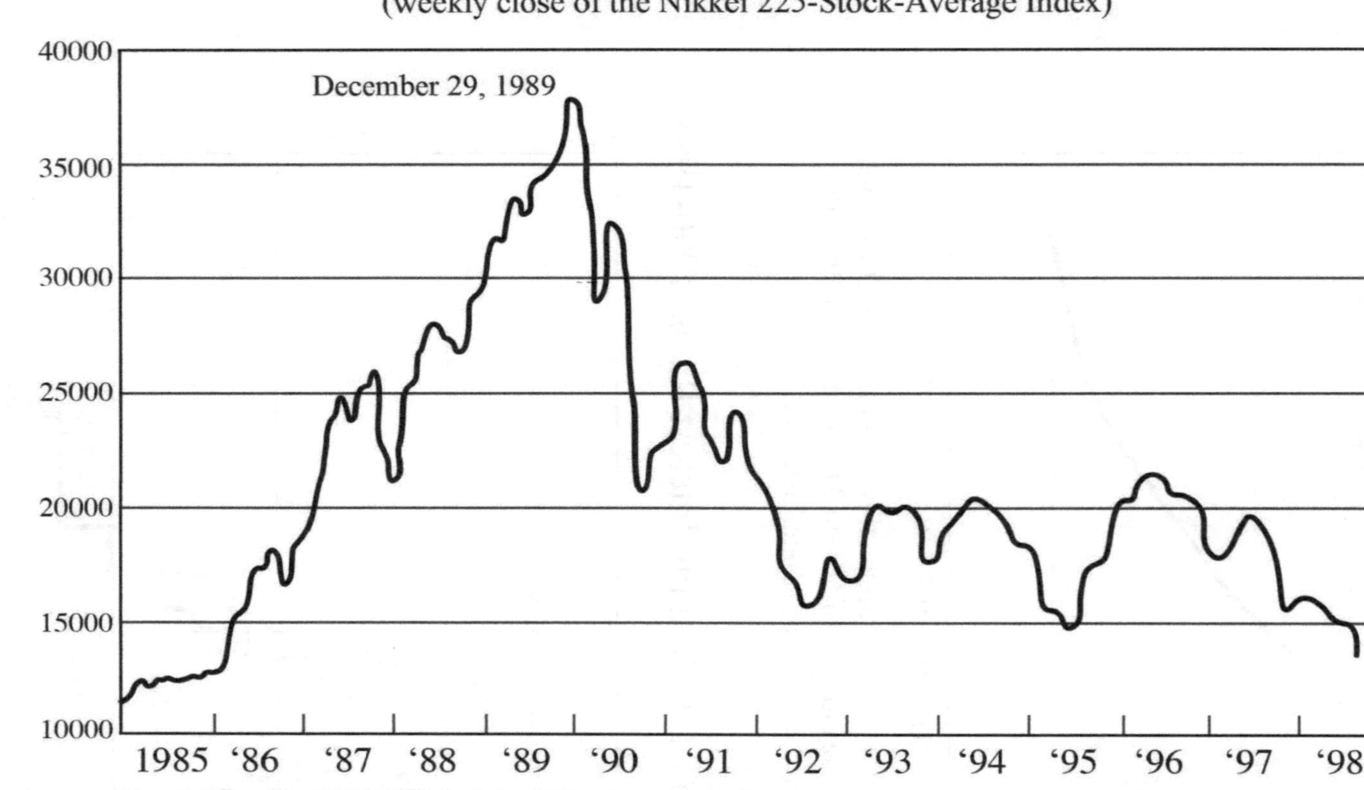

Source: Reprinted by permission of Dow Jones & Company, Inc. via the Copyright Clearance Center.

Exhibit 1.3 Plummeting Property, 1990-1998

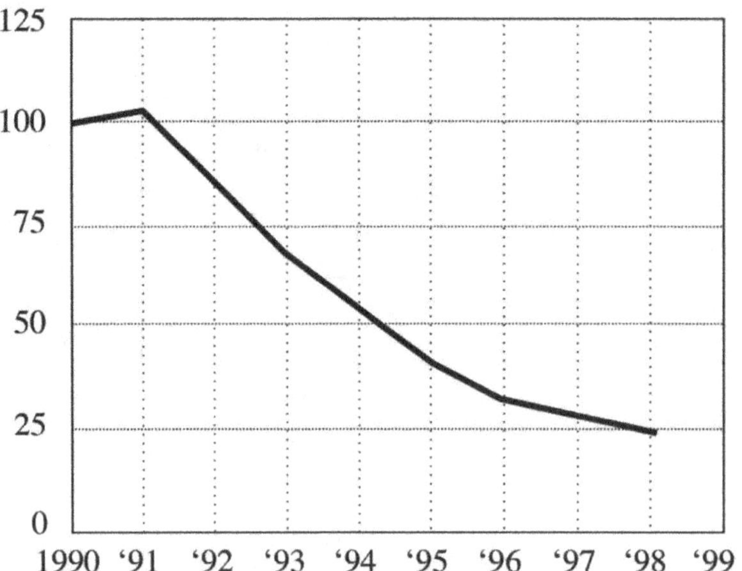

Note: Index of commercial real-estate values in six major Japanese cities as of March 31; March 31, 1990=100.
Source: Japan Real Estate Institute.

Exhibit 1.4 Plunging Interest Rates, 1990-1998

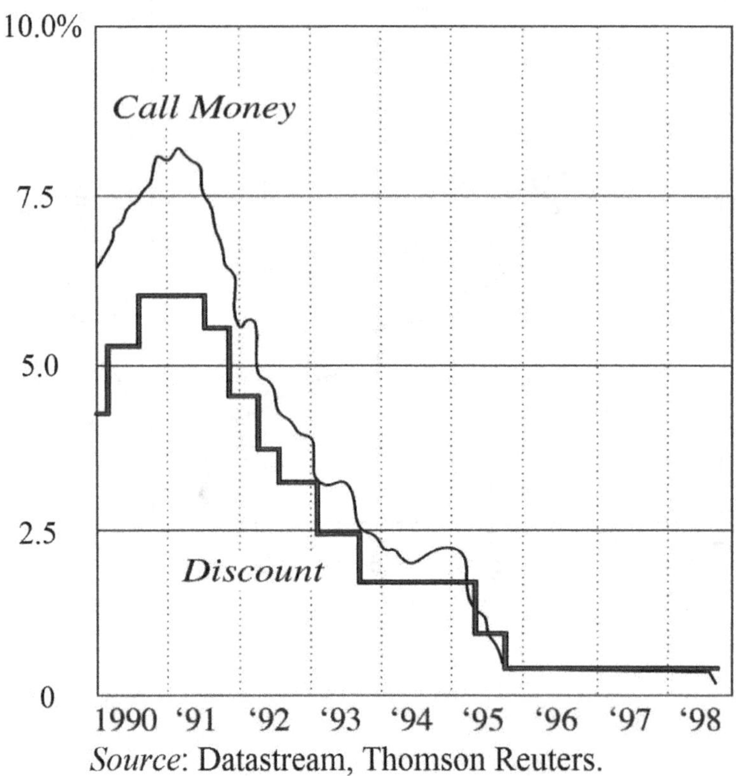

Source: Datastream, Thomson Reuters.

then globally unprecedented level of 0.25 percent in (September) 1998. The call money rate, although higher in early 1991, followed suit by declining steadily to the same level.

Japan's deflationary spiral was not reversed until 2002, when moderate growth set in as a result of a global boom led by US consumption and the robust growth of the emerging economies. In the time that has lapsed since, media and academic attention has focused on the lessons learned from the bubble crisis and how to avoid the mistakes that led to the lost decade. In Japan, the length, cost, and consequence of the financial crisis continue to challenge the country's policymakers.

Regional Contenders in the 1990s

As the 20th century drew to a close, there was a noticeable change in the international economy--global integration, supported by advances in technology combined to result in the freest flow of goods, services and capital in human history. Further, acceleration in the growth rate of world output and the spread of increased living standards in most other parts of the globe contributed to the emergence of a number of key players of regional stature, in the international economy. Such was, for example, the case of East Asian economies which in the course of the 1980s attracted sizable amounts of foreign investments and registered some of the most impressive growth rates in the world. Development of high-tech manufacturing contributed to the technological transformation of the East Asian economies within a decade--a process that took Japan 50 years to accomplish. Thus, while the 1960s and 1970s belonged to the U.S. banks, and the 1980s to the Japanese banks, the 1990s was the decade of the East Asian banks. The East Asian "tigers" included Hong Kong, Malaysia, Singapore, South Korea and Taiwan. As exports of high-tech products expanded rapidly, the Asian tigers realized significant trade surpluses that were funneled into the Eurocurrency market, the standard source of funds for major corporations. A large part of these funds went to finance corporate restructurings in the United States and Europe, where the pace of consolidation was gaining momentum. The international activity of East Asian banks came to an end with the expansion of domestic investment bubbles, financed mainly with borrowed money. Collapse of the Thai baht in mid 1997 initiated a financial crisis that spread quickly to the economies of the region (contagion) raising concerns of an international meltdown.

Another group of key players of regional stature that became a strong contender for global dominance at the turn of the century were European banks. Their strengths included solid capital bases, strong balance sheets, and control of the home market. The Second Banking Directive of 1989, which went into effect on January 1, 1993, permitted banks to operate throughout the European Economic Community (EEC) with a single banking license issued by the their home country. Establishment of the Economic and Monetary Union (EMU) created additional incentives for consolidation of the financial sector and contributed to the global preeminence of European banks.

CONTEMPORARY CHALLENGES

As evidenced from the historical overview of international banking in the preceding section, each period presented its own challenges. Extension of international loans to lesser developed countries has always carried considerable country risk. European bankers of the nineteenth and early twentieth century, for example, faced the periodic defaults and financial panics of borrowing countries in more than one occasion. Exhibit 1.5 identifies some of the loan defaults and crises of this era and their underlying causes. During the twentieth and early twenty-first century, international bankers faced some of the same challenges although in the context of a new economic order established in the immediate post-World-War-II era. Establishment of two new institutions--the IMF and the World Bank--helped provide a new policy framework for economic development and financial assistance to countries.

The international bankers of today are yet witnessing some new, contemporary challenges that cause the industry to undergo important changes more rapidly than at any other time in its history. The combined forces of technology and globalization have altered both the nature of commercial banks and the competitive environment within which they operate. These forces have broken down the traditional barriers that both restricted the activities in which banks could engage and protected their position within the prescribed areas of activity. As a result, banks can now offer a wide array of services and compete directly with a variety of other financial and nonfinancial institutions both at home and abroad.

Exhibit 1.5 Selected Crises, 1875-1914

Country	*Description*	*Cause*
Turkey (1875)	Debt default	Fiscal deficits were funded by foreign borrowing that eventually could not be sustained.
Peru (1876)	Debt default	Falling guano exports and stagnation of other revenues combined with increasing fiscal deficits to generate a crisis.
Egypt	Debt default	Increased foreign borrowing to finance consumption led to unsustainable debt growth.
Argentina (1890)	Debt crisis and institutional failure	Inability of the country to meet debt-service payments led to the bailout of Barings Brothers.
United States (1873)	Financial crisis	Bank runs and failures and fears about U.S. commitment to gold parity followed by a stock market crash.
Greece (1893)	Debt default	Increased borrowing to finance consumption led to unsustainable debt growth.
United States (1894-1896)	Speculative attack	Speculation against the U.S. gold standard parity followed the Sherman Act (1890) and increasing fiscal deficits.
Brazil (1898)	Debt default	A 64 percent decline in coffee prices over the preceding five years generated an external crisis.
United States (1907)	Financial crisis	Banking panic and suspension of cash payments followed interest rate hikes and bank failures.
Canada (1907)	Speculative attack/banking crisis	High interest rates in Canada (in response to hikes in the United States) led to excessive credit expansion that generated speculation against the Canadian dollar.
Brazil (1914)	Debt default	A sharp decline in coffee prices in the preceding two years generated a debt crisis.

Source: International Monetary Fund, *International Capital Markets: Developments, Prospects, and Key Policy Issues* (Washington, D.C.: International Monetary Fund, November 1997), p.238. Reprinted by permission of the publisher via the Copyright Clearance Center.

Technology and Globalization

Advances in technology during recent decades have tied together financial centers as widely dispersed as London, New York, Singapore, Tokyo, and Sydney. These advances have made possible the functioning 24/7 of a global business network to attract savings and extend credit, accommodate cross-border financial transactions, and support a growing stream of information. The relative importance of technology to international banking may be sensed when considering a communication system such as SWIFT (Society for Worldwide Interbank Financial Telecommunications) which facilitates the wire transfer of trillions of dollars daily for major international banks and multinational companies around the world.

Globalization enabled capital to gravitate to the freest markets thereby exerting pressure on countries to build modern, efficient economies. Capital mobility contributed in the development of a global money and capital market, and increased the dependence of countries and corporations on this market. Technology and globalization broke down geographical and functional barriers among banks and between banks and nonbank financial institutions increasing international competition and convergence of the financial service industry. As consolidation began to develop, entrenched financial structures became obsolete dictating the development of new financial products and services and the implementation of new strategies.

In the United States the financial sector experienced the development of large financial holding companies that entered aggressively into new lines of business with new products and services which they extended in foreign markets throughout the world. The growth of derivatives, the unbundling of financial services and outsourcing, and the large number of foreign-owned financial holding companies in the United States are a few examples of the changes experienced during this period. These developments, together with the need to control the spread of financial fraud, mandated a new public policy to ensure the safety and soundness of the industry while sustaining a reasonably competitive level playing field at the regional and global levels.

Technology and globalization have effectively tied what used to be isolated national financial systems into a true international financial market system. Liberalization of money and capital markets took place first in Europe and then in

Asia. Launched by United Kingdom's enactment of financial reforms, deregulation of financial institutions and markets was followed by similar moves on the continent including the creation of the EMU and the introduction of a single currency (1999). Outside Europe, financial reforms were implemented in Australia, Canada, New Zealand, Japan, and Korea. The obvious consequence of these measures was that they enabled international banking services to experience expansion and sustained growth unknown to their history. But things changed.

Beginning in mid-2007, a series of crises began to undermine the U.S. economy. Several large financial institutions, including commercial banks, investment banks, and insurance companies, experienced significant losses from an excessive financial leverage position during a period of declining home prices and real estate values. As a result, credit availability suffered and borrowing terms stiffened. By the end of that year the U.S. economy fell into recession and the global economy followed. To contain the effects of the crisis, the U.S. government approved a sizable bank bailout program (e.g., in the form of equity investment, purchase of loans, and issuance of guarantees) for institutions at risk and enacted a massive stimulus plan of tax cuts and increased government spending to jump start the stalling economy and bolster consumer and business confidence. Similar actions were taken by the governments of foreign countries that were affected by the U.S. crisis and underwent similar experiences. International bank bailout programs at year-end 2008 stood at €3.1 trillion ($4.19 trillion).

The disproportionate impact of the crisis on advanced economies and their stuttering recovery caused a reversal of past trends by turning emerging and developing economies into leading contributors to global economic growth in the post-crisis period. China's overtaking of Japan as the world's second biggest economy made Chinese banks figure prominently among the world's top banking institutions. Another impact of the crisis was the transformation of the financial services industry through consolidation and public policy. U.S. investment banks as traditionally structured no longer exist as independent organizations. Many banking firms in the United States and abroad failed, were acquired by stronger surviving institutions, or have come under government control. The financial crisis underscored the need for a new approach to supervision and regulation to safeguard the financial system and restore market confidence. From an operational perspective, breakdown of the loan origination and distribution model prompted banks to revert to conservative loan underwriting by refocusing on debtors' ability and willingness to repay. The move to strong risk management systems and controls renewed bank emphasis on capital adequacy, quality of assets, and the availability of adequate liquidity.

Although international banking services have come a long way from the days of the Italian and German merchant banking houses of the Medici and the Fugger, respectively, the industry's reconfiguration has still some way to go. The driving forces of change--technological innovation and globalization--will continue to be among the main catalysts to impact money and capital markets which are central to international banking services. Indeed, with capital and technology flowing directly and easily between countries, world economic expansion will sustain the further growth of international banking. As the global marketplace expands and encompasses a multinational clientele with increasingly diverse and complicated financial needs, large international banks--both American and foreign--will find themselves forced to create increasingly distinctive and attractive financial service packages in order to acquire and maintain a share of the market. Some of the challenges that will confront international banks will be altogether new, others a variation of those encountered in the past. Whatever the nature of these challenges, international bankers will need to manage risk to take advantage of the opportunities for growth and profits in the global marketplace.

Risks in Banking

The primary objective of bank management is shareholder wealth maximization. Essentially, the institution should strive to maximize the return to shareholders by maximizing the market value of the bank's common stock. Profit maximization differs from wealth maximization in that instead of pursuing long term value maximization, management seeks to maximize growth in short term earnings. A bank's profitability will generally vary directly with the riskiness of its portfolio and operations. Although some risks can be sought out or avoided, others are inherent in the prevailing economic environment and the specific markets served. For example, a bank that operates internationally, would be exposed to the risks inherent in the global environment. Some of the more important risks confronting an internationally active bank are identified below.

- *Credit risk* is the likelihood of borrower default (inability to repay principal and interest when due)
- *Liquidity and funding risk*, inability to meet ordinary operating requirements or fund maturing liabilities
- *Settlement/payment risk*, payment of money or delivery of assets by one party prior to receipt of cash or assets by another
- *Interest rate risk*, effect of interest rate changes on the volume and maturity of interest-sensitive assets, liabilities and off-balance items
- *Market risk*, the risk of losses arising from adverse movement in market rates or prices
- *Foreign exchange risk*, the risk of losses in on- and off-balance sheet positions from fluctuations in foreign exchange rates
- *Operating risk*, risk of losses resulting from fraud, legal, and environmental developments, or failure of internal controls and systems
- *Country risk*, the risk of losses arising from the economic, social and political environments of a given foreign country where a bank operates
- *Sovereign risk*, when a national government defaults on debts, or alters unilaterally debt service payments, or seizes bank assets without adequate compensation

Increasingly in recent years, the focus of bank management has been to manage risk. Assessment, monitor and control of the risks associated with particular business activities has become a formidable task. The growth in the range and complexity of financial products has made risk management more difficult to attain. Thus, risk management has become a central function of all banks, especially in recent years that banking has evolved into a more globalized industry.

2 BANKS IN THE GLOBAL MONEY AND CAPITAL MARKETS

The financial market performs a vital function within a national economic system. It is the conduit for the channeling of funds between the various groups of market participants. The financial market has been the heart of every national financial system, attracting and allocating savings and setting interest rates and the prices of financial assets (securities). Advances in technology and communication have integrated national financial markets into a global system at work 24 hours a day attracting savings, extending credit and fulfilling other vital cross-border financial transactions. The integration process of national financial systems contributed in turn to the development of international communications network markets that have come to dominate physical marketplaces in the trading of standardized products (e.g., suppliers and users of capital do not need to see the "commodity" before entering into a transaction).

Conceptually, depending upon the parties to financial transactions, financial markets may be distinguished into domestic markets, where a large body of suppliers and demanders of funds are domiciled in the same country, and international markets, where one of the component groups (suppliers or demanders of funds) are foreign. When both groups are foreign but transact via a third market mechanism, the financial market is called an offshore market. These differentiations have given rise to the distinction between international (or entrepôt) financial centers (e.g., New York and Tokyo), and offshore financial centers (e.g., Panama, Cayman Islands and Singapore).

Suppliers of funds are attracted to international financial centers because of their well-functioning economies--capital will flow efficiently from those who supply it to those who demand it. Suppliers may use their funds to purchase debt and equity securities or if they are risk averse they may just place them with financial intermediaries which, in turn, use these funds to make loans and buy and hold securities. An alternate venue for these same transactions are the offshore centers. Suppliers of funds, whether investors or depositors, may opt to transact through offshore centers to benefit from their bank confidentiality laws and favorable tax environment.

As follows from the preceding, demanders of funds in international markets have access to two sources of capital--debt and equity. Debt capital may be sourced through bank loans or the issue of debt securities, with each one of these comprising alternate types of debt financing. Equity, on the other hand, may be raised typically through a share issue which constitutes a corporate option (governments do not issue equity). Banks play a major role in the operational efficiency of international markets both through their credit extension and investment banking functions (e.g., as underwriters and traders of securities, discussed in Chapter 6). The sections that follow provide an overview of sourcing debt and equity in global markets.

SOURCING DEBT IN GLOBAL MARKETS

Recent decades have experienced a vast need for funds denominated in dollars, British pounds, euros, yen and other convertible currencies. Although bank loans represent the oldest and largest source of financing, issue of debt securities has made a considerable leap forward with borrowers' use of a variety of securities of different quality, maturity, pricing structure, and subordination or linkage to other debt instruments. Foreign bank loans at the end of the first quarter of 2016, according to the Bank for International Settlements (BIS), stood at $26.9 trillion compared to international debt securities of $21.7 trillion. The basic attributes of each of these debt markets is described below.

International Bank Loans

International loans are extended to multinational corporations, sovereign governments, international institutions and banks. Denominated in foreign currency, these loans are known as *Eurocredits* because they are funded by deposits in the same foreign currency. The pricing of these loans is tied to the London Interbank Offered Rate (LIBOR). Administered by the Intercontinental Exchange (ICE) since 2014, the LIBOR is based on the quotes of less than 20 global banks and represents the daily benchmark rates for loans in five currencies (CHF, EUR, GBP, JPY and USD) and seven tenors (overnight, one week, and 1, 2, 3, 6 and 12 months). The spread charged over LIBOR for loans to nonbank borrowers is known as the *risk premium* and reflects the risk associated with the credit. Most loans are for a fixed term with no provisions for early repayment. LIBOR priced loans are usually of short- or medium-term tenor.

Short term loans may be made for a period up to a year. They may take the form of "lines of credit" which rating agencies, such as Standard and Poor's and Moody's, require issuers of commercial paper to have in place to assure investors of repayment when the paper matures. The practice to backup the paper with lines of credit (liquidity enhancement) secures quality ratings and consequently a lower cost of borrowing. Other instances of short term lending include the financing of mergers, acquisitions and leverage buyout transactions.

Medium term loans are an intermediate type of credit with an original maturity of more than one year and up to seven or eight years, sometimes longer. They can take a number of forms, one of which is the *revolving credit* (or revolver), which runs from one to three years. It is a formal contractual agreement which permits clients to draw down funds as needed, over an agreed period of time, under an agreed interest formula. Funds are repaid at the borrower's option with the bank committed to continue lending up to the maximum amount stated in the revolving-credit agreement until its expiration. The flexibility associated with this type of credit renders it useful in cases where the client cannot be certain of the precise timing of the needed funds or their repayment. Revolving credits usually finance such needs as working capital, expansion of operations, and purchase of fixed assets. At maturity, the revolving credit may be paid off or extended over and over, in response to the particular needs of individual borrowers. Often, revolving credit arrangements include a provision that at their expiration, the entire amount borrowed will be incorporated into a term loan.

A *term loan* may be made for a period of seven or ten years although not infrequently it may exceed this limit. This type of facility has been used to fund the credit needs of a sovereign entity or a multinational corporation whose ability to repay is related to its anticipated earning power. Typical business borrowers include firms that have heavy fixed capital requirements (e.g., petroleum refining, mining, chemicals and rubber, and public utilities). Term loans are used for a number of purposes including the financing of working capital increases, and the purchase or improvements of fixed assets (plant, equipment and machinery).

Term loans, and revolving facilities may be extended directly, or may take the form of a *syndicated credit* whereby several banks are assembled by a lead bank, or syndicate manager, to participate in the financing of the loan. This process enables the participating banks to spread the risk involved in large specialized loans, and it permits the borrower to obtain funds well in excess of a single bank's lending limit. The syndicate manager originates the transaction, structures it, assembles the syndicate, supervises the documentation, and in most cases services the loan after signing. Its position is the most crucial and, from a legal perspective, the most exposed. It owes duty to the borrower to arrange a syndicate, and a duty to the other banks not to mislead them or misrepresent any aspect of the credit. Syndicated credits are made at floating rates (some premium over LIBOR) and provide for a fee structure--management fee for managing the participating banks, an agency fee for servicing the loan, and in the case of a revolving facility a commitment fee on the unused portion of the credit. Exhibit 2.1 shows a bank syndicated term loan to the sovereign state of Belgium.

Debt Securities Issued or Traded in International Markets

Financial institutions, government and state agencies, and corporations rely on alternate types of debt issues to finance their activities. Exhibit 2.2 lists the value of international debt securities outstanding at the end of March 2015, by maturity (money market versus capital market), issuer, currency, and type (floating-rate, fixed-rate and equity related debt). As seen in this Exhibit the largest value of securities in global markets is fixed-rate debt, dollar-denominated, issued by financial corporations. Euro-denominated debt trailed in importance. The various types of debt issues are addressed below under the headings of money and capital markets.

Money Markets. The global money market is a broad and diverse market made up of a variety of instruments. Reliance on the alternate type of instrument to address funding needs varies by type of borrower. Banks, for example, rely heavily on Euro time and

Exhibit 2.1 Syndicated Medium Term Loan

This announcement appears as a matter of record only

KINGDOM OF BELGIUM

U.S. $1,000,000,000

MEDIUM TERM LOAN

MANAGED BY

BANQUE BRUXELLES LAMBERT S.A / BANK BRUSSEL LAMBERT N.V

BANQUE DE PARIS ET DES PAYS-BAS BELGIQUE S.A / BANK VAN PARUS EN DE NEDERLANDEN BELGIE N.V.

KREDIETBANK N.V.

SOCIÉTÉ GÉNÉRALE DE BANQUE S.A / GENERALE BANKMAATSCHAPPIJ N.V.

PROVIDED BY

ALGMENE BANK NEDERLAND N.V.
AMSTERDAM-ROTTERDAM BANK N.V.
THE BANK OF NOVA SCOTIA C.J. LIMITED
BANK OF TOKYO, LIMITED
BANQUE BRUXELLES LAMBERT S.A.
BANQUE DE PARIS ET DES PAYS-BAS BELGIQUE S.A.
BANQUE EUROPEENNE DE CREDIT (BEC)
BANQUE NATIONALE DE PARIS
BARCLAYS BANK INTERNATIONAL LIMITED
BAYERISCHE LANDESBANK INTERNATIONAL S.A.
BERLINER HANDELS- UND FRANKFURTER BANK
CANADIAN IMPERIAL BANK OF COMMERCE
CHASE MANHATTAN BANK N.A.
CREDIT COMMERCIAL DE FRANCE
CREDIT LYONNAIS
DEUTSCHE BANK (ASIA CREDIT) LIMITED
EUROPEAN AMERICAN BANK (LUX. BRANCH)
THE FIRST NATIONAL BANK OF CHICAGO
FUJI BANK, LIMITED
KREDIETBANK N.V
LLOYDS BANK INTERNATIONAL (BELGIUM) S.A.
MIDLAND BANK LIMITED
MITSUBISHI BANK (EUROPE) S.A.
NATIONAL WESTMINSTER BANK GROUP
NEDERLANDSCHE MIDDENSTANDSBANK N.V.
ORION BANK LIMITED
THE ROYAL BANK OF CANADA (LONDON) LIMITED
SFE BANKING CORPORATION LIMITED / SFE GROUP
SOCIETE GENERALE / SOGENAL
SOCIETE GENERALE DE BANQUE S.A.
THE SUMITOMO BANK LIMITED
WESTDEUTSCHE LANDESBANK GIROZENTRALE

AGENT

KREDIETBANK N.V.

Source: Reprinted by permission of Euromoney.

Exhibit 2.2 International Debt Securities Outstanding, March 2015
(in billions of U.S. dollars)

Total Issues	**$20,890**
Money Market Instruments	**888**
Financial corporations	784
Non-financial corporations	45
Government and state agencies	24
U.S. dollar	380
Euro	288
Other currencies	220
Capital Market: Bonds and notes	**20,002**
Financial corporations	14,211
Non-financial corporations	2,868
Government and state agencies	1,539
U.S. dollar	8,628
Euro	7,763
Other currencies	3,611
Floating rate	5,037
Fixed rate	14,570
Equity-related	395

Source: Bank for International Settlements, *Quarterly Review*, March 2015
http://www.bis.org/publ/qtrpdf/r_qs1506.pdf

Euro certificates of deposit compared to multinational corporations that rely on other types of instruments such as the Euro-commercial paper, Euronote facilities and Euro medium-term notes. The sale and distribution of these instruments may, or may not, entail underwriting facilities. Before addressing the various types of instruments it is important to clarify the functioning of the Eurocurrency market, the major component on the global money market, and a key linkage between the global money and capital markets.

The domestic currency of one country on deposit in another country is known as

Eurocurrency. The Eurocurrency market is an efficient and convenient market for banks to attract excess corporate liquidity and finance loans. The dominant currency in the market is the Eurodollar--a U.S. dollar deposited in a bank outside the United States. The term "Eurodollar" originated during a time when the market was almost exclusively located in principal European financial centers. Over time the market expanded and Eurodollar deposits are also held in major financial centers around the world. The market's reference rate of interest for the trading of Eurodollars is the LIBOR, the interbank rate at which banks would lend these funds to each other. The LIBOR is the rough equivalent of the U.S. federal funds rate (interbank rate) in the Euromarket and has evolved into a benchmark rate for the pricing of short term loans and deposits. In addition to Eurodollars, banks also quote rates for any other convertible currency on deposit outside its home country. Some of the quoted rates refer, for example, to British pound-denominated deposits in banks outside the United Kingdom (Eurosterling), Japanese yen-denominated deposits outside Japan (Euroyen), euro-denominated deposits outside the Eurozone (Euroeuros), and Canadian-dollar denominated deposits outside their home country (Eurocanadian dollars). Thus the prefix "Euro" denotes the nature and function performed by these deposits rather than the European location of these funds. The reference rate of interest for foreign currency deposits traded in major financial centers around the world is expressed in relation to the specific center's interbank rate. In Hong Kong, for example, the interest rate in which Eurocurrency deposits are traded is the Hong Kong Interbank Offered Rate (HIBOR). In Singapore, it is the Singapore Interbank Offered Rate (SIBOR). Given the global dimension of this market any attempt to gauge its exact size has been challenging at best because of the variability of the day-to-day decision of its depositors--e.g., the corporate treasurers with temporarily idle funds.

The origins of the Eurocurrency market, and the Eurodollar in particular, go back to the immediate post World War II period, when Iron Curtain countries were afraid to deposit their dollar balances in the United States out of concern that those deposits might be attached by U.S. residents with claims against their Communist governments. Mounting Soviet friction with the United States convinced a number of these countries, such as China, to place their dollar balances in a select number of banks in Europe. As European banks had accepted limited amounts of dollar deposits before the war they became a natural choice for the holding of such balances in the postwar period. Growth of the postwar dollar market in Europe precipitated the influx of additional funds seeking higher yields than were available in the United States. Some of these funds came from European-based commercial banks and central banks, others came from insurance companies, and still others from international refugee funds. Although the development of the Eurocurrency market was an outgrowth of its economic efficiency, several events in the postwar decades were of particular importance, such as the imposition of British controls in the use of the sterling for credits to nonresidents (1957), U.S. balance of payment deficits (1960s), suspension of purchases or sales of gold by the U.S. Treasury (1968), and the recycling of the petrodollars (early 1970s). These events led to the active solicitation of dollar deposits by banks in Western Europe and contributed to the sustained development of the Eurocurrency market into a global money market relatively free from governmental control and interference.

Banks that intermediate in the Eurocurrency market are identified as "Eurobanks." These institutions (essentially the departments of large commercial banks), bid for foreign-currency deposits to finance foreign-currency loans. For example, if the loan is to be denominated in U.S. dollars, the Eurobank may bid for a Eurodollar time deposit or issue a Eurodollar certificate of deposit.

Eurodollar time deposits (TDs) are U.S. dollar-denominated time deposits with a maturity range from call money and overnight funds to longer periods. However, most of these deposits mature in anywhere from one week to six months. An important difference between Eurodollar time deposits and their domestic counterparts is that Eurodollar time deposits are to a large extent interbank liabilities, are nonnegotiable and pay a fixed rate of return for the term of the deposit. Quoted rates are determined competitively.

Eurodollar certificates of deposits (CDs) are U.S. dollar-denominated CDs offered by banks outside the United States (or within the United States itself but via international banking facilities or IBFs). They are issued in bearer form, are negotiable, and are free from withholding tax on interest. First introduced in the U.S. market by

Citibank in 1961 they were issued abroad by the same institution, five years later, as Eurodollar CDs. They were a major innovation that encouraged over time the development of a secondary market in dollar instruments and contributed to the growth of the Euromoney market. Bank-issued CDs are sold to clients and correspondent banks, and on occasion through dealers for a modest commission. Issuing banks maintain a secondary market in their own CDs, assisted by dealers (who trade bank CDs for their own account) and brokers who function as agents for the bank or individual investors. Banks may issue single Eurodollar CDs on "as required" basis in order to tap the market for funds. As a result this type of CDs is known as tap CDs; their denomination usually ranges from $250,000 to $5 million. By contrast, tranche CDs (from the French tranche) are sizable Eurodollar CD issues--in amounts of $10 million to $30 million--marketed in several smaller portions to appeal to investors with a need for smaller instruments. Tranche CDs are usually offered in $10,000 certificates, each bearing the same interest rate, issue date, interest payment dates, and maturity. In order to minimize interest-rate risks for both the borrower and the lender, Eurodollar floating-rate CDs have come into use. The interest rate is reset at a marginal spread above the LIBOR approximately every three to six months.

Conceptually, a Eurodollar CD would pay a higher interest rate than its domestic counterpart of the same maturity because, by virtue of its being offered abroad, it is not subject to U.S. regulatory costs (e.g., reserve requirements and FDIC insurance). Further, being an online product it does not carry much overhead, and lastly, it includes a risk premium to compensate depositors for the perceived risk of the host government or the government whose currency is being used. On the lending side, a Eurodollar loan rate would be lower than the corresponding U.S. domestic rate for the same loan maturity because of the wholesale nature of the Eurodollar market (e.g., transactions are usually in excess of half a million dollars), perceived high quality of nonbank borrowers (e.g., multinational corporations and governments), and broader competitive environment. The Eurodollar market's higher CD rates and lower lending rates imply that Eurobanks operate on narrower margins or spreads than banks in the United States. The size of the spread (often less than 1 percent) has been a key factor in attracting both depositors and borrowers to the Eurodollar market.

As the Eurocurrency market is an informal, over-the counter market made up of banks and other professional dealers from around the world, it is unregulated--it functions outside the regulatory framework of any monetary authority. The monetary authority of the host country where the deposit is made is not concerned with the non-resident deposit or borrowing of foreign currencies as they do not affect the domestic money supply. It is also outside the control of the monetary authority of the home country of the currency because the transaction takes place in a foreign market.

Euro-Commercial Paper (ECP) is a standard financing instrument by strong corporate borrowers. The Euro-commercial paper may be issued in markets around the world. It is a short term promissory note issued to sophisticated investors, usually other corporations, mutual funds and pension funds. Maturities are typically one, three, and six months. The paper is usually sold at a discount from its face value or occasionally with a stated coupon. The issue (denomination and maturity) is tailored to investor preferences and may be placed with the investor directly (directly placed issue) or through a dealer (dealer placed, non-underwritten). Although commercial paper is essentially a substitute for bank loans, banks play an active role in this market as underwriters and guarantors. U.S. dollar-denominated commercial paper accounts for over 90 percent of the ECP market. Exhibit 2.3 identifies select bank issuers in ECP market.

Euronote Facilities represent a family of revolving credit facilities, also known as note issuance facilities (nifs), revolving underwriting facilities (rufs), and standby note issuance facilities (snifs). Provided by a bank, or a group of banks, the credit facility allows a borrower to issue short term Euronotes over a given period of time. The underwriting banks are committed to place the notes directly with the institutional investors market. In the event the notes cannot be placed in the market at previously guaranteed rates, banks stand ready to purchase unsold notes. Just as commercial paper is an alternative to short term bank lending, Euronotes may be viewed as a substitute for syndicated lending. From the bank's point of view syndicated lending entails use of bank funds while Euronote facilities generate fee-based income from underwriting and distribution services.

Euro medium-term notes (EMTNs) may be issued for as little as nine months to

Exhibit 2.3 Select Issues of Euro-commercial Paper

AskSz(M)	Issuer	Maturity	Days To M	Dsc/Cpn	S&P	M	Reg Type
4,600	SOC GENERALE	3/14/2017	1	0.63	A-1	P-1	4.2
3,078	BK OF CHINA/HK	3/29/2017	16	0.97	A-1	P-1	3a3
8,500	CNPC FINANCE HK	3/30/2017	17	0.89	A-1	P-1	3c7A
38,980	HYDRO-QUEBEC	3/31/2017	18	0.64	A-1+	P-1	4.2A
26,850	OEST KONTROLLBK	3/31/2017	18	0.82	A-1+	P-1	3a3
5,800	TOYOTA IND COMM	4/4/2017	22	0.82	A-1+	P-1	4.2A
5,000	TOYOTA IND COMM	4/4/2017	22	0.79	A-1+	P-1	4.2A
5,900	MACQUARIE BK LTD	4/5/2017	23	0.77	A-1	P-1	4.2A
1,498	MIT UFJ T&B SG	4/7/2017	25	0.77	A-1	P-1	4.2A
2,500	MACQUARIE BK LTD	4/10/2017	28	0.82	A-1	P-1	4.2A
1,500	CREDIT AGRI CIB	4/11/2017	29	0.82	A-1	P-1	3a3
10,500	BANK NED GEMEENT	4/13/2017	31	0.77	A-1+	P-1	4.2A
22,125	SWEDISH EXP CRED	4/17/2017	35	0.92	A-1+	P-1	3a3
2,750	NESTLE FIN INTL	4/18/2017	36	0.74	A-1+	P-1	3a3
19,800	SUMITOMO MITSUI	4/20/2017	38	0.87	A-1	P-1	4.2A
2,150	TOTAL CAP CANADA	4/20/2017	38	0.74	A-1	P-1	4.2A
16,430	MITSUB UFJ T&B	4/26/2017	44	0.87	A-1	P-1	4.2
2,400	MITSUB UFJ T&B	4/26/2017	44	0.82	A-1	P-1	4.2
5,800	SOC GENERALE	5/1/2017	49	0.92	A-1	P-1	4.2
2,500	NESTLE CAP CORP	5/4/2017	52	0.71	A-1+	P-1	4.2A
30,500	MITSUB UFJ T&B	5/12/2017	60	0.90	A-1	P-1	4.2
98,000	DBS BANK LTD	5/15/2017	63	0.91	A-1+	P-1	4.2A
1,800	MIZUHO BK LTD/NY	5/18/2017	66	0.97	A-1	P-1	4.2A
12,500	STANDARD CHART	6/5/2017	84	1.02	A-1	P-1	4.2A
6,750	SWEDBANK	6/7/2017	86	0.97	A-1+	P-1	3a3
8,800	BANCO DE CHILE	6/9/2017	88	1.12	A-1	P-1	4.2A
85,150	MACQUARIE BK LTD	6/12/2017	91	1.09	A-1	P-1	4.2A
146,500	CAISSE AMORT DET	7/5/2017	114	1.14	NR	P-1	3c7A
84,850	SWEDBANK	7/12/2017	121	1.07	A-1+	P-1	3a3
2,500	CAISSE AMORT DET	7/17/2017	126	1.07	NR	P-1	3c7A
1,500	SOC GENERALE	7/17/2017	126	1.12	A-1	P-1	4.2
1,750	LANDESBK HESSEN	7/24/2017	133	1.07	A-1	P-1	4.2A
22,000	BANQ CAISSE EPAR	8/7/2017	147	1.14	A-1+	P-1	3a3
1,075	NATL AUSTRALIABK	9/1/2017	172	1.11	A-1+	P-1	4.2A
125,000	BANQ CAISSE EPAR	9/7/2017	178	1.21	A-1+	P-1	3a3
1,150	SOC GENERALE	9/27/2017	198	1.32	A-1	P-1	4.2
15,000	SWEDBANK	9/28/2017	199	1.17	A-1+	P-1	3a3
33,648	SOC GENERALE	10/2/2017	203	1.32	A-1	P-1	4.2
1,750	MACQUARIE BK LTD	10/4/2017	205	1.27	A-1	P-1	4.2A
34,700	SOC GENERALE	10/23/2017	224	1.37	A-1	P-1	4.2
2,500	NATL AUSTRALIABK	2/8/2018	332	1.47	A-1+	P-1	4.2A

Source: Street run of offerings, March 13, 2017.

a maximum of 10 years. Thus it bridges the maturity gap between ECP and the longer-term international bond. EMTNs are issued by large corporations and governments and their agencies from all around the world. Exhibit 2.4 illustrates the advertisement (prospectus) for a $1 billion 100-year EMTN issued by the United Mexican States. EMTNs are sold to investors directly or through dealers (dealer placed, non-underwritten). The EMTN carries many of the basic characteristics of a bond, e.g., principal, maturity, interest rate and coupon structure (coupons are typically paid semiannually). However, this instrument possesses three unique characteristics. First, unlike a bond which is sold at once, it allows for continuous issuance over a period of time. This practice reflects the U.S. Securities and Exchange Commission (SEC) rule 415 which allows a corporation that has obtained a shelf registration earlier on to issue notes continuously without need for a new registration. Another difference with bonds lies in debt service. As EMTNs are sold continuously, to make debt service practicable, coupons are paid on set calendar dates regardless of the date of issue. Lastly, EMTNs are issued in relatively small denominations (e.g., from $2 million to $5 million) which renders their acquisition more flexible than the large minimums required for the purchase of bonds in international markets.

Capital Markets. Capital markets trade equity (discussed in the following section) and long term debt (bonds) instruments. Straight fixed-rate securities dominate the market mainly because of the strong demand for dollar and some euro currency assets and the historically low interest in the U.S. and Eurozone markets. Typically the major supplier of international bonds are financial institutions that, together with other issuers (corporations and governments), seek to secure long term financing. International bond issues may be grouped in two generic classifications--foreign bonds and Eurobonds--depending upon the residence of the borrower and the currency of denomination of the issue.

Foreign bond is an issue of a foreign borrower in a target country, underwritten by a syndicate of firms in the host country, sold to investors within that country, and denominated in the currency of that country. For example, a Brazilian company issuing a dollar-denominated bond in the United States, underwritten by U.S. investment

Exhibit 2.4 Euro Medium-Term Note Offering

Final Terms
To Prospectus dated September 2, 2010 and
Prospectus Supplement dated September 2, 2010

United Mexican States

U.S. $80,000,000,000 Global Medium-Term Notes, Series A
Due Nine Months or More From Date of Issue

U.S. $1,000,000,000 5.750% Global Notes due 2110

The notes will mature on October 12, 2110. Mexico will pay interest on the notes on April 12 and October 12 of each year, commencing April 12, 2011. Mexico may redeem the notes in whole or in part before maturity, at par plus the Make-Whole Amount and accrued interest, as described herein. The notes will not be entitled to the benefit of any sinking fund.

The notes will contain provisions regarding acceleration and future modifications to their terms that differ from those applicable to Mexico's outstanding public external indebtedness issued prior to March 3, 2003. Under these provisions, which are described beginning on page 7 of the accompanying prospectus dated September 2, 2010, Mexico may amend the payment provisions of the notes with the consent of the holders of 75% of the aggregate principal amount of the outstanding notes.

Mexico will apply to list the notes on the Luxembourg Stock Exchange and to have the notes admitted to trading on the Euro MTF market of the Luxembourg Stock Exchange.

Neither the Securities and Exchange Commission nor any other regulatory body has approved or disapproved of these securities or passed upon the accuracy or adequacy of these final terms or the accompanying prospectus supplement or prospectus. Any representation to the contrary is a criminal offense.

The notes have not been and will not be registered with the National Securities Registry maintained by the Mexican National Banking and Securities Commission ("CNBV") and may not be offered or sold publicly in Mexico. The notes may be offered or sold privately in Mexico to qualified and institutional investors, pursuant to the exemption contemplated under Article 8 of the Mexican Securities Market Law. As required under the Mexican Securities Market Law, Mexico will give notice to the CNBV of the offering of the notes under the terms set forth herein. Such notice does not certify the solvency of Mexico, the investment quality of the notes, or that the information contained in these final terms, the prospectus supplement or the prospectus is accurate or complete. Mexico has prepared these final terms and is solely responsible for their content, and the CNBV has not reviewed or authorized such content.

	Price to Public [1]	Underwriting Discounts	Proceeds to Mexico, before expenses
Per note	94.276%	0.40%	93.876%
Total	U.S. $942,760,000	U.S. $4,000,000	U.S. $938,760,000

(1) Plus accrued interest, if any, from October 12, 2010.

The notes will be ready for delivery in book-entry form only through the facilities of The Depository Trust Company ("DTC"), the Euroclear System ("Euroclear") and Clearstream Banking, société anonyme, Luxembourg ("Clearstream, Luxembourg") against payment on or about October 12, 2010.

Joint Lead Managers

Deutsche Bank Securities **Goldman, Sachs & Co.**

October 5, 2010

Source: https://www.gob.mx/cms/uploads/attachment/file/29239/Emisi_n_D_lares_vencimiento_2110_.pdf

banking firms and sold in this country would be a foreign bond. U.S.-issued foreign bonds are often referred to as "Yankee bonds," while foreign bonds sold in Japan are called "Samurai bonds." UK-issued bonds are known as "Bulldogs." Exhibit 2.5 shows the tombstone ad for a 10- and 20-year Yankee bond issues by the Republic of South Africa. As these issues constitute foreign-government debt, they are commonly known as sovereign bonds.

Eurobond is an issue underwritten by an international syndicate and sold outside the country of the currency in which they are denominated. For example, a dollar denominated bond issued by a foreign government and sold in foreign markets (e.g., Europe and Asia) would be a Eurobond (see tombstone ad on a two-part offering by the Republic of Italy, Exhibit 2.6). Most Eurobonds are straight debt offerings with maturities in the 10-15 year range, are issued by financial institutions, and are generally not secured (they are senior debt with issuers prohibited from creating security interests on their assets). Although Eurobonds are listed in organized exchanges, most trading activity takes place in the international over-the-counter market made up of dealers around the world linked by computers and electronic networks. Communications network markets dominate physical market places. Eurobonds are widely bought by banks for their retail investors (e.g., middle class professionals and wealthy individuals) and other financial institutions (e.g., pension funds, insurance companies and investment companies). The first Eurobond was a $15 million issue, offered in 1963 by an Italian motorway network (Autostrade); it had a 15-year maturity and was listed on the Luxembourg Stock Exchange.

Although Eurobonds vary widely in characteristics the most common types include the following:

- **Straight fixed-rate bonds.** These pay an annual coupon rate that is fixed over the term of the bond.
- **Floating-rate notes (FRNs).** FRNs are usually offered with a fixed medium term maturity. However, a number of FRNs are perpetuities (as the principal is not repaid these issues provide the same financial functions as equity). In addition to corporations and governments many banks have

Exhibit 2.5 Yankee Bond Issues

Merrill Lynch
on the value of integration in the new South Africa.

October 1996

US $300,000,000

Republic of South Africa

Inaugural 10-year Yankee Bonds

Lead Manager

Merrill Lynch & Co.

June 1997

US $500,000,000

Republic of South Africa

20-year Yankee Bonds

Lead Manager

Merrill Lynch & Co.

When the new Republic of South Africa started working on social integration, they asked Merrill Lynch to participate in the task of reintegrating the country into the global financial markets. Their first sovereign Yankee bond issue in Autumn 1996 gave South Africa a crucial foothold in the US Capital markets. In Spring 1997, Merrill Lynch was awarded the lead manager role on the second issue – and assisted the Republic with the ratings agencies to achieve an investment grade rating.
As South Africa moves towards a more open society, opening doors to the world's investors makes a difference.
The difference is Merrill Lynch

A tradition of trust

Source: Reprinted by permission of Euromoney.

Exhibit 2.6 Two-part Offering: Notes and Bonds

US $5,500,000,000

Republic of Italy

US $2,000,000,000	US $3,500,000,000
6% Notes due 2003	6⅞% Debentures due 2023
Price 99.851%	Price 98.725%
Plus accrued interest, if any, from September 27th, 1993	Plus accrued interest, if any, from September 27th, 1993

Upon request, a copy of the Prospectus Supplement and the related Prospectus describing these securities and the issuer may be obtained within any State from any Underwriter who may legally distribute it within such State. The securities are offered only by means of the Prospectus Supplement and the related Prospectus, and this announcement is neither an offer to sell nor a solicitation of any offer to buy.

Goldman, Sachs & Co. **Salomon Brothers Inc.**

CS First Boston **Deutsche Bank AG London** **IBJ International plc**

Merrill Lynch & Co. **J.P. Morgan Securities Inc.** **Morgan Stanley International**

UBS Limited

Banca Commerciale Italiana
Banca di Roma
Gruppo Cassa di Risparmio di Roma
Banca Nazionale del Lavoro
Banco di Napoli
BNP Capital Markets Limited
CARIPLO S.p.A.
CREDITO ITALIANO
Daiwa Europe Limited
Dresdner Bank Aktiengesellschaft
IMI Bank (Lux) S.A.
Istituto Bancario San Paolo di Torino S.p.A.
Lehman Brothers
Monte dei Paschi di Siena
Nomura International
Paribas Capital Markets
Swiss Bank Corporaion
S.G. Warburg Securities
Westdeutsche Landesbank Girozentrale

Source: Reprinted by permission of Euromoney.

used the FRN market to fund their activities in the Euromarket. FRNs pay a semiannual coupon rate reset regularly, usually every 3 or 6 months, at some fixed spread over LIBOR. Continuous resetting of the rate at regular intervals ensured that the price of the note would trade at par (100%). As with all variable-rate instruments, FRNs allowed investors to transfer more of the interest-rate risk to the borrower. This feature rendered it a popular instrument in the 1980s when world markets experienced high and unpredictable interest rates in response to the inflationary pressures of this period. Since then the market appeal of FRNs has weakened.

- **Zero-coupon bonds.** These pay no interest but sell instead at a deep discount. At maturity they are redeemed at full face value. For the issuing corporation the advantage is that no cash is actually paid out until final maturity, while providing for tax savings from the annual deductible amortization of the discounted amount.
  Zeros can be also created by detaching the interest payment from the principal, treating the coupons and the body as separate securities (**stripped bonds**). This concept has been widely used on U.S. Treasury bond issues.
- **Equity bonds.** These have either attached warrants, which give the holder the right to buy shares of the issuing corporation at a specified price; or they are convertible into shares of the issuer at a specified ratio or at a specified price per share.
- **Other types.** Some of the different types of bonds issued include **callable bonds** where the issuer reserves right to redeem these bonds before maturity; **partly-paid bonds** with partial payment upon subscription and the balance to be paid at a later date (down payment of 30% and the balance due in six months); **indexed bonds** with the payment of interest tied to a specific price index (e.g., consumer price index), or the price of a commodity (e.g., oil); **reverse floaters** with coupon payments that rise when the underlying reference rate falls, and vice versa; and **capped bonds** where interest rates are capped at a preset level.

Innovations in the Eurobond Market. With the global Eurobond market very competitive, innovations to appeal to issuers and investors with particular needs have not been uncommon. Three such innovations include the dual currency bonds, catastrophe bonds, and currency cocktail bonds.

Dual currency bonds were introduced in the early 1980s and enjoyed significant investor appeal because of the two different currencies involved. The currency of issue (base currency) is the currency the investor would pay to purchase the bond and is the same currency in which coupon payments are denominated. However, at maturity the principal redemption value is fixed in a second currency. The investor's appeal of the issue lies in the prospect of gain if the exchange rate moves in his favor at bond maturity when the principal is repaid. Appreciation of the exchange rate will translate into a gain while depreciation will result into a loss. For the issuer, the motivation for a dual currency bond is the attractively priced debt service cost of capital, and the potential availability of the second currency in which the firm' future operating revenues will be generated. The most recent issuers of such bonds include Chinese state-owned companies--such as the Export-Import (Exim) Bank of China, and the State Grid Corporation of China both with 2016 issues, and the Three Gorges with a 2015 issue.

Catastrophe (Cat) bonds were introduced in the mid-1990s to enable an issuer or a sponsor (often an insurance or reinsurance company) mitigate a stipulated set of risks by transferring it to capital markets. The rationale behind this move was the need by insurance companies to hedge the risk they would face if a major catastrophe occurred and damages exceeded collected premiums and returns from investments. Despite cat bonds' early start, it was not until a decade later that these instruments exploded in popularity. The financial crisis ushered in a period of ultralow interest rates that sent institutional investors scrambling for higher yields. Investment banks and insurers' own securities-brokerage operations started churning out billions of dollars in catastrophe bonds to meet the growing demand for higher returns by pension plans, investment companies and wealthy families. The bonds pay high interest rates and diversify an investor's portfolio because their returns are largely uncorrelated with the returns on other investment instruments (natural disasters occur randomly and are independent of economic factors). These considerations induced investors to take on the risks of a specified catastrophe, or event occurring, in return for attractive rates of return on their investment. Investors' risk exposure depends on how the bond is structured. Should the qualifying catastrophe or event occur and losses exceed a certain threshold specified in the bond offering, the investor may lose all or part of the principal and unpaid interest, and the issuer will use that money to cover losses (this is what happened to funds that owned hurricane-linked cat bonds when hurricane Katrina struck). Otherwise, the investor will earn a bond yield that would equal the risk free rate plus a premium reflecting the expected probability of risk occurrence.

Inherently risky (rated below investment grade), cat bonds have maturities up to four years or less, and are usually issued through a separate legal structure (a special purpose vehicle) that invests the proceeds in low risk securities. Cat bond sponsors include insurers, reinsurers, corporations, and government agencies. The World Bank issued its first catastrophe bond (2014) to cover natural hazard risks (tropical cyclone and earthquake) in sixteen Caribbean countries. The only national sovereign to issue cat bonds has been Mexico (in 2006 to cover against earthquake risk and in 2009 and 2012 against both earthquake and hurricane risk). It secured insurance coverage by issuing notes directly to bond investors. At year-end 2015, a total of $72 billion of cat bonds and similar investments were outstanding with this amount expected to double in the next several years, a sign that the transfer of risk from the insurance industry to capital markets has opened up access to a seemingly limitless source of funding.

Currency cocktail bonds are bonds tied to a basket of currencies. Interest in these bonds stemmed from issuers' concern for fluctuating exchange rates and their effect on the cost of debt service for foreign currency denominated securities. Indexed to a basket of currencies, currency cocktail bonds offered a more stable cost of debt service than would be true for a single currency issue. Conceptually the same diversification principle that produces a lower standard deviation of expected returns in a portfolio of securities applies to the portfolio of currencies that make up a currency cocktail bond.

A major currency cocktail basket for the denomination of bonds has been the Special Drawing Rights (SDR). The SDR was created by the International Monetary Fund (IMF) in 1969 and was allocated to member countries as a supplementary international reserve asset to support the expansion of world trade and financial flows. The SDR is defined by the IMF as the value of a basket of five currencies--the U.S. dollar, the pound sterling, the Japanese yen, the euro, and, as of October 1, 2016, the Chinese renminbi (RMB). The relative weights for each currency is broadly proportionate to each country's share in international transactions. These weights, reviewed every five years, are used to determine the amounts of each of the five currencies included in the SDR basket until the next valuation period (2021). The value of the SDR in terms of the U.S. dollar is determined daily and posted on the IMF's website. It is calculated as the sum of specific amounts of each basket currency valued in U.S. dollars, on the basis of exchange rates quoted at noon each day in the London market. Exhibit 2.7 identifies the component currencies and respective amounts, and the dollar value of the SDR at the set date.

SDR-denominated bonds were first issued in 1975 and reached a peak in the early 1980s. A recent offer of such bonds has been that of the World Bank in China (2016) in the amount of 2 billion yuan (approximately $2.8 billion). Separately, the China Development Bank, a state-owned bank, is scheduled to follow up with an issue between $300 million and $800 million of SDR notes. Outside of the bond market, SDR-denominated CDs were issued by such banks as Barclays, and Hongkong and Shanghai Banking Corporation (HSBC) while Chase accepted both time deposits and granted loans in SDRs.

In addition to international bond issues in SDRs, financial markets also experienced the offer of bonds denominated in the European Currency Unit (ECU), the precursor to the Euro. Created in March 1979, the ECU represented the weighted index of the currencies of the then European Economic Community member countries.

Unique Attributes of the Eurobond Markets. The Eurobond market owes its existence to several distinct characteristics, the most important of which include market breadth--availability of a wide variety of issues in terms of desired issuer, maturity, quality, currency of denomination and yield; absence of foreign registration and disclosure requirements such as applied in the United States by the Securities and Exchange Commission; greater flexibility in dealing with national authorities given

Exhibit 2.7 SDR Rates as of Thursday, December 1, 2016

Currency	Currency amount under Rule 0-1	Exchange Rate[1]	U.S. dollar equivalent	Percent change in exchange rate against U.S. dollar from previous calculation
Chinese Yuan	1.0174	6.89770	0.147498	0.041
Euro	0.38671	1.06230	0.410802	-0.221
Japanese Yen	11.900	114.38500	0.104035	-0.988
U.K. Pound Sterling	0.085946	1.26210	0.108472	1.357
U.S. Dollar	0.58252	1.00000	0.582520	
			1.353327	
		U.S.S1.00 = SDR	0.738920[2]	0.032[3]
		SDR1 = USS	1.353330[4]	

Footnotes

1 The exchange rates for the Japanese yen and the Chinese renminbi are expressed in terms of currency units per U.S. dollar; other rates are expressed as U.S. dollars per currency unit. Chinese renminbi refers to the name of the currency, while Chinese yuan refers to the currency unit.

2 IMF Rule O-2(a) defines the value of the U.S. dollar in terms of the SDR as the reciprocal of the sum of the equivalents in U.S. dollars of the amounts of the currencies in the SDR basket. Under current IMF procedures, each U.S. dollar equivalent is calculated on the basis of the mid-market rates, as provided to the IMF by the Bank of England, based on spot exchange rates observed at around noon London time (see Bank of England website); the value of the U.S. dollar in terms of the SDR is rounded to six significant digits. The Federal Reseve Bank of New York and the European Central Bank serve as backup providers for these exchange rates. For further details see Method of Collecting Exchange Rates for the Calculation of the Value of the SDR for the Purposes of Rule O-2(a).

3 Percent change from previous calculation.

4 The reciprocal of the value of the U.S dollar in terms of the SDR, rounded to six significant digits.

Source: International Monetary Fund SDR Valuation. http://www.imf.org/external/np/fin/data.rms_sdrv.aspx

that Eurobonds are denominated in foreign currencies and few of the local residents possess such currencies to invest. Two additional attributes of this market are the issue of Eurobonds in bearer form which ensures the anonymity of the investor and his country of residence; and the fact that interest earned by the investor is not subject to a withholding tax.

SOURCING EQUITY IN GLOBAL MARKETS

International transactions in the equity markets remained in the backwater of international finance through the late 1970s. Very few shares traded outside their home markets, and those that did were basically of multinational corporations and as such of interest to arbitrageurs and some institutional investors. However, from the 1980s on international transactions expanded enormously as a result of such factors as deregulation and reforms of local markets, advances in market information and communications technology, privatizations, cross-border mergers and acquisitions, and globalization of stock distribution techniques. These factors expedited the process toward the integration of capital markets around the world. Thus, gross purchases of U.S securities by foreigners increased drastically, as did purchases of foreign securities by U.S investors.

Availability of capital and market depth exhibit significant variation among markets. In terms of overall liquidity, stock markets may be distinguished into the most liquid (e.g., London, NYSE, NASDAQ), the semi-liquid (e.g., Mexico, Taiwan, Australia, Hong Kong, Philippines, and Chile), and the least liquid which offer very little liquidity to their own domestic firms, let alone foreign. Thus, promising firms resident in less liquid markets (emerging markets and many smaller industrial country markets), are motivated to "internationalize" their capital structure by tapping liquid markets to attain the global cost and availability of capital. With London Stock Exchange (LSE), NYSE and NASDAQ the most liquid and prestigious markets, many foreign companies seek to list and trade their shares in these markets.

In developing a strategy to access a foreign equity market, a path usually followed by many publicly traded firms is to first cross-list their shares in a less prestigious foreign market. The next step would be to issue equity in that market. This move affords greater market visibility and larger potential investor audiences which may translate into higher share prices and a pathway to cross-list, and eventually issue, shares on a highly liquid prestigious foreign stock exchange. This strategy accomplishes two objectives--it enables firms to escape dependence from their domestic market and benefit from the lower cost and increased availability of capital in global markets. Over the past decade, many foreign firms raised equity capital outside their home markets by pursuing alternate pathways to the highly liquid prestigious foreign stock exchanges, such as the LSE, NYSE, or NASDAQ. Cross-listing, the initial stage of the process, has several advantages. For the firms that face high cost, or limited availability, of capital in their home capital markets, cross-listing would have a favorable impact on the pricing of the stock. Further, it enhances the corporate image of the firm, it increases the potential for acquisitions through (tax-free) share swaps, and allows use of the stock for compensating local management and employees (e.g., through option plans).

Cross-listing is initiated through the registration and trading of a company's shares on the stock exchange of a foreign country. Compared to shares traded in the domestic market, **Global Registered Shares** (GRSs) have the additional benefit of being traded on equity exchanges in different countries and currencies. For example, the shares of Sony were listed, and traded, in 19 exchanges around the world.

Depositary Receipts constitute an alternate conduit of cross-listing in a foreign equity market. Depositary receipts are negotiable certificates issued by a bank against the underlying shares of the foreign firm held in trust at a custodian bank in the firm's home country. If these certificates are denominated in U.S. dollars, and are issued and traded in the United States, they are referred to as American Depositary Receipts (ADRs). Exhibit 2.8 identifies the types of ADR programs available in the United States--level 1 ADRs can only trade in the over-the-counter (OTC) market, level 2 can be listed on the major stock exchanges, and level 3 permits the direct issue of equity in the U.S. markets. Unlike level 1 which is subject to minimal regulation, level 3 calls for an increased amount of regulatory requirements (e.g., annual reports that comply with GAAP standards, filing of a disclosure form, and prior SEC registration required at level 2). The top three banks that are actively engaged in the issuance of ADRs in the United States are the Bank of New York Mellon, Citigroup and J.P. Morgan Chase.

Exhibit 2.8 American Depositary Receipt (ADR) Programs

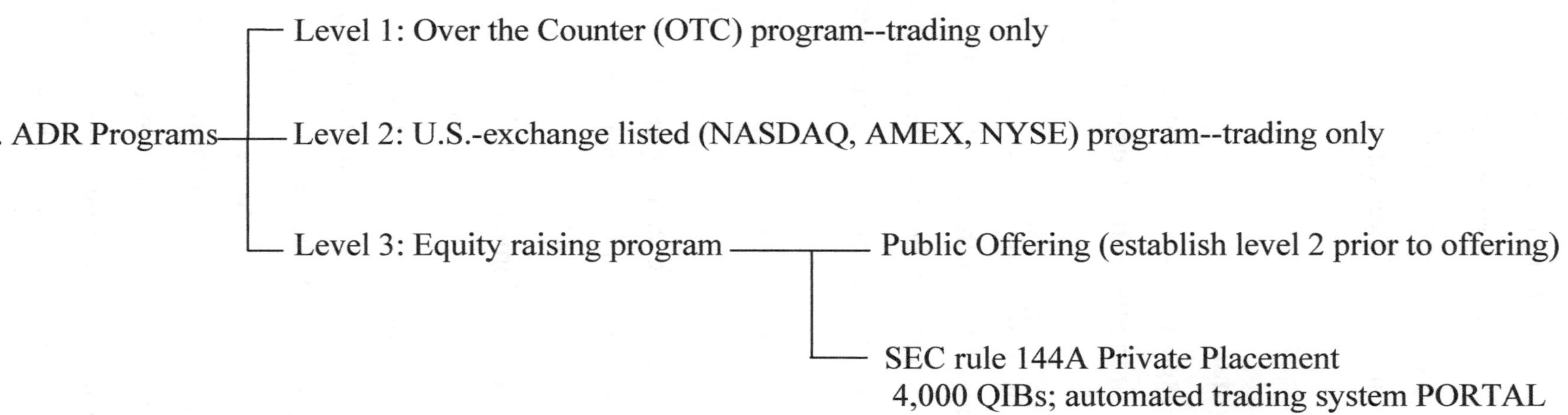

Source: Developed by the author.

Two other forms of depositary receipts are the European Depositary Receipts (EDRs) and Global Depositary Receipts (GDRs) aimed at non-U.S. resident investors and traded mainly in markets outside the United States. Wherever traded, if are created at the initiative of the foreign firm they are referred to as sponsored depositary receipts, to distinguish from unsponsored receipts initiated by interested investors with the consent of the firm whose shares are to be traded.

Alternate Approaches to Raising Equity Capital

A firm raising equity capital in global markets has two alternatives, to go public or private. As seen in Exhibit 9 each of these alternatives involves different strategic options.

Directed Public Share Issue represents one of the two venues for the public sale of shares. Under this strategy the company needs to target the investors of a particular foreign country to market its shares. Company shares may be underwritten in whole or in part by local investment banking firms and may or may not be denominated in local currency.

Euroequity is the alternate option for a public share issue. This venue calls for the underwriting of company shares by an international syndicate of investment banking institutions and entails the simultaneous sale of shares to foreign investors in more than one national market. It may be an initial public offering (IPO) as opposed to a follow-on, a new offering by a firm that has shares already trading in the secondary market. Euroequity provides for the financing of issuers whose domestic markets are too small or inactive to accommodate large distributions. Government privatization of state-owned enterprises is an example of the latter because of the large size of these issues and the need to attract major institutional investors in liquid markets. The UK privatization model of British Telecommunications in 1984 gave prominence to this approach. Since then a number of other government privatizations were implemented through Euroequity issues, including the Telefonos de Mexico $2 billion offer (1991), Yacimientos Petrolíferos Fiscales (YPF) of Argentina $3 billion offer (1993), and Deutsche Telecom $13 billion offer (1996). The world's largest Euroequity offering was the 2010 sale of $78 billion in shares by Petrobras, with Banco Bradesco the lead

Exhibit 2.9 Sourcing Equity Globally: Strategic Options

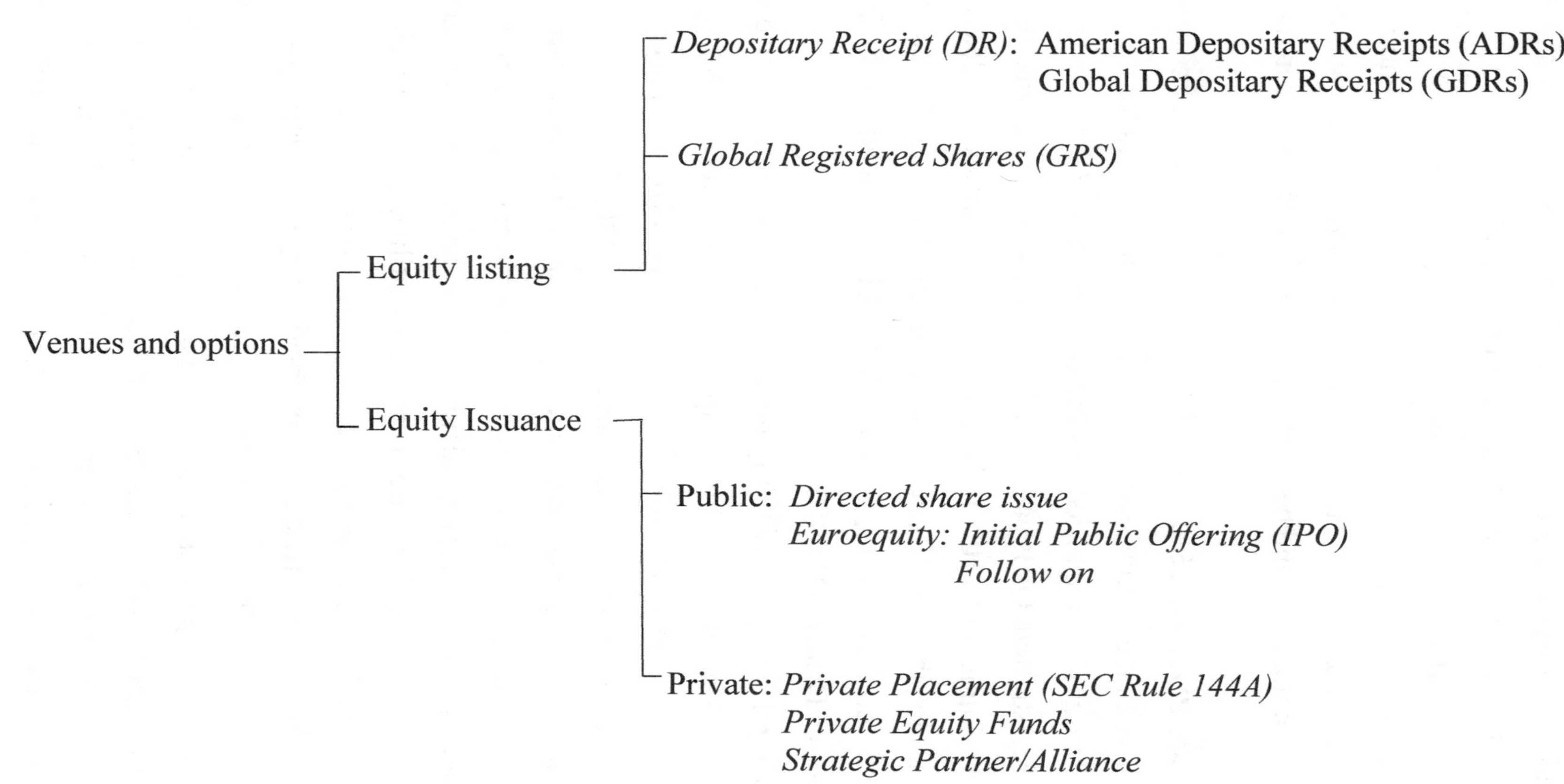

Source: Developed by the author.

underwriter and Bank of America Merrill Lynch, Citigroup, Banco Itau and Morgan Stanley acting as global bookrunners (book-running managers).

Private Placement provides for the raising of equity capital privately. An investment banking firm, acting as an agent for a fee, may help identify a large institutional investor or a group of such investors, to purchase the whole issue. Traditionally, insurance companies and pension funds are major investors in the private placement market.

Rule 144A Private Placement Sale is a private placement named after Rule 144A of the Securities and Exchange Commission. This regulation provides for the sale of an issue (domestic or foreign), to Qualified Institutional Buyers (QIBs) in the United States, without SEC registration. QIBs cannot be individuals, only nonbank institutions that own and invest a minimum of $100 million or more in securities on a discretionary basis. QIBs may trade their positions among themselves, facilitated through establishment of an automated trading system (PORTAL) operated by the National Association of Securities Dealers (NASD).

Private Equity funds is a professionally managed pool of funds invested in firms with the intention of taking them private, improving their management, and then reselling them, in one to three years, privately or publicly. Private equity funds are usually limited partnerships made up of institutional and wealthy investors.

Strategic Alliance is an organizational and legal construct wherein two or more firms act in concert to attain a common objective. Whether because of the globalization momentum, the rapid pace of technological innovation, or corporate constraints of capital and managerial resources, firms are increasingly utilizing strategic alliances to explore opportunities outside core business lines. The urge to collaborate in the sharing of risk and resources is intense worldwide and covers virtually every aspect of economic activity (e.g., heavy engineering and defense, business and financial services, entertainment and media, and pharmaceutical companies). Strategic alliances include different types of contractual collaborations, such as joint marketing and servicing agreements (with each partner representing the other in certain markets), shared resource and core competencies arrangements (pilot projects and R&D funding agreements), and joint ventures (two or more companies form a new entity to exploit a business opportunity that neither could do alone-- e.g., enter into a foreign market or introduce a new product or service). Another form of strategic alliance is when two firms that view each other as stable and friendly may exchange shares of ownership between themselves to defend against a possible takeover. Although all alliances across industries are not equity linked, recent years have experienced a dramatic surge in equity-based alliances wherein each of the partners in the alliance acquires an equity stake in the other partner firm. These equity investments are typically made through a direct purchase of the shares in the firm via a private placement.

3 PATTERNS AND TRENDS IN OFFSHORE BANKING

Recent decades have witnessed the proliferation of offshore banking markets in different parts of the world. Functioning as conduits for the flow of foreign capital, offshore banking markets have been among the fastest-growing venues in international finance. This chapter reviews the forces responsible for the development of offshore banking centers, distinguishes among the different types of offshore markets, and identifies the financial standing of the most important amongst them.

GLOBAL FINANCIAL TRENDS

The 1990s experienced an explosion in international banking activity. From primarily a domestic enterprise, banking has become an increasingly global business. Total international bank claims that stood at $442 billion in 1975 grew to over $10 trillion (a twenty threefold increase) by the turn of century. Some of the developments that contributed in the international expansion of banking activity include the growth of multinational corporations and their demand for international financial services, the collapse of the Soviet Union and the globalization of the market for financial services, reduced and streamlined bank regulation worldwide, and advances in technology and communications. The drastic decrease in the cost of recording, transmitting, and processing financial information made it cheaper for banks to extend and maintain real-time control of their international operations. While some banks responded to the new environment by focusing on core or niche business, others followed strategies aimed at providing fully integrated global financial services to benefit from synergies between various products. These banks positioned themselves to handle a sizable portion of the growing flow of capital among nations.

Although the financial crisis (2008) and the ensuing recession dealt a setback to cross-border financial flows, they have since bounced back and surpassed their pre-crisis level, reaching a record of $27.5 trillion by the end of the first quarter of 2016. The growing momentum of cross-border financial flows over time has contributed to the development of international financial centers in various parts of the world. These centers have come to play an important role in facilitating the flow of capital around the globe. The conditions and practices that can make an international financial center a successful, competitive offshore banking center (OBC) are many and varied.

ORIGINS AND GENERAL CHARACTERISTICS OF OBCs

The origin of international financial centers may be traced to tax havens. The earliest historical reference to this concept dates from the second century B.C. when the Romans, to undercut the Greek island state of Rhodes, setup the nearby island of Delos as a tax free port. Rhodes' commanding geographic location in Eastern Mediterranean sea lanes caused the island to impose a tax of 2 percent on all trade that passed through it. For that tax, Rhodes was to keep sea routes free from pirates. The Roman move to grant Delos a tax free status proved detrimental for Rhodes' tax revenues; within a year's time they declined precipitously causing the eventual collapse of the island's economy.

In the less distant past, European powers (Dutch, English, and Spanish) presented early America as a tax haven to entice its colonization. Historians contend that for many of the early settlers avoidance of European taxes was a major cause for their drive to immigrate. Interestingly, the impetus for the American Revolution originated in the endeavor of English authorities to increase taxes on colonial America.

In more modern times, the traditional dominance of financial capitals, led by London and New York, has been complemented by the development of international financial centers in new corners of the world. These evolved from domestic centers as they set out to assist their clientele in trade and investment activities. In some instances, the transformation process was set in motion when individual governments took action to establish an environment free from the regulatory framework that governed their domestic financial market. A few jurisdictions complemented these measures with the offer of banking licenses with relatively little scrutiny. However, it was not until the

1970s and the onset of the oil crisis that these measures grew in appeal and gave recognition to offshore financial centers. Banks' active role in the recycling of the petrodollars during that crisis contributed to the growth of offshore centers, in size and importance, and led to the expansion of their international network to include current or former British colonies or Crown Dependencies some of which were successful tax havens. The presence of banks with an established reputation of integrity added to the sophistication of these centers and led to their reference as OBCs.

While the term originates from the Channel Islands being "offshore" from the United Kingdom, and while most offshore banks are located in island nations to this day, the term is used figuratively to refer to banks in any location. Thus, banks in landlocked Switzerland, and Luxembourg are described as offshore banks. The comprehensive definition of an OBC may be attributed to McCarthy, who identified it as:

> "cities, areas or countries which have made a conscious effort to attract offshore banking business, i.e. nonresident foreign currency denominated business, by allowing relatively free entry and by adopting a flexible attitude where taxes, levies and regulations are concerned."[1]

The distinction between an OBC and other financial centers may be emphasized by reference to the alternate modes of borrower/lender transactions that may occur in a financial marketplace. Conceptually, there are four possible transactions: between domestic borrowers and domestic lenders, between domestic borrowers and foreign lenders, between domestic lenders and foreign borrowers, and between foreign borrowers and foreign lenders. While the first is purely domestic situation, the three remaining cases are examples of international banking transactions. By definition, traditional financial capitals permit all three types of international transactions. Offshore banking, on the other hand, is a term usually applied only to the last category in which transactions are conducted between two or more foreign parties. Essentially,

[1] Ian McCarthy, "Offshore Banking Centers: Benefits and Costs," Finance and Development, December 1979, Vol. 16, No. 4, p. 45.

offshore centers function as channels through which foreign funds pass. That is, these markets serve as financial intermediaries between nonresident suppliers of funds and nonresident users of funds. Unlike traditional centers, offshore centers have been subject to minimal regulation, taxation, or governmental controls over portfolio decisions by banking units. Exhibit 3.1 identifies some of the more important OBC locations by geographic area. As seen in this Exhibit the competition for offshore banking is very intense, and the market is crowded throughout.

TYPES OF OBCs

In terms of legal format, three distinct types of offshore centers have emerged over the years. The first and most common type (traditional OBC) provides for the establishment of an offshore sector alongside the domestic financial market by creating an environment free from the taxation and regulation imposed upon the latter. A second type, introduced by the United States in 1981 in the form of international banking facilities (IBFs), provides for special institutional arrangements within established financial centers. The third kind, integrated market, makes no distinction between the foreign and domestic transactions. Exhibit 3.2 distinguishes OBCs based on alternate criteria--geographic size, function (market of origination of funds versus market of their use) and legal format.

Traditional OBCs

In the most common type of OBC, residents in the host country are prohibited from conducting offshore transactions. These centers attract foreign banks by offering low or no taxes, minimal regulation, sophisticated telecommunications networks, and a local supply of skilled labor. In addition to enjoying the financial advantages OBCs offer, foreign banks seek strategic time zone locations that enable them to capitalize on the opening and closing of international markets, stable governments that can provide safe havens for funds from politically unstable countries, banking secrecy and client confidentiality.

In the 1960s, the Bahamas and Cayman Islands established the first OBCs in order to attract offshore investments from the United States and Europe. (Prior to that date,

Exhibit 3.1 Offshore Banking Centers

Europe

Channel Islands	Liechtenstein
Cyprus	Luxembourg
Gibraltar	Malta
Ireland	Switzerland
Isle of Man	United Kingdom

The Americas

Anguilla	Curacao
Antigua	Grenada
Aruba	Montserrat
Bahamas	St. Kitts and Nevis
Barbados	Saint Lucia
Belize	Saint Vincent and the Grenadines
Bermuda	Turks and Caicos Islands
British Virgin Islands	United States: IBFs
Cayman Islands	Uruguay

Asia

Bahrain	Nauru
Hong Kong	Philippines
Japan: JOM	Seychelles
Macau	Singapore
Malaysia (Labuan)	Taiwan
Mauritius	Thailand
Samoa	Vanuatu

Source: Developed by the author.

Exhibit 3.2 Offshore Banking Centers by Size, Function and Legal Format

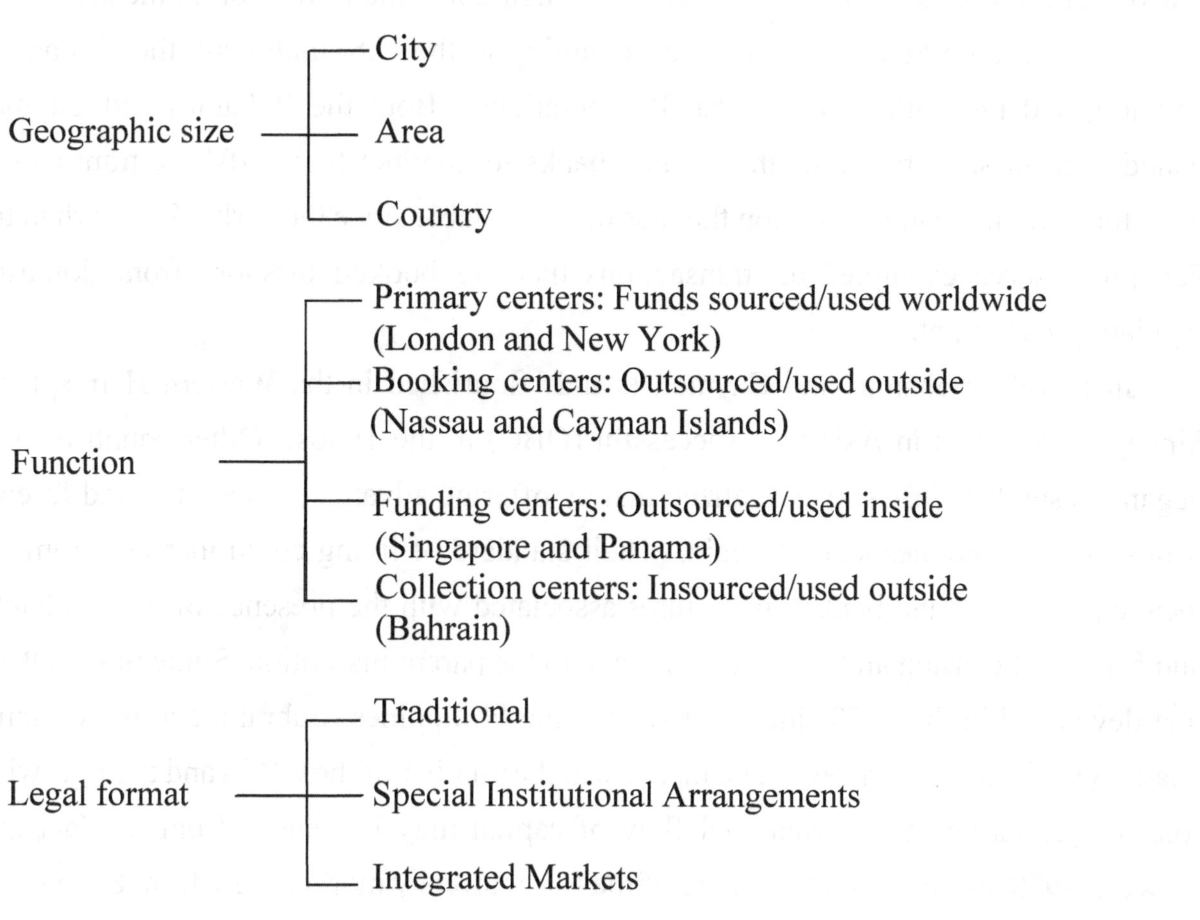

Source: Developed by the author.

most international transactions took place in London, New York, or Zurich.) The Caribbean centers have succeeded because of their convenient location in the same time zone as the United States, their easy accessibility to the U.S. mainland, the absence of taxation, and their allowance of "shell" operations. Both the Bahamas and Cayman Islands permit shell branches that enable banks to conduct their offshore transactions from the U.S. mainland, an option that has been available since the early 1970s, when the Federal Reserve exempted all transactions that are booked offshore from domestic regulatory constraint.

Just as the Bahamas and Cayman Islands flourished in the Western Hemisphere, Singapore emerged in Asia as a successful (OBC) in the 1960s. Other countries then began to establish OBCs; they realized that by offering advantages that attracted foreign banks, their economies stood to gain. Their standard of living could increase from the local employment and bank expenditures associated with the presence of foreign banks and from the licensing and other fees charged to the parent institution. Some of the OBCs that developed in the 1970s include Panama, the Philippines, Bahrain, and the Channel Islands (Jersey and Guernsey). The increase in the number of the OBCs and their growing role in facilitating the international flow of capital may be sensed from the fact that between 1970 and 1981, OBCs' share of the Eurocurrency market grew from 8.7 percent to 28.5 percent. This growth contributed to the decentralization of the Eurocurrency market, which until 1970, had existed almost exclusively in London and a few Western European centers.

In the 1980s and 1990s the number of OBCs proliferated. As the world economy continued to grow and international trade expanded, so did the size of the Eurocurrency market and the role of the OBCs. Among the more important OBCs to be established during this period were Aruba, Cyprus, Grenada, the Isle of Man, Labuan (Malaysia), Malta, Nauru and Vanuatu. Some of the more recent providers of offshore banking services include Mauritius, Seychelles and Vietnam.

For traditional OBCs to be successful they must satisfy certain conditions identified in Exhibit 3.3. Some of these conditions can be met through enactment of legislation and other deliberate governmental policies. Others depend on factors beyond a country's

Exhibit 3.3 Conditions for the Development of Traditional OBCs

---

Crucial conditions are of such importance that in their absence offshore financial activities would be impossible to undertake

- political stability
- confidentiality of records
- flexible banking laws and regulations
- no currency conversion limitations
- low, or no, domestic taxes.

Significant conditions aid in the development and maintenance of offshore financial services

- possession of adequate infrastructure, such as electronic and telephone communication
- availability of qualified personnel
- advantageous geographical location

Desirable conditions can greatly enhance the attractiveness of a specific offshore financial center

- low cost of operation
- favorable government policies
- mentality of the general population toward the offshore business
- reasonable fees and levies
- languages and other

Source: Developed by the author.

control, such as geographic location, time zone, international political developments, policies of neighboring countries. Based upon their relative importance for the successful establishment and operation of an OBC, Exhibit 3.3 distinguishes these conditions into crucial, significant and desirable.

The IBF Model

Late in 1981, in an attempt to attract Eurodollar business into the United States from offshore locations, the Federal Reserve introduced what developed into a second model of offshore banking market. It authorized U.S. banks, including U.S. branches and agencies of foreign banks, to establish international banking facilities (IBFs). IBFs are located mainly in the major U.S. financial centers and operate as record keeping entities. They are permitted to conduct international banking business (such as receiving foreign deposits and making foreign loans) largely without restrictions that apply to the domestic market (for example, reserve requirements and insurance assessment on deposits). IBF deposit and loan customers are limited to foreign residents, including banks, other IBFs, and the parent bank. All nonbank deposits must be nonnegotiable time deposits with a maturity of at least two business days and a minimum size of $100,000. Time deposits offered to other banking institutions (e.g., foreign banks, foreign central banks, official institutions, other IBFs, and the parent bank) can have maturities of one day or longer. Issuance of negotiable instruments, such as certificates of deposits (CDs), is prohibited. In addition to these restrictions, IBFs are not able to offer secret trust accounts and they are subject to federal income taxes.

The establishment of IBFs attracted a significant portion of offshore business away from other centers, especially from jurisdictions in the Caribbean. However, this development did not threaten the existence of these centers because the latter can legally transact business with U.S. residents, an activity not permitted for the IBFs. IBF growth received significant impetus from foreign-bank owned IBFs because depositors prefer--from a risk perspective--to hold their balances within the political and legal jurisdiction of the United States rather than offshore. IBFs' share of total international assets grew over time to a little over one-third of U.S. banks' external positions in all currencies. This suggests that IBFs have had the intended effect of shifting international banking business from offshore to onshore U.S. locations.

In 1986 Japan established its own offshore market, to promote liberalization and internationalization of its financial markets. The Japanese Offshore Market (JOM) is similar in concept to the U.S. IBFs. Japanese banks may establish a set of segregated accounts that are exempt from specified domestic regulations. The main depositors and borrowers in this market are the Japanese banks, themselves, and their foreign branches. The Euroyen is their currency of denomination for their interbank transactions. The JOM has proven popular particularly among regional and small banks that previously had no direct access to international markets. Since its establishment, the JOM has expanded rapidly, with more than half of the international assets of Japanese banks held in this market. Both the U.S. and Japanese arrangements offer an alternative model of an offshore market, by providing special institutional provisions within established financial centers, such as New York and Tokyo. This model has also been used in other financial centers, such as Bangkok (Thailand) and Taipei (Taiwan).

Integrated Markets

Centers where financial transactions are liberalized for both residents and non-residents constitute a third type of offshore market. In this type of model, domestic and foreign transactions are integrated and hence there is no distinction between onshore and offshore transactions between non-residents. Switzerland and centers like London and Hong Kong are examples.

GROWTH RECORD

With the exception of Bahamas and Cayman Islands, where banks may operate through shell branches, an offshore banking presence in other markets usually takes the form of a branch office or a subsidiary of the parent bank. The primary goal of most offshore banks is to attract deposits and grant loans in international markets (e.g., placement of funds in the interbank market and syndicated credits). In traditional OBCs, some offshore banks specialize in attracting foreign deposits to fund the credit needs of their home country.

The ability of banks to attract deposits is a key factor in their success. Depositors choose to conduct their business in particular OBCs for a variety of factors, including personal, cultural, and emotional reasons, as well as more purely financial considerations, such as the costs of banking services, the regulatory environment, and tax laws. The availability of banking personnel who speak their language is another important concern for many depositors. Others seek to achieve safety for their investments by spreading their funds among several centers throughout the world. As a result of their diversified clientele, some banks have established offices in more than one center in order to appeal to a broader spectrum of depositors.

Exhibit 3.4 shows the volume of cross-border claims of by banks in select major offshore banking centers at the end of the first quarter of 2016. As seen in this Exhibit, the JOM held $3.4 trillion in foreign assets, the largest share held by any single OBC. This amount represented a nine fold increase over its 2011 stake and portrayed a surge in the business conducted at offices of Japanese banks in centers outside Japan. Trailing in importance were the U.S. IBFs with holdings of worldwide assets valued at $3.1 trillion. This is all the more impressive when considering that in 2011 the corresponding amount stood at $52 billion. The rapid increase in worldwide assets reflected the robust growth in the share of U.S. banks in external banking activity.

Hong Kong, a leading offshore financial center in Asia, held $1.3 trillion in foreign assets. Its liberal banking regulation and prime location in the Asia-Pacific region contributed to the influx of substantial numbers of local and foreign banks, international investment banking houses, and portfolio managers, all of which turned Hong Kong into a highly active international financial center. Over time it has grown into a major hub for the arrangement, syndication and management of eurocredits to Asian Pacific borrowers. A key concern has been its political stature. Expiration of a 99-year lease on June 30, 1997, marked the end of British rule in Hong Kong and its return to China at the status of Special Administrative Region. It has been the general belief that China will adhere to its commitment in a 1984 agreement with Britain that provides for Hong Kong to keep its present status for a period of 50 years. The sustained financial prominence of Hong Kong is of great importance to China.

Exhibit 3.4 Cross Border Positions of Banks in Select Markets
(in billions of dollars, Quarter 1, 2016)

Market	Amount
Bahamas	$197.9
Bahrain	138.7
Cayman Islands	1,160.9
Cyprus	26.1
Guernsey	142.9
Hong Kong	1,259.1
Isle of Man	55.4
Japan	
Offshore Market	3,371.6
Jersey	62.5
Luxembourg	649.2
Macao	104.2
Panama	57.0
Singapore	708.9
Switzerland	804.4
United States	
IBFs	3,106.4
All reporting countries, total	**$27,507.8**

Source: Bank for International Settlements, *Statistical Bulletin*, September 2016, p. 8. http://www.bis.org/statistics/bulletin1609.htm

The Cayman Islands with $1.2 trillion in foreign assets has played an important role in offshore banking. A British Overseas Territory the Caymans are attractive to outside banks because they possess a number of the attributes identified in Exhibit 3, including a location in the same time zone as the United States, easy accessibility to the U.S. mainland, allowance of shell operations, and absence of taxation. American banks are a major force in the Caymans and the Caribbean offshore markets in general.

Switzerland, with foreign assets of $804 billion, has been a preeminent offshore center with a long-established reputation for its sophisticated financial services. A federal republic of 26 cantons, it draws its origin from a loose confederation of states that forged a protective alliance at the end of the 12th century. Landlocked and mountainous it is distinguished for its linguistic and cultural diversity and its political neutrality which was internationally recognized at the Congress of Vienna (1815). Its long-standing economic stability together with Swiss bank confidentiality (nondisclosure of customers' financial information) have proved instrumental in attracting considerable amounts of foreign funds. This has been especially true during periods of international crises--political, or economic--when the Swiss franc turns into a refuge currency; much as it did during both World Wars. Some of the issues that have eroded Swiss bank secrecy in recent years include the claims for reparations by descendants of holocaust survivors and their out-of-court settlement (1999), criminalizing money laundering (e.g., enactment of anti-money laundering legislation), and the qualification of tax fraud as predicate offense to money laundering (2016) following the Union Bank of Switzerland (UBS) enticement of its clients to defraud the United States (2009).

Singapore, with foreign asset holdings of $709 billion, is a major OBC in the Asia-Pacific region. Like Hong Kong, it enjoys a strategic location and a British-influenced efficient civil service and a well-developed service (e.g., legal and accounting) infrastructure. However, its early development as an OBC diverged from that of Hong Kong because of key differences in the operating environments for banks. The Monetary Authority of Singapore (MAS), the island-state's central bank, has pursued a policy of active regulation of banking activity, and it was its calculated policy decision that launched Singapore as an OBC. Singapore has evolved into the fifth largest global trader in derivatives, the fourth major foreign exchange market in the world, the dominant center for the issue of international bonds in Asia, a principal communications center for the region (e.g., for Disney, and HBO), and a prime base for high tech manufacturing companies.

Luxembourg (formally the Grand Duchy of Luxembourg) held $649 billion in foreign assets in 2016. Landlocked, it is one of the oldest and most established OBCs in Europe dating its origin to a 1929 law that exempted holding companies from significant taxation. Revised in 1983 to expand its scope, it was later replaced by a new tax regime (2007) that complied with the EMU guidelines. In addition to holding companies, Luxembourg is the home to such financial institutions as banks, investment companies, insurance and reinsurance companies, and Clearstream, a clearing house for transactions in marketable securities. Growth of Luxembourg's external banking activity reflects a variety of factors, such as its political stability, good communications, easy access from other European centers, strict bank secrecy laws, multilingual professional personnel, absence of reserve requirements for banks, and a comparative tax advantage over neighboring countries.

Bahamas share of foreign assets was close to $200 billion in 2016. A former British colony and an independent nation since 1973, Bahamas' offshore sector experienced rapid growth from the 1960s onward. It has been the home of many international corporations, and such financial institutions as banks, trust companies, and investment companies. Some of the island-state's key attributes include its easy access from the U.S. mainland, location in the same time zone as New York, the absence of taxation, allowance for shell operations, excellent communications networks, and strict bank secrecy laws. As a result of money laundering activity in the early 1980s, the country enacted comprehensive anti-money laundering legislation (1996), and its central bank has been monitoring compliance of financial reporting requirements.

Numerous other jurisdictions provide offshore banking to a greater or lesser degree. Exhibit 4 identifies some of these jurisdictions along with their respective shares of foreign assets. Cyprus, the smallest of the centers cited, exhibited unprecedented growth in the last two decades. Despite a 1974 Turkish invasion that partitioned the island into separate Greek and Turkish communities, the Greek-dominated Republic of Cyprus emerged as the principal offshore banking center in eastern Mediterranean. It is close to Eastern Europe, the Middle East, and Africa and its time zone straddles the closing of the financial centers in the East and the opening of financial centers in the West. This location, seven hours ahead of New York and seven hours behind Tokyo, gave Cyprus a desirable trading window for portfolio transactions by banking units. Like other major international financial centers where offshore banking activities have flourished, Cyprus offers a favorable regulatory and tax environment, efficient telecommunication and transportation facilities, banking secrecy and client confidentiality.

OECD TRANSPARENCY STANDARDS

With the growth of offshore banking, problems have become inevitable. Some of them were induced by differences in national regulation and regulatory oversight while others emanated from illegal practices, such as fraud, political corruption and money laundering. The monetary authorities of the major industrialized countries sought to address these issues through collaborative action in the framework of the Organization for Economic Cooperation and Development (OECD). A major step in this direction was OECD's 2000 report *Towards Global Tax Co-operation: Progress in Identifying and Eliminating Harmful Tax Practices*,[2] which identified 47 jurisdictions as tax havens based on their preferential tax regimes for financial services and the absence of procedures for the exchange of tax information. The immediate result of this report was that within two years (2000-2002), 31 of these jurisdictions made formal commitments to implement OECD's standards of transparency and exchange of information and were removed from the list of tax havens. However it was not until the onset of the financial crisis (2008) that economic and political pressure on offshore centers started to come to a head. The shortfall of tax revenues to support social programs and the accompanying bailout of banks and other firms, caused sizeable fiscal problems for nearly all countries. In the United States alone tax evasion by businesses and individuals was estimated by the U.S. Senate to account for tax revenue losses of $100 billion a year.[3] In many other

[2]http://www.oecd.org/ctp/harmful/2000progressreporttowardsglobaltaxco-operationprogressinidentifyingandeliminatingharmfultaxpractices.htm

[3]OECD, "Fighting Tax Evasion." https://web.archive.org/web/20120413120533/http://www.oecd.org/document/21/0,3746,en_2649_37427_42344853_1_1_1_37427,00.html

An anti-tax haven pressure group estimated the annual cost of tax evasion worldwide at $3.1 trillion, with an aggregate between $21 trillion and $32 trillion in financial assets sheltered in unreported tax havens worldwide. These estimates do not include real estate and other non-financial assets owned through offshore structures. Tax Justice Network, "Size of the Problems," November 2011. http://www.taxjustice.net/topics/more/size-of-the-problem/

http://www.taxjustice.net/cms/upload/pdf/The_Price_of_Offshore_Revisited_Presser_120722.pdf

See also "The Cost of Tax Abuse"

http://www.tackletaxhavens.com/Cost_of_Tax_Abuse_TJN%20Research_23rd_Nov_2011.pdf

countries the cost of tax evasion run into billions of euros. The loss in tax revenues combined with the need to crackdown on money laundering increased the pressure on offshore centers and undermined the value of financial secrecy.

Since 1998, the OECD has led a charge against harmful tax practices, by targeting mainly the activities of tax havens. OECD-issued guidelines define tax havens, provide a framework of cooperation with countries seeking to administer their tax statutes, and impose sanctions on the "uncooperative tax havens." The defining criteria put forward were the following[4]

- *No or nominal taxes.* Jurisdictions that impose zero or nominal taxes (generally, or in special circumstances) and offer (or are perceived to offer) themselves as a place to be used by nonresidents to escape high taxes in their country of residence.
- *Protection of personal financial information.* Jurisdictions that have laws or administrative practices under which businesses and individuals can benefit from strict rules and other protections against scrutiny by foreign tax authorities. This prevents the disclosure of information about taxpayers who are benefiting from the low tax jurisdiction.
- *Lack of transparency.* Jurisdictions that lack transparency in the operation of related legislative, legal or administrative provisions. The OECD is concerned that laws should be applied openly and consistently, and that information needed by foreign tax authorities to determine a taxpayer's correct tax liability is available. Lack of transparency in one country can make it difficult, if not impossible, for other tax authorities to apply their laws effectively. Examples of lack of transparency include "secret rulings," negotiated tax rates, limited regulatory supervision, and government's lack of legal access to financial records.

As follows from the preceding, the three key factors that characterize a tax haven, as per OECD criteria, are zero or nominal taxes on foreign investors, no disclosure or exchange of information, and lack of transparency. In determining whether or not a jurisdiction is a tax haven, the initial consideration is whether it has no or nominal taxes. In the affirmative, the other two considerations--whether or not there is an exchange of information and transparency--must be evaluated. Having no or nominal taxes is not

[4]OECD, Countering Offshote Tax Evasion, September, 2009. https://www.oecd.org/ctp/harmful/42469606.pdf

sufficient, by itself, to describe a jurisdiction as a tax haven. The OECD recognizes the right of every jurisdiction to decide on the administration and enforcement of its domestic tax law--e.g., whether to impose direct taxes and if so to determine the appropriate tax rate.

Mounting international pressure on tax havens prompted several countries to revise, or agree to revise, their policies to have their names removed from OECD's blacklist. By early 2009 the number of countries remaining on the list was down to three. Yet, the prospect of sanctions by an upcoming meeting of the Group of 20 (G-20) countries (the world's most advanced economies), produced a consensus and staved off any retaliatory measures. One of the last three was Liechtenstein (formally the principality of Liechtenstein), which consented to avail data on bank clients but only in response to specific tax fraud investigations by foreign governments.[5] Officially it became the 62nd signatory (2013) of the *Multilateral Convention on Mutual Administrative Assistance in Tax Matters (the Convention)* which provides a comprehensive framework of tax cooperation against tax evasion and avoidance, a top priority for all countries.[6] A 2016 count of the convention signatories amounted to 107 and include a wide range of countries, e.g., all G-20 countries, all BRICS (five major emerging national economies), all OECD countries, major financial centers and an increasing number of developing countries.

Development of the standards of transparency and information exchange in tax matters is attributed to OECD's premier international body the Global Forum on Transparency and Exchange of Information for Tax Purposes ("Global Forum"). Established in 2000 and restructured in 2009, the Global Forum works under the auspices of the OECD and the G-20 and its membership now includes 137 jurisdictions and the European Union. Through an in-depth two-stage peer review process, the

[5]The Liechtenstein Declaration, March 12, 2009.
https://www.oecd.org/countries/liechtenstein/42826280.pdf
[6]A Boost to Transparency and International Tax Co-operation
http://www.oecd.org/tax/exchange-of-tax-information/a-boost-to-transparency-and-international-tax-cooperation.htm

Global Forum monitors that its members abide by the standard of transparency and exchange of information they have committed to implement. A crucial part of the peer review process has been the use of ratings to recognize progress in essential elements and the overall standing of a jurisdiction.

A major impetus for international tax cooperation was the enactment by the U.S. Congress of the Foreign Account Tax Compliance Act (FATCA) of 2010. Aiming to combat tax evasion by U.S.-based businesses and individuals, this law forces foreign financial institutions to disclose their American clients. Highlights of this law are presented in Appendix 3A.

APPENDIX 3A

FOREIGN ACCOUNT TAX COMPLIANCE ACT (FATCA)

Enacted in 2010 as part of the U.S. legislation Hiring Incentives to Restore Employment (HIRE), FATCA aims to combat tax evasion by U.S. taxpayers with investments in offshore accounts. To this end the law calls on foreign financial institutions to identify such taxpayers by reporting them to the U.S. Internal Revenue Service. Specifically, the law requires

(a) U.S. taxpayers with financial assets outside the United States in excess of $50,000 to report these assets to the IRS (beginning with 2012 for assets held in taxable years on or after January 1, 2011). Failure to report will result in a penalty of $10,000 (and a penalty of up to $50,000 for continued failure).

(b) Foreign financial institutions (FFI) to report directly to the IRS information about financial accounts held by U.S. taxpayers, or by foreign entities in which U.S. taxpayers hold a substantial ownership interest (FFI reporting begins in 2013). If there is no sufficient information about the identity of the taxpayer or the foreign entity, the FFI must identify the direct and indirect owners' status and determine whether they are U.S. accounts.

IMPLEMENTATION BY FOREIGN FINANACIAL INSTITUTIONS

FATCA requires FFIs to enter into an agreement with the IRS to disclose this information (become a "participating institution"). FFIs that do not agree to do this will suffer a 30 percent withholding tax on all U.S. payments (including gross proceeds from sale of securities) made to:

(a) Non-participating FFIs

(b) Individual account holders that fail to provide sufficient information whether or not they are a U.S. person

(c) Foreign entity account holders that fail to provide sufficient information about the identity of its U.S. owners.

FATCA provisions apply to all U.S. financial and non-financial entities abroad, foreign financial institutions (FFIs), and non-financial foreign entities (NFFEs). FATCA's definition of FFIs is broad to include hedge funds, private equity funds, and investment companies (e.g., insurance firms that sell cash value products).

FATCA EFFECTS

The scheduled implementation of FATCA on January 1, 2013, triggered some noteworthy international developments.

Select Western European Countries

France, UK, Italy, Spain, and Germany issued a joint statement with the U.S. Treasury for an intergovernmental approach to improving international tax compliance and implementation of FATCA. The FATCA partners agreed to pursue the necessary legislation to require the FFIs in their jurisdiction to identify US accounts and transmit information about those accounts to the IRS.

The US Treasury, on its part, has asserted that it is willing to reciprocate on an automatic basis the collection and exchange of information on accounts held in US financial institutions by residents of the other countries. The statement does not contemplate exemption from FATCA of any jurisdiction.

The US Treasury has stated that it intends to use this agreement as a model to work with other countries.

Switzerland

The assault of foreign laws and regulations on Swiss banks, including the imposition of huge fines and criminal charges, has prompted the following course of action.

(a) Swiss government has been negotiating with the US government to pay a fine in billions of dollars to settle all claims and charges against the leading Swiss banks without admitting guilt or singling out individual banks. It is hoped that such a deal would allow the Swiss banking system to move forward under the new rules without being on the defensive. It has already signed direct deals with England and Germany.

(b) Swiss banks, in turn, have taken several measures including
- Adoption of informal rules that prohibit members of the senior staff and wealth management group to travel to the United States, even to change planes or go to Disney World on a holiday.
- Closing down of branches and offices in the United States.

- Refusal to take accounts of US citizens anywhere in the world, even if there is a very legitimate reason for these accounts. Swiss banks are not alone in this move. It is almost impossible for an American to open an account with any bank, in any jurisdiction, outside the United States.
- Tightening up on spying by not issuing working permits for Americans to work with Swiss banks.

Other Offshore Centers

The reaction of West European countries and Switzerland to FATCA has prompted clients that consider absolute secrecy essential, to seek safer jurisdictions. Given the mobility of capital, strong competition has been developing for funds by Singapore, Mauritius, and Dubai. Developing trends indicate that:

- Eighty percent of US dollars outside of the United States are held in Asia.
- Luxembourg and Jersey still have a foothold in Europe, and
- Panama is growing in the Americas.

4 OVERVIEW OF SELECT BANKING SYSTEMS

As the repercussions from the financial crisis of the last decade faded out, commercial banks around the world resumed their growth momentum, thriving again. The assets of the world's ten largest banks experienced marked growth reaching a combined total of $26.61 trillion in 2016. With the exception of two U.S.-based banks, the rest institutions in the list are located in foreign countries. As seen in Exhibit 4.1, Chinese banks occupy four of the top five places. Based on capitalization criteria, the top ten banks had a combined total market capitalization of $1.65 trillion and included four U.S. banks, 4 Chinese banks a UK and an Australian bank. Wells Fargo was the world's largest bank with market capitalization of $254 billion.

Although Chinese banks figured prominently among the world's top ten institutions, the country's slowing momentum has been a concern for its banking industry. In 2016, China's gross domestic product grew by 6.9 percent, the slowest reported rate in a quarter century. Economic deceleration caused profits to plateau at the country's top banks. A 6.7 percent GDP growth rate in 2016, supported by an increase in government spending, was in line with market expectations and indicated that the country's lenders may be entering a consolidation phase after years of world beating growth.

Despite China's slowdown and economic transition, IMF's World Economic Outlook forecasts global economic growth of over 3.4 percent for 2017 sustainable through most of the late teens. Emerging markets are projected to experience a strong growth of about 4.5 percent while the outlook for advanced economies is a 2 percent rate of growth. These economic forecasts indicate improved prospects for global financial markets and the banking industry through the closing years of this decade.

Exhibit 4.1 Top 10 Banks in the World by Asset Size and Market Capitalization, 2016
(in billions of dollars)

Rank	Institution	Country	**Assets**	Rank	Institution	Country	**Market Capitalization**
1	Industrial and Commercial Bank of China	China	$3,549.88	1	Wells Fargo Bank	USA	$254.19
2	China Construction Bank Corporation	China	2,981.85	2	Industrial and Commercial Bank of China	China	226.55
3	Mitsubishi UFJ Financial Group	Japan	2,901.34	3	J.P. Morgan Chase & Co.	USA	217.79
4	Agricultural Bank of China	China	2,818.89	4	China Construction Bank Corporation	China	155.97
5	Bank of China	China	2,656.07	5	Agricultural Bank of China	China	155.04
6	HSBC Holdings	UK	2,608.15	6	Bank of China	China	144.16
7	J.P. Morgan Chase & Co.	USA	2,466.10	7	Bank of America	USA	142.39
8	BNP Paribas	France	2,417.00	8	HSBC Holdings	UK	128.91
9	Bank of America	USA	2,186.61	9	Citigroup, Inc.	USA	126.74
10	Japan Post Bank	Japan	2,022.02	10	Commonwealth Bank of Australia	Australia	99.69
Total Assets			**$26,607.91**	**Total Market Capitalization**			**$1,651.43**

Source: Top 10 Banks in the World, 2016, http://www.relbanks.com/worlds-top-banks/assets
World's Largest Banks, 2016, http://www.relbanks.com/worlds-top-banks/market-cap

Exhibit 4.2 shows IMF's projected nominal gross domestic product (GDP) for the five largest economies of the world--the United States, China, Japan, Germany, and United Kingdom--for 2016 and 2020. With the world's biggest banks located in the largest economies of the world, the section that follows reviews the prevailing banking structures and operating models in each of these countries as shaped by respective challenges for greater efficiency and competitiveness. A second section addresses two banking systems in distinct geographic regions and variant economic frameworks--that of an emerging market in Latin America (Mexico), the other encountered in the Islamic countries of the Middle East and Asia.

Exhibit 4.2 Five Largest Economies of the World:
Projected Nominal GDP, 2016 and 2020
(in billions of dollars)

Countries	2016	Share %	2020	Share %
United States	$18,561.934	24.70	$21,927.00	23.43
China	11,391.619	15.10	16,458.00	17.58
Japan	4,730.300	6.29	5,506.00	5.88
Germany	3,494.898	4.65	4,008.00	4.28
United Kingdom	2,649.893	3.52	2,928.00	3.13
World Total	**$75,213.000**		**$93,599.00**	

Source: International Monetary Fund, *World Economic Outlook*.
http://statisticstimes.com/economy/countries-by-projected-gdp.php

BANKING SYSTEMS IN THE WORLD'S FIVE LARGEST ECONOMIES

The United States

Unlike their European counterparts, banks in the United States had a late start. Although the first commercial bank was chartered in 1781, lack of a central bank and a supervisory and regulatory framework impeded the development of the banking industry. In fact as late as the pre-World War I era, the private sector was so busy developing the country's resources and satisfying the needs of an immense domestic market that the financing of international trade by U.S. banks was quite negligible. Also, the great majority of U.S. banks suffered from lack of capital, a development that undermined their ability to expand the scope of their operations. Last but not least, U.S. national banks were prohibited from branching abroad or accepting drafts arising from international transactions (bankers' acceptances), a prohibition that automatically excluded a large segment of the banking system from financing international trade. Enactment of the Federal Reserve Act in 1913, permitted national banks to finance foreign trade (through bankers' acceptances). Also, national banks with $1 million in capital and surplus were allowed to establish foreign branches, subject to the approval of the Federal Reserve. The first U.S. bank to receive such approval was Citibank which established a branch in Buenos Aires in 1914. By then, European banks operated a network of 2000 foreign branches.

The turning point in the development of the financial sector came with World War I. The United States entered the War as a debtor nation and emerged as a creditor. The growth of exports to the Allied and neutral nations together with the influx of flight capital from Europe propelled New York into an international financial center and laid the foundations for the development of international banking. Exhibit 4.3 identifies some of the important legislative milestones in the development of the commercial banking industry in the United States.

While each of the above enactments exerted important influence on the structure of the U.S. commercial banking system, special reference must be made to the last two, and most recent, pieces of legislation. Enactment of the Gramm-Leach-Bliley (GLB) Act was touted as the biggest change in the regulation of financial institutions in nearly 70 years. This law repealed the 1933 Glass-Steagall Act barriers that prohibited commercial banks from engaging in investment banking activities. Although a Section 20 amendment of the Glass-Steagall allowed a number of bank holding companies to

Exhibit 4.3 Key Legislative Milestones in the Development of the U.S. Banking Industry

---

State legislation:

- Pennsylvania's state-chartering of the Bank of North America, Philadelphia (1781)
    - First state to charter a commercial bank to serve colonial America

Federal legislation:

- ***National Bank Act 1863, 1864***
    - Created the OCC and authorized it to grant national charters (dual banking system)
    - Provided for the issue of a safe and uniform currency
- ***Federal Reserve Act 1913***
    - Established the central banking system partially due to concerns about recurrent banking crises.
- ***Banking Act of 1933 (Glass-Steagall Act)***
    - Provided for the implementation of a plan of federal deposit insurance
    - Introduced Regulation Q which prohibited interest payment on demand deposits and set maximum interest rates on time and savings deposits
    - Prohibited commercial banks from underwriting corporate securities and engaging in investment banking.

  Interpretation of Section 20 allowed establishment of "Section 20 subsidiaries" (as a result of court rulings, the Federal Reserve started granting such authority to money center banks in 1987)
- ***Interstate Banking and Branching Efficiency Act of 1994 (Riegle Neal Act)***
    - Allowed a BHC to acquire an out-of-state bank and consolidate it into its branch network
- ***Financial Services Modernization Act of 1999 (Gramm-Leach-Bliley Act)***
    - Provided for establishment of a Financial Holding Company
- ***Wall Street Reform and Consumer Protection Act of 2010 (Dodd-Frank Act)***
    - Sweeping revision of the U.S. financial system and the rules that govern it

---

Source: Developed by the author.

form a (so-called Section 20) subsidiary to engage in limited investment banking, GLB broadened the regulatory framework by providing for the creation of a full-service investment banking institution under a **financial holding company** (FHC). Furthermore, it modified portions of the Bank Holding Company Act (1956) to allow the FHC to undertake, through full-service subsidiaries, a range of additional financial activities including underwriting and selling insurance, commercial and merchant banking, investing in and developing real estate, and "complementary activities." Exhibit 4.4 depicts a general configuration of a FHC and the subsidiary institutions under its control. These may include a thrift holding company as well as a bank holding company (BHC) which may, in turn, own other financial institutions. GLB opened the door to the consolidation of the U.S. financial services industry and the development of financial supermarkets to offer their corporate clients a full range of financial products and services similar to those offered by Europe's universal banks. Should a FHC be allowed to expand to nonfinancial services, through additional subsidiaries, its structure could accommodate it. Establishment of a FHC is subject to the prior approval of the Federal Reserve which requires any one of its insured depository subsidiaries to be well capitalized, or well managed, or to have received at least a satisfactory rating in their most recent Community Reivestment Act (CRA) exam.

The Dodd-Frank Act, touted as the most far-reaching Wall Street reform, sought to overhaul the financial regulatory system to prevent recurrence of the financial crisis of 2008. The major features of this law include vigorous supervision and regulation of financial institutions and markets, protection of consumers and investors from financial abuse, tools to manage financial crises, and support for international cooperation and regulatory standards. Despite its 2010 passage, Dodd-Frank has not been fully implemented as part of the rules called for have yet to be formalized. Six years later, of the 390 new rules required by this law, 274, or 70 percent, have been written and finalized.

Exhibit 4.5 shows the development of the U.S. bank regulatory system. As seen in this Exhibit, supervisory and regulatory functions in this country are carried out by a number of different agencies each with its own particular mandate, yet working in tandem with each other. The Office of the Comptroller of the Currency (OCC), attached

Exhibit 4.4 Structure of a Financial Holding Company

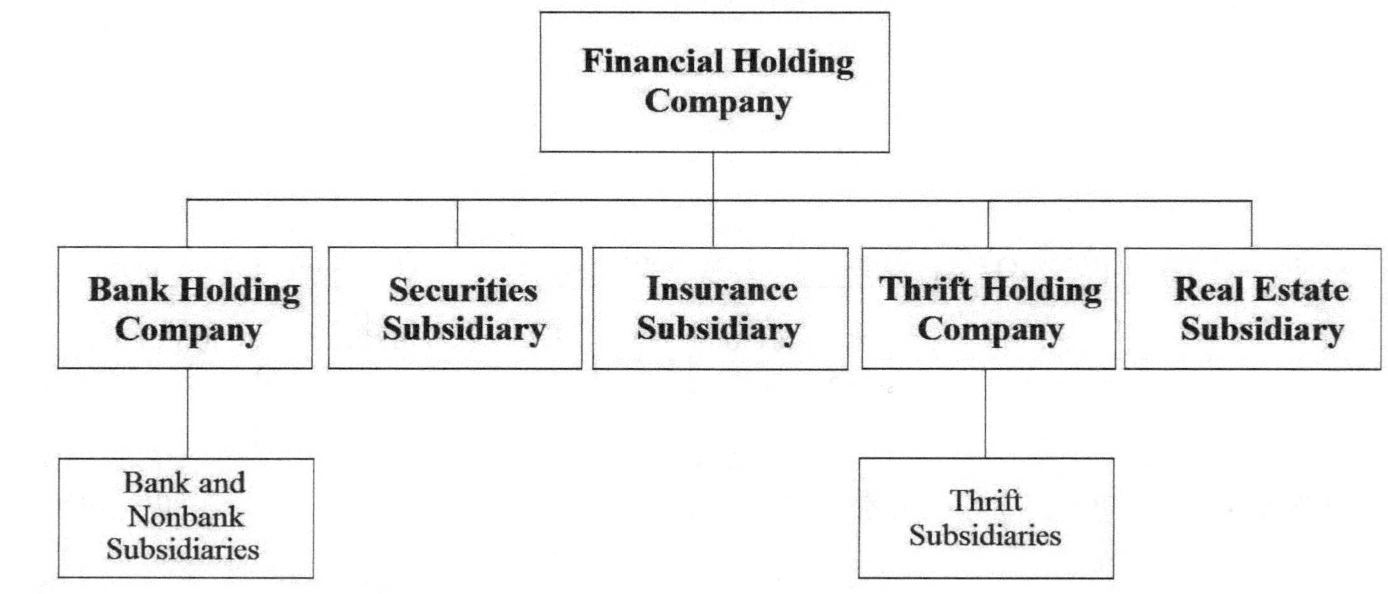

Source: Developed by the author.

Exhibit 4.5 Primary Supervisors of U.S. Banks and Thrifts

Institution	Regulator
National banks	Office of the Comptroller of the Currency (OCC)
State member banks	Federal Reserve and state authority
Insured nonmember banks	FDIC and state authority
Noninsured banks	State authority
Insured federal savings associations	OCC*
Insured state savings associations	FDIC and state authority*
Uninsured state savings associations	State authority
Federal credit unions	National Credit Union Administration Board
State credit unions	State authority
Bank holding companies	Federal Reserve
Savings and loan holding companies	Federal Reserve*

*Dodd-Frank Wall Street Reform and Consumer Protection Act 2010 abolished the Office of Thrift Supervision and reassigned the oversight of the affected institutions to the designated regulators.
Source: Developed by the author.

to the U.S. Treasury Department, is the primary supervisory agency for nationally chartered banks. The Comptroller is a presidential appointee and as such he operates with a high degree of autonomy. The OCC works with the Federal Reserve Board, which has authority over bank holding companies.

State-chartered banks are supervised by state bank supervisory agencies, while their holding companies fall under the jurisdiction of the Federal Reserve Board. The Dodd-Frank Act abolished the Office of Thrift Supervision and subjected federally chartered savings and loan associations and savings banks to the OCC. All federally chartered banks, savings and loan associations and savings banks, together with state member banks are also subject to the supervision of the Federal Deposit Insurance (FDIC). Under the GLB repeal of the Glass-Steagall Act, it was agreed that the Treasury Department (including the OCC) and the Federal Reserve will share supervision of new financial conglomerates while the SEC will continue to oversee securities subsidiaries.

Foreign banks operating in the United States fall under the jurisdiction of federal and state authorities and comply with the statutes and laws to which U.S. banks must adhere. In theory, foreign banks are given a level playing field with their U.S. counterparts.

China

Redefinition of the Communist ideology to incorporate reforms has initiated the transformation of China from central planning to a free market economy and propelled it into one of the fastest growing countries in the world for over 30 years. This economic momentum set in motion the gradual streamlining of the banking system from a statist orientation to commercialized institutions. Established in the late 1980s, commercial banks underwent significant changes to begin functioning more like western banks. Measures to transform them to competitive market driven institutions were introduced simultaneously with legal and regulatory reforms to improve supervision. As a result, the country's banking system has been in transition toward the establishment of an efficient financial services industry. The institutional composition of the banking system is made up of the following six groups: 3 policy banks, 4 state commercial banks, 12 national joint stock commercial banks, 140 city banks, credit cooperatives, and foreign banks.

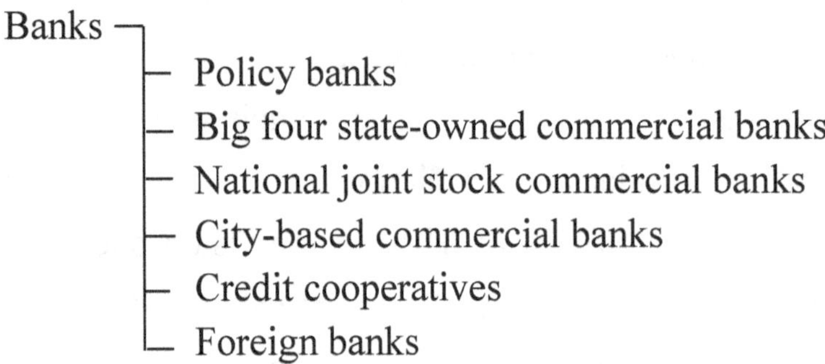

Policy banks, created in 1994, consist of 3 development banks, the Agricultural Development Bank of China (ADBC), China Development Bank (CDB), and Exim Bank of China. As implied by their names, each of these institutions has a distinct area of funding responsibility--agricultural projects in rural areas, infrastructure and industrial projects, and trade financing.

Big four state-owned commercial banks comprise the Bank of China, the Agricultural Bank of China, the China Construction Bank and the Industrial and Commercial Bank of China. A major government step in the restructuring of the banking industry was the disposal of sizeable amounts of bad debts held by the Big Four and the move to boost their capital base. As a result all four have recapitalized by going public, with the Agricultural Bank of China issue surpassing all others through a $22.2 billion offering (2010) listed in the Shanghai and the Hong Kong Stock Exchanges. Trailing in importance was the issue of the Industrial and Commercial Bank of China with a $21.9 billion offering (2006), also listed in the Shanghai and the Hong Kong Stock Exchanges. Tradable shares represent only a fraction of the equity of the recapitalized banks with state ownership still a dominant component. All four, taken together, control about 50 percent of the country's banking assets and constitute a major source of credit.

National joint stock commercial banks amount to 12 institutions and account for 15 percent of China's total banking assets. They exhibit a sound financial record of asset quality and profitability and a much lower non-performing loan ratio than the big four.

City-based commercial banks, as their name suggests, were formerly allowed to operate only within the city in which they originated. However, as a result of a change in regulation (2004), they may now expand their operations beyond the area of their home market. Another important trend has been the merger of some of the smaller city banks to form larger regional institutions and their drive to go public by raising capital and listing their shares. City commercial banks number about 140 and account for approximately 5 percent of total banking assets.

Credit cooperatives date from the 1950s and were created essentially to develop a rural financial system through the provision of financial services to rural enterprises and individuals. By the turn of the century there were about 42,000 rural credit cooperatives compared to 3,200 urban. Sizeable amounts of bad debts caused since the failure of many rural credit cooperatives and prompted the reform of the rural financial system. The resulting reorganization has led to the establishment of a new institutional order made up of rural commercial banks, rural cooperative banks and credit cooperatives. Collectively they amount to 3,274 rural financial institutions with a total of 76,000 branches spread across the country. Urban cooperatives and rural financial institutions account for 8 and 0.5 percent, respectively, of total banking assets.

Foreign banks account for a limited participation in the banking system. This reflects to a large extent earlier operational restrictions which confined the scope of their permissible activities. There are about 41 locally incorporated foreign banks operating in China while at least 20 foreign banks have shareholdings in domestic banks subject to the 20 percent investment ceiling regulation (less restrictive ownership rules apply on shareholdings in mid-sized banks). A large number of foreign banks maintain branches in Shanghai, the financial capital of the country. Foreign banks command a market share of only 2 percent of banking assets.

Over the years there has been a marked improvement in the performance of banking institutions and in the level of sophistication of their products and services. All of the above institutions offer their customers the basic commercial banking products and services, such as deposits, loans, payment and clearance. Some of the more sophisticated institutions cater to the needs of corporate clients through value added services (e.g., cash management, treasury and securities clearance), while large retail-focused institutions engage in the provision of banking services to individual customers (e.g., credit cards, mortgage loans and other retail products). An even smaller group of institutions are providers of Internet banking services (e.g., account access and transaction services) by appealing to younger, more affluent professionals.

Up until the turn of the century, bank supervision and regulation was largely in the hands of the country's central bank, the People's Bank of China. As the need to separate bank regulatory authority from monetary policy became essential, reforms in 2003 led to the establishment of the China Banking Regulatory Commission (CBRC). An independent authority, CBRC has been the supervisory agency for the country's financial institutions.

Japan

Up until World War II, Japan's banking system operated in a financial environment devoid of any regulatory barriers. Commercial banks were members of large family-controlled financial and industrial combines, known as ***zaibatsu***. This model encouraged banks to fund industrial development and play a significant role in addressing the financial needs of the particular conglomerate. After Japan's surrender, U.S. occupation authorities sought to make competition the supreme law of an economy in which concentration had always been the official policy of the government. Inspired by the Glass-Steagall Act provisions at home, occupation authorities enacted legislation that introduced duplicate restriction (Article 65, Securities Exchange Law of 1947) to separate commercial and investment banking.

Once the occupation forces departed and a reasonable time interval elapsed some of the old groupings reconstituted themselves. The new form of business group that emerged, termed ***keiretsu*** ("business affiliations"), was more loosely organized with controlling ownership being replaced by cross-ownership of smaller blocks of shares, cross-directorships, and informal business ties. Each business group had a diverse composition made up of firms that engaged in such activities as manufacturing, commercial banking, trust, insurance, leasing, investment banking and real estate. This system of close linkages left a legacy of a weak credit culture in which banks gave little concern to credit risk in making loans. Asset growth was in some ways more important than profitability.

The system of close linkages and the pivotal role of commercial banks in the economic and financial infrastructure were preserved throughout most of the postwar era. The same may be said for the separation of commercial banks from investment banks. The need for financial reforms became apparent when the bubble economy of the late 1980s gave way to the crash of the early 1990s. The opening up of the Japanese financial markets received important impetus from the collapse of Yamaichi Securities (1997), which together with Nomura, Nikko and Daiwa constituted Japan's Big Four brokerages. Additional momentum came from the failure and subsequent nationalization (1998) of two other troubled institutions the Nippon Credit Bank and Long-Term Credit Bank, both prestigious specialized banks in the extension of long term loans to the Japanese industry. Successive reforms (1994, 1997, and 1998) provided for the dismantling of the barriers imposed by Article 65, the restructuring and consolidation of the banking system, and the creation of a new bank supervisory agency.

Japan's commercial banking system consists of three categories of institutions-- city banks, regional banks and specialized banks. **City banks** are the most significant category of commercial banks with operations both nationwide and internationally. As

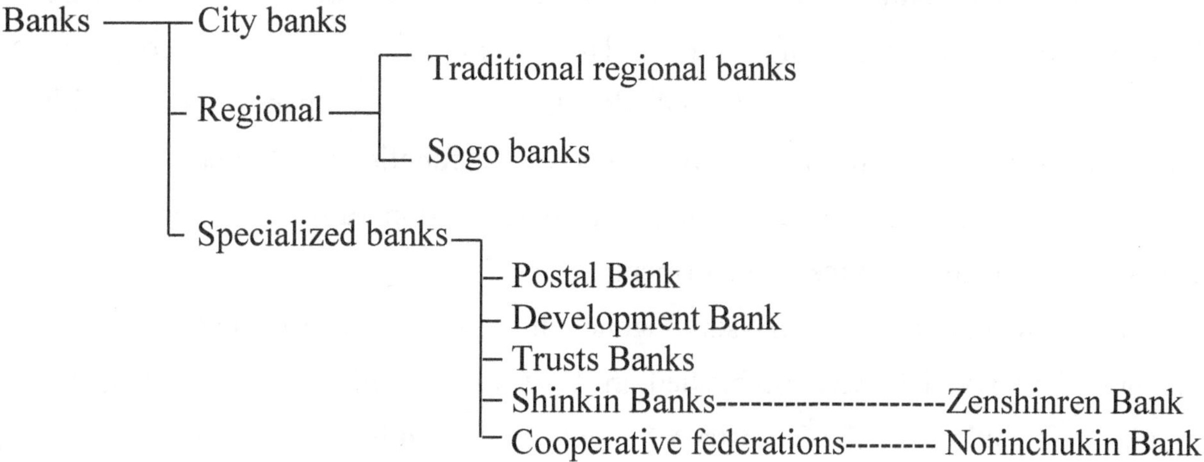

was the case with the country's corporate sector, banks came under considerable pressure to consolidate in the aftermath of the protracted recession of the 1990s. Global competition was an additional impetus to the consolidation process. The most significant city banks are members of financial holding companies, e.g., the Sumitomo Mitsui Financial Group, the Mitsubishi UFJ Financial Group, and the Mizuho Financial Group, created through the combine of different banking institutions.

Regional banks are made up of two subgroups--the former sogo banks and the traditional regional banks. Established as mutuals in the postwar period through enactment of the Sogo Bank Law, sogo banks specialized in the financing of small and medium-sized enterprises. However because of the changing needs of their clients they gradually converted themselves into ordinary banks joining in 1989 the ranks of the regional banks. The traditional regional banks have been located in Japan's prefectures, and their operations have been generally tied to the local economy. As a reasult, during the 1990s they experienced significant losses from loans to the troubled real estate, construction, and retail serctors. In recent years some of these institutions have expanded their operations beyond the bounds of their prefectures and in some cases they have extended them to the international domain. However, the recent negative interest rate policy of the Bank of Japan and more importantly the drastic drop in Japan's urban population is triggering a merger movement among the 34 regional banks in the overly congested prefectural markets.

Specialized banks is a broad category that includes a variety of institutions focusing on different types of activities. The Shinkin banks are credit cooperatives catering to the financial needs of small--locally oriented--companies and individuals under the oversight of the Zenshinren Bank which functions as the central bank for these instritutions. Agricultural, fishing, and forestry cooperative federations function under their own central bank, the Norinchukin Bank.

The principal bank supervisory agency in Japan is the Financial Supervisory Agency (FSA) which was established in 1998 as a result of restructuring of the regulatory functions of the Ministry of Finance. In addition to commercial banks, FSA's oversight authority extends to insurance companies and the securities markets through its control of the Securities and Exchange Surveillance Commission. Its expanded authority is deemed necessary to ensure the stability of the country's financial system. The agency operates with a commissioner and reports to the Minister of Finance.

Europe

European banks have been strong contenders for global dominance. An early impetus in their drive for such dominance were the First (1977) and Second (1989) Banking Directives of the EEC which provided respectively for home country control and a single banking license by the bank's home country. The move toward economic integration and the establishment of a monetary union created additional incentives for the consolidation of the financial sector. Banks were seen as the catalysts for this consolidation. The model for banking under the European Union (EU) regime has been the ***universal banking*** system of Germany. A universal bank is a fully integrated financial institution that may extend to its customers at home and abroad commercial and investment banking, leasing, and insurance services under one roof as a financial supermarket. Absence of any national regulatory constraints has been a decisive factor in the development and growth of universal banking in Europe.

In addition to internationally active banks, the universal banking model has been adopted by institutions that have a nationwide scope of operations in their respective countries. By contrast institutions with a regional or a strong local orientation are less likely to operate as universal banks. Cantonal banks and community banks are examples of institutions with limited functions and products and a strong orientation to their respective markets.

Germany

Germany's banking system is made up of four categories of institutions--commercial banks, savings banks and their regional giro institutions, cooperative banks and their regional giro institutions, and other banking institutions. This classification is depicted below.

The first three categories of institutions dominate the national banking system and constitute the major groups of universal banks in the country. **Commercial banks**

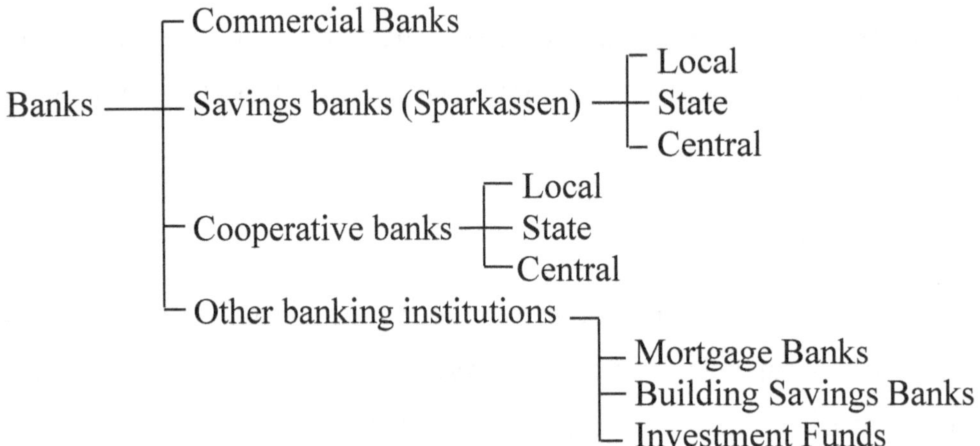

command a significant percentage of the country's total banking assets and are the most actively engaged in international banking. Deutsche Bank leads this group and is followed by Commerzbank which, after its acquisition of Dresdner Bank (2009), has a proven securities expertise and an extensive network of offices at home and abroad.

Catering to the public interest, **savings banks** operate in three levels: local savings banks, state savings banks and the central savings banks. **Cooperative banks** are mutual institutions with their operations exhibiting the same three-level structure. Both savings banks and cooperative banks have their own regional giro institutions (giro is an electronic system that facilitates consumer bill payments and credit transfers). **Other banking institutions** is an assortment of institutions that includes specialized banks (e.g., mortgage banks), building savings banks and investment funds.

Two developments in recent years have been noteworthy in striving to strengthen the competitive climate among German banking institutions. One of these developments was the phase out of state guarantees for Landesbanks and Sparkassen institutions (savings banks) in an effort to make publicly owned banks more market driven in raising funds from financial markets. The second was the enactment of a law (2000) for the divestiture of equity cross-holdings between banks and large companies. The intention of this law was to put an end to the traditional influence or control associated with the ownership of large holdings of equity.

With the exception of the credit institutions that meet the criteria of the Single Supervisory Mechanism of the EMU and are subject to the oversight of the European Central Bank (ECB), all other German banking institutions are under the statutory and regulatory oversight of the country's Federal Financial Supervisory Authority (BaFin). Operating under the authority of the Federal Ministry of Finance, BaFin's supervision extends to insurance companies, other financial services institutions, and capital markets to safeguard the viability, integrity and stability of the financial system. Besides the direct supervision of credit institutions by the ECB or by BaFin, the country's central bank, Deutsche Bundesbank, is responsible for receiving and analyzing data submitted by all banks. The ECB and/or BaFin and the Bundesbank cooperate closely and share observations and findings which are necessary for the performance of their tasks.

United Kingdom

Over 500 banks operate in the United Kingdom with virtually all of the world's major institutions maintaining a physical presence in London, the country's dominant financial center and a leading international hub. The banking institutions operating in the United Kingdom may be classified into the following four major groups:

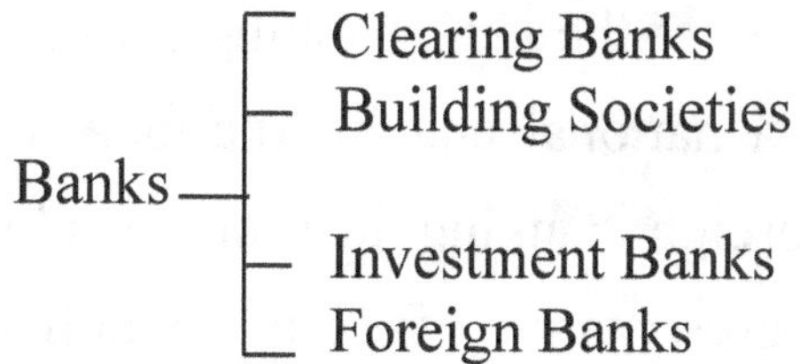

Clearing banks, similar to commercial banks in the United States, were primarily engaged in accepting deposits and making loans. They derive their name from membership and control of clearing houses. Following regulatory changes they moved into other non-deposit products and began to expand gradually into the securities business through merchant banking subsidiaries. Barclays, HSBC, and Royal Bank of Scotland are examples of clearing banks.

Building Societies originated as residential mortgage lending institutions. Regulatory changes in the mid1980s allowed them to demutualize (by issuing shares) and expand into banking services, life insurance, pensions, and investment products. Over time, some of these societies merged to form larger ones, others were acquired by financial groups, while still others converted into banks. Abbey National and Halifax are examples of former building societies that converted into banks, currently operating as an integral part of the Santander Group and Lloyds Banking Group, respectively.

Investment banks trace their origin to the eighteenth century merchant banking houses and their underwriting and export financing activities. While there were no official prohibitions against commercial banking functions, merchant banks tended to forego straightforward lending concentrating instead on wholesale financial transactions to the UK corporate sector through such activities as financial advisory services, mergers and acquisitions, leasing, securities underwriting and other specialized form of financing. Financial reforms in the mid-1980s enabled merchant banks to become full-service investment banks by broadening the scope of their operations to include security trading and brokerage services. The number of firms in this group has declined significantly in recent years because of acquisitions by large, well-capitalized foreign entrants. S.G. Warburg, Kleinwort Benson, and Barings are examples of institutions that were acquired by UBS, Dresdner Bank, and International Netherlands Group (ING), respectively.

Foreign banks constitute a major component of the U.K. banking sector because of the financial eminence of London both as a national and international financial center. The organizational structure of the foreign banking institutions physically present in the London market ranges from a representative office to a wholly-owned subsidiary. In addition, there is a large number of foreign securities houses that have set up offices in London to provide their clients with the full range of investment banking products and services demanded.

Perceived bank supervisory failure during the financial crisis of 2008, prompted a new UK regulatory framework for financial services. The responsibilities of a single supervisory agency were split (2013) between two regulatory institutions, the Financial Conduct Authority (FCA), and the Prudential Regulation Authority (PRA). The FCA, an independent agency financed by charging fees to members of the financial services industry, is responsible for protecting investors, policing financial markets, and promoting competition. The PRA, an arm of the Bank of England, has prudential regulation and supervision of commercial banks, building societies, credit unions, insurers and large investment firms.

TWO ALTERNATE MODELS

Mexico

Nationalized in the aftermath of the Mexican debt moratorium in 1982, the country's banking system was reprivatized in the early 1990s in resoponse to the economic reforms and market-oriented policies associated with the resolution of the debt crisis. Operating in a deregulated environment, the new ownership and management of the Mexican banks focused on the credit needs of the private sector which had been underserved during the preceding period. However, the absence of a strong values driven credit culture--evidenced by the lack of risk management systems and controls--led to aggressive loan underwriting which undermined bank performance and fed into a bubble economy. The consequences of the policies pursued and the magnitude of exposure assumed by the banking sector became apparent in the failed peso devaluation of December 1994 and the ensuing major economic crisis commonly referred to as the tequila crisis.

As many Mexican banks had raised dollar denominated loans to finance local firms, the foreign exchange risk sustained by borrowers in the aftermath of the devaluation converted to a credit risk for the banks that had extended the foreign currency loans. But bank balance sheets detriorated further as the economic slump undermined the operations of businesses and forced the rescheduling of many loans to the corporate sector. The level of nonperforming loans rose significantly reaching 30 percent of total loans. These developments made it very hard for banks to raise new capital at a reasonable cost, leading them instead to cut back on their lending in order to shrink their asset base and thereby restore their capital ratios. The consequent decline in bank lending led in turn to a further contraction in economic activity.

Bail out of the banking industry came at a cost of $100 billion, or about 20 percent of the country's GDP. Government response to the banking crisis consisted essentially of measures to support both the debtors and the banking industry through recapitalization and help in loan restructuring. Further, bank supervision was enhanced and regulatory controls were eased to open up the banking sector to foreign investments. The latter move proved instrumental resulting in the acquisition of more than 80 percent of the assets of the banking system by major foreign financial institutions. Foreign ownership has strengthened banking sector competition and improved the asset quality of Mexican banks. Citibank, HSBC, Banco Santader, and Banco Bilbao Vizcaya Argentaria (BBVA) are just a few of the foreign banks with ownership interests in Mexican institutions.

Bank supervision and regulation is shared between the Ministry of Finance, the National Banking and Securities Commission (NBSC), and the Bank of Mexico, the country's central bank. The Ministry of Finance is concerned with institutional issues, such as licensing and credit policies, NBSC, a semi-autonomous government agency, is responsible for supervision of the financial system, and the Bank of Mexico implements these policies and also operates the country's electronic funds transfer system. Both increased foreign bank ownership and enhanced supervision and regulation have contributed to a more prudent banking system.

Islamic Banking

An inherent part of the Muslim world since its very beginning, Islamic banking did not receive much attention until the petrodollar boom of the 1970s. Islamic banking is a model practiced in the Middle East and in such Asian countries as Bangladesh, Indonesia, Kuwait, Malaysia, Pakistan, Saudi Arabia, and Sudan. In 2012 there were about 300 Islamic financial institutions with $1.3 trillion in assets operating in more than 75 countries. It is estimated that over the last decade these institutions enjoyed an average growth rate of 15 percent per annum. While many of these institutions follow strictly Islamic principles, many also follow Western practices catering to both markets. Interestingly, many of the internationally larger banks (with HSBC, Lloyds TSB, UBS and Citigroup as notable examples) have Islamic banking operations both in Muslim countries and the West.

Although the Western banking model has long sidestepped the religious dimesion of financial issues, these are still prevalent in the Muslim world. Such, for example, is the case of usury (the charging of interest on money loans) which remains an important issue for much of the Islamic world. Sharia, the Islamic law, prohibits the fixed or floating payment, or acceptance, of interest or fees for money loans, but allows profit sharing--share participations to be paid out at some date as earnings.

Western financial institutions have been relying increasingly on Islamic scholars (sharia boards) to certify that their banking products and services are in accord with sharia principles. This is all the more important given the size of investible funds at stake, estimated to amount to $1 trillion. The pursuit of sharia-compliant assets is contributing to the transformation of Islamic finance into an effective force in Muslim countries.

SUPRANATIONAL BANKS

"Supranational" is a term that denotes a cluster of intergovernmental institutions and development banks that operate in the international domain. With the exception of a select few that may operate on a global basis, the vast majority of these institutions are of a regional nature. Exhibit 4.6 identifies the makeup of this group and the size of financial resources in their disposal at year-end 2015.

What all these institutions have in common is that they have been established (or chartered) by more than one country. As a result, their membership is composed of individual countries, often along regional lines, and their mission is tied to economic development. Their initial capital is derived from member country subscriptions, with additional funds raised through the issuance of bonds on the local markets of member countries and in the Eurobond market. These issues enjoy a top rating (Moody's has usually rated these issues as Aaa).

Supranational institutions extend badly needed capital to developing countries in the form of medium- and long-term financing, and at interest rates and terms that would not be available elsewhere. The World Bank (IBRD), is the oldest and most widely recognized institution of this group. Established at the end of World War II to help Europe rebuild, it commenced operations in 1946. It is owned by the governments of 189 member countries and works closely with the rest of the World Bank Group to provide loans and other assistance primarily to developing countries. As seen in Exhibit 4.6, its balance sheet size of $343 billion is the second largest of the supranational organizations. The European Investment Bank (EIB), established in 1958 under the Treaty of Rome, is the world's largest supranational institution with assets of $619 billion. EIB shareholders, are the EU member countries which are also the principal beneficiaries of its financing activities. The bank has also funded projects to some non-EU member countries.

Exhibit 4.6 Select Supranational Institutions, 2015

Institution	Assets (in billions of dollars)
African Development Bank	$35.1
Asian Development Bank	117.4
Black Sea Trade and Development Bank	1.4
Caribbean Development Bank	1.3
Central American Bank for Economic Integration	8.8
Corporacion Andina de Fomento	32.5
Council of Europe Development Bank	27.3
Eurasian Development Bank	2.9
EUROFIMA*	22.7
European Bank for Reconstruction and Development	59.7
European Investment Bank	619.4
European Investment Fund	2.4
Inter-American Development Bank	111.0
International Bank for Reconstruction and Development	343.2
International Finance Corporation	87.5
Islamic Development Bank	22.3
Nordic Investment Bank	29.7

*European Company for the Financing of the Railroad Rolling Stock of member countries.
Note: Depending upon the geographical scope of their operations, these institutions may be distinguished into global, regional and subregional, a classification that determines country membership.
Source: Standard & Poor's, *Global Ratings: Supranationals*, Special Edition, October 2016. https://www.spratings.com/documents/20184/86957/Supranationals+Special+Edition+2016/f4676dd6-0822-4e02-a5ce-e8a6dc2e36f4

INSTITUTIONAL DIVERSITY

With the exception of supranationals that constitute multinational organizations with a developmental mission, review of the banking systems in the five largest economies and select regions of the world shows that invariably every country has its mix of commercial banks, savings banks, credit unions and specialized banks, alongside its nonbank financial institutions. Not all of these have the same structures and functions, nor they operate with the same business objectives. The largest firms have fully integrated the financial services offered (e.g., banking, securities, insurance, and other services) and have transformed themselves into global banks. Whether structured as universal banks or financial holding companies, these institutions cater to their customers in major products and geographical markets around the world. As a result these institutions are characterized by internationally diversified asset structures and earnings flows. A second tier of institutions operate on a national scale targeting their functions and products to the domestic market. A third tier of banks has a regional, or super regional, focus in the delivery of their products and services. A fourth tier of banks has a strong local orientation. A separate category includes the specialized institutions which may be product focused or customer oriented.

5 ENGAGING IN INTERNATIONAL BANKING: KEY OBJECTIVES

A bank's decision to engage in international banking may involve the pursuit of one or more objectives. Although factors such as bank size and degree of international sophistication may affect individual perspectives, most institutions active in international banking seek to attain certain broad objectives. A principal objective is to provide international banking services to domestic corporate customers who expand and improve the scope of their activities abroad. The emergence of multinational corporations in the United States and Japan sharply increased the demand for international financial services in the respective countries and induced the expansion of banks' international operations and presence abroad. The initial ventures of banks overseas were defensive in nature, designed to accommodate the needs of their domestic customers. In time, however, increased competition and narrowed profit margins abroad prompted many banks to seek new markets, among them the large and medium-size local companies.

Profit, too, has been a major objective in the initiation of international services. Entry into new markets often entails greater profit potential than is available in the domestic market. A bank may extend to foreign markets the expertise, or competitive advantage, it has developed in its home market for the purpose of generating additional income. U.S. penetration of foreign consumer-banking markets is a case in point. With their consumer lending experience in this country dating from the 1920s, U.S. banks enjoy a competitive advantage in this field abroad. Indeed, personal financial services constitute an attractive niche in foreign markets, and many U.S. banks have gained a major share of the consumer-loan and deposit markets of Europe and Asia.

Escaping burdensome regulation has been another important reason for banks' international expansion. Just as burdensome regulation has been a cause for financial innovation, so it has also been a spur to international banking. Restrictive domestic regulation offered both U.S. and Japanese banks limited opportunities for growth; international banking was a substitute. Indeed, U.S. banks have faced considerable restrictions regarding securities, insurance, and commercial activities, and their operations at home have been subject to a host of regulatory controls. Expansion abroad allowed banks to circumvent some of these controls (particularly reserve requirements, ceiling interest rates on deposits, and deposit insurance premiums), and in certain offshore locations to benefit in addition from a favorable tax treatment.

Diversification is still another reason for international banking. As with expansion in the domestic markets, international activities potentially enhance the opportunity for a bank to improve diversification of its assets and earnings flows. Domestic earnings flows from financial services are linked to the state of the economy. With the economies of the world growing at different rates and subject to different business cycles, international expansion holds the potential for greater earnings diversification.

Other objectives in international expansion include the increased visibility and prestige associated with such a move, and taking advantage of improvements in technology and communications that have allowed the extension and maintenance of real-time control over overseas operations at a decreasing cost.

STRATEGY

Strategy refers to the measures a bank may take to realize the established objectives. In weighing the decision to engage in international banking and determine the appropriate strategy, management must address the structuring of the international function at home and abroad in the context of such considerations as available resources (human and financial), projected volume of international business, and knowledge of--and experience with--foreign markets. At the home market, structuring of the international function calls for deciding between two alternate organizational structures, a formal and an informal one. An informal structure would require a staff of specialists to offer the very basic services related to trade finance, e.g., collections, letters of credit and foreign exchange. By contrast, a formal structure would require establishing an international banking department and deciding between two types of models, the traditional and the functionally integrated. The traditional model, shown in Exhibit 5.1, is also known as a bank-within-a-bank concept because of its duplication of the domestic banking functions. This type of model is widely used by banks in the United States.

A key aspect of the traditional model is the geographic focus of the lending function supported by the economics, money market (e.g., funds management) and operations sections. Reporting to the senior management of the bank, it is a self-contained structure. Its key strengths are twofold--it enables a cost/benefit analysis of the departmental performance and it provides for clear lines of authority and accountability. Its weakness is the duplication of domestic functions which impacts the efficient use of resources. The alternate model, functionally integrated, is shown in Exhibit 5.2 and is used mostly by banks in foreign countries (e.g., Japan). In this model, the only activities conducted by the international department relate to foreign trade and supporting operations. All other international functions are integrated with their domestic counterparts (e.g., credit analysis, economics, corporate/multinational, funds management and loan servicing). The strength of this model is efficiency and economies of scale while its weaknesses are the difficulty of a cost/benefit assessment of the international function, and cluttered lines of authority and accountability. Given the divergent strengths and weaknesses of the two models, choice of the appropriate configuration would depend upon such considerations as the existence and effectiveness of the current international structure, the evolving state of international operations, and the perceived needs of the bank at any given point in time. Availability of human resources to staff duplicate functions is an additional consideration that would weigh significantly in this decision.

Equally important are the challenges associated with the structuring of the international function abroad. Some of the issues to be addressed include choice of foreign markets to serve, regulatory and tax environment of the candidate

Exhibit 5.1 Organization of the International Department at the Head Office: Traditional Structure

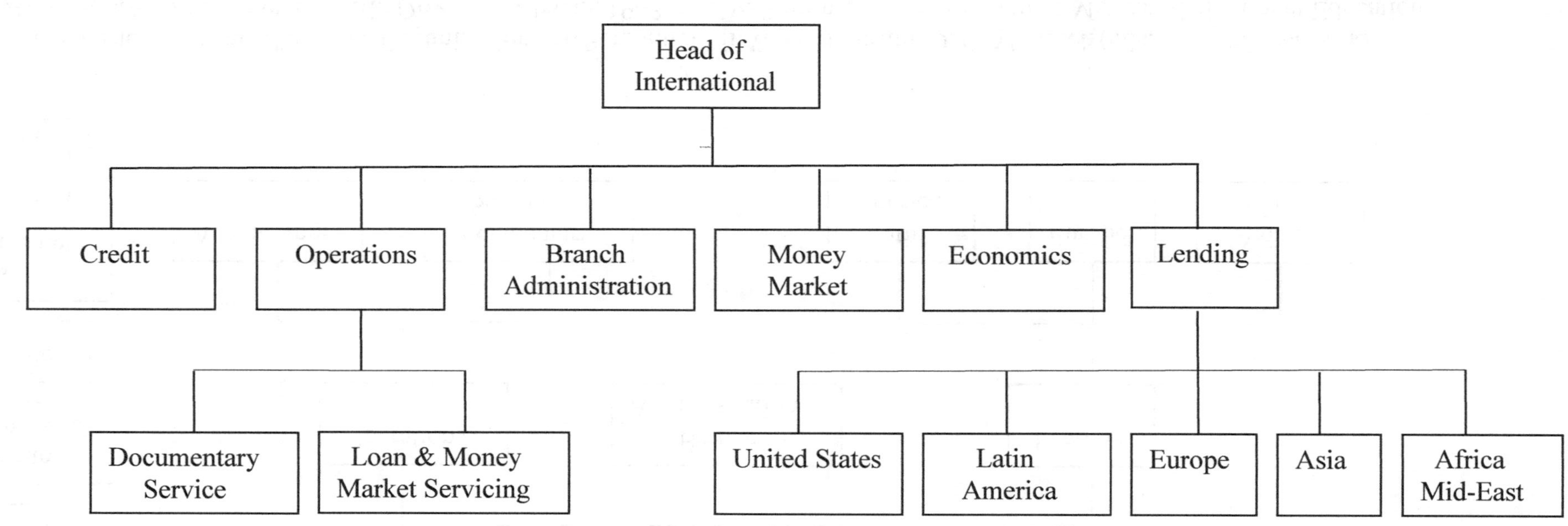

Source: Charles F. Turner, "Internal Organization and Personnel," in W.H. Baun and D. R. Mandich (eds.), *The International Banking Handbook*, Homewood, Ill.: Dow Jones-Irwin, 1983, p. 617. Reprinted by permission of McGraw-Hill Global Education Holdings, LLC.

Exhibit 5.2 Organization of the International Department at the Head Office: Functionally Integrated Structure

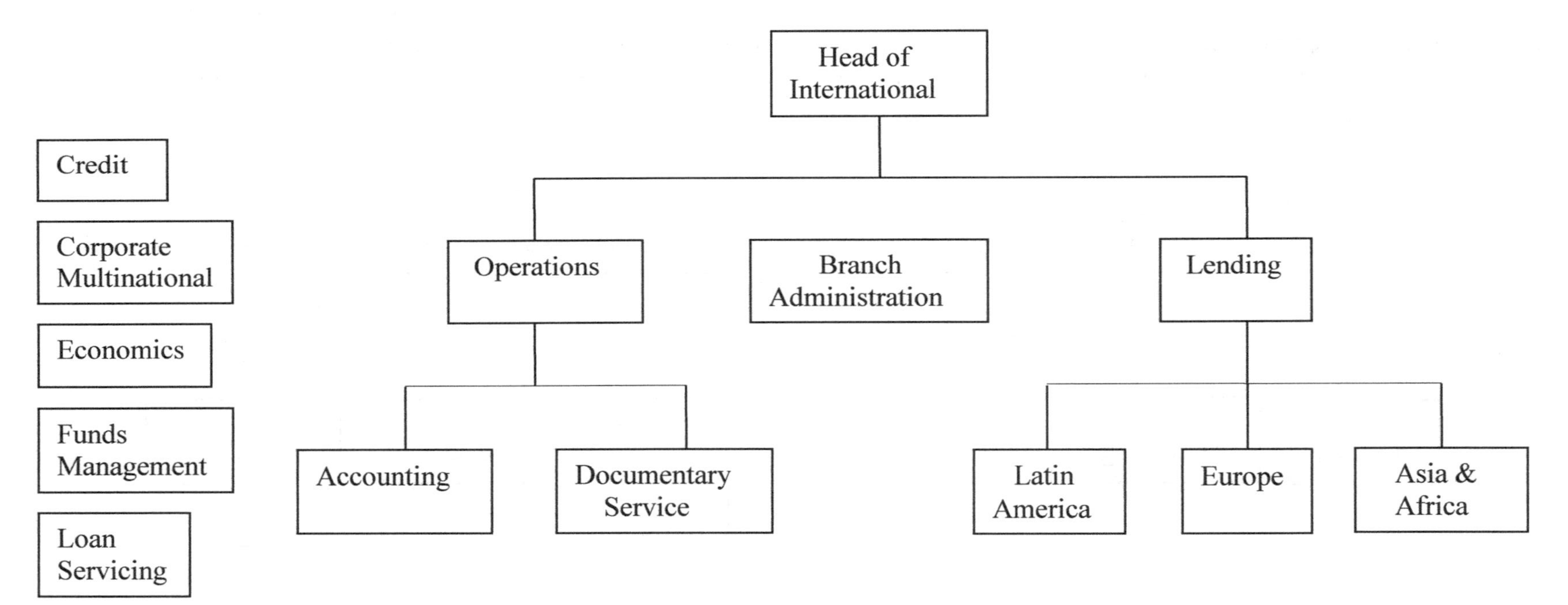

Source: Charles F. Turner, "Internal Organization and Personnel," in W.H. Baun and D. R. Mandich (eds.), *The International Banking Handbook*, Homewood, Ill.: Dow Jones-Irwin, 1983, p. 619. Reprinted by permission of McGraw-Hill Global Education Holdings, LLC

countries, prevailing banking structures, and customer profile. A key issue of the decision process is the type of vehicle to be used in the delivery of international services. Most U.S. banks use anyone or a combination of vehicles to access foreign markets. By the same token, the foreign banks that have a presence in this country rely upon a combination of the same vehicles for the conduct of their U.S. business. The alternate vehicles available are described below.

Correspondent Banking

Correspondent banking involves the use of a bank native to a foreign market to offer the desired international services. Candidate banks are usually located in their country's national or regional money centers. Not infrequently a bank may rely on a network of correspondent banks abroad to handle its foreign transactions. Under this arrangement a U.S. bank, for example, may have a prior agreement with a foreign bank to the effect that each will function as the agent of the other in their respective countries. Correspondent banking entails no foreign investment, no salaries for staff or any other related expenses. The banks may carry deposit accounts with one another or charge direct fees for the services rendered. Correspondent services include accepting drafts, honoring letters of credit, collecting or paying funds, furnishing credit information, and buying or selling securities for the account of the U.S. bank or its customers.

Representative Offices

A bank establishes a representative office (also known as a rep office) in a foreign country primarily to assist its clients that conduct business in that country or in neighboring countries. A representative office cannot engage in general banking activities; that is, it cannot accept deposits nor make loans, but it can generate business for the head office. Some banks establish representative offices as an interim step prior to direct establishment of a full-fledged branch. Additionally, these offices are utilized for entry into countries where the presence of foreign commercial banks is either limited or prohibited (e.g., Saudi Arabia and India). As they are a low budget vehicle, rep offices may also be used in countries with low per capita income (e.g., Haiti), strong banking institutions (e.g., Switzerland), or high risk (North Korea).

Agencies

Unlike a rep office, a foreign bank agency may engage in limited banking activity. In the United States, an agency is not allowed to accept domestic deposits but may engage in full scale lending operations. These are essentially sustained through the resources of the parent bank and the branch offices in the parent network. An alternative source of loanable funds may be the domestic interbank market (federal funds market) and/or the offshore dollar-denominated interbank market (Eurodollar market). Foreign bank agencies are generally used for wholesale international commercial transactions--their customers are chiefly banks and other nonbank businesses rather than individuals. Like rep offices, agencies are an integral part of their parent banks.

Branches

A foreign branch is a banking office owned by the parent bank, and therefore does not constitute a separate legal entity. It is subject to two sets of regulations--those of the home country and those of the host country. Although branching abroad calls for a sizable investment, it enables a bank to offer more personalized services than through a representative office or a correspondent relationship. Thus, it can provide full banking services, including large loans based on the size of the parent bank's capital. Deposits are a legal obligation of the parent bank, not of the branch. From the customer's viewpoint, the branch organization is most accommodating because branch services are based on the worldwide value of the customer relationship rather than on the relationship to any specific office.

Foreign branches constitute the principal vehicle used by U.S. banks in the conduct of their international activities; they account for the largest concentration in foreign assets. Most of the foreign branches of U.S. banks are located in Latin America, Asia, the Caribbean and Europe. However, the majority of foreign assets are held by branches in Europe (particularly in the United Kingdom, because of London's preeminence as the center of the Eurodollar market), followed by branches in the

Caribbean. The two primary Caribbean banking centers are the Bahamas and the Cayman Islands. Since the early 1970s, the Federal Reserve has allowed U.S. banks to establish *shell branches* (also known as "brass plate" branches) in these islands for the purpose of "booking" offshore transactions that took place on the U.S. mainland. Since the Fed's intention was to promote competition among U.S. banks in international markets, all offshore-booked transactions are exempt from reserve requirements, the cost for FDIC insurance, and other regulations.

Subsidiaries and Affiliates

When entry into a foreign market through a branch is restricted or prohibited, a bank may choose to enter that market through the de novo formation of, or stock acquisition in, a locally incorporated institution. If the investment results in a majority ownership position of the foreign institution it is termed a *subsidiary;* if it results in a minority ownership position, it is known as a foreign *affiliate.* In essence, then, the difference lies in the size of equity investment in--and, hence, extent of control of--the foreign institution.

Complete or partial investment in foreign institutions has been an important avenue in the international activities of U.S. banks. In general, as vehicles for implementing an international banking program, subsidiaries and affiliates provide the parent bank with an entry into foreign markets with only minimal demands on its manpower resources while adding international expertise to the domestic experience of the nationals managing the subsidiary or affiliate. The major advantage for the parent bank, however, is that the potential for developing new business and fruitful connections in the foreign country is far greater than might be possible through the establishment of a branch. The key disadvantage for the parent is that unlike a branch which requires no separate capitalization, a subsidiary, being a distinct legal entity, must possess adequate capital stock under host-country rules.

Subsidiaries constitute the second most important vehicle used by U.S. banks. Most of their assets are held in Europe, particularly in the United Kingdom.

One special type of subsidiary is an *Edge Act corporation.* Drawing its origin from a 1919 amendment to the Federal Reserve Act, an Edge Act corporation is a domestic subsidiary that may be owned by a U.S. bank or (since enactment of the International Banking Act in 1978) by a foreign bank. An Edge Act corporation may function as a commercial bank accepting deposits and making loans to companies engaging in international business. Moreover, it may function as an investment company, taking equity positions in foreign financial organizations, such as merchant banks and finance companies. Because Edge Act corporations can be located anywhere in the United States, they have become an established vehicle for banks to engage in interstate banking. Some Edge Act corporations operate offices overseas. The state-chartered and supervised counterparts to Edge Act corporations are known as *agreement corporations* because they must agree to the same restrictions that govern Edge Act corporations.

A special type of affiliate is a *consortium bank.* A group of banks, not necessarily of the same nationality, may establish abroad a joint venture, known as a consortium bank, to undertake activities they are restricted from engaging in their respective countries. The consortium bank has its own name and functions as an independent corporate entity in the framework of the policies developed by its shareholding banks represented on the board. Its activities include medium- and long-term credits, facilitating corporate mergers and acquisitions, taking equity participations, and performing underwriting or private placements of public and private issues. Since their heyday in the 1960s and early 1970s, consortium banks have declined in importance. Antagonism with their bank owners has led to the restructuring of many consortia into single-parent banks (subsidiaries). Some of those in existence operate as merchant and investment banks and are often located in offshore tax havens.

International Banking Facilities (IBFs)

Like shell branches, IBFs were created by the Federal Reserve to encourage American banks to do more international business in the United States rather than abroad. Introduced in December 1981, IBFs have been exempted from regulatory costs (reserve requirements and deposit-insurance premiums) and many states have exempted them from state and local taxes. An IBF is a record-keeping entity (accounting entity) similar to an offshore shell branch; that is, a separate set of asset and liability accounts segregated from the regular bank books. As such, IBFs may be maintained by a U.S. bank, an Edge Act corporation, or U.S. offices of a foreign bank. IBF facilities are limited to time deposits (negotiable CDs are prohibited) that must be in minimum amounts of $100,000 and may originate from non-U.S. residents and other IBFs. Deposits so obtained cannot be used domestically but may be used to make foreign loans. Of the IBFs in this country, about half are located in New York and the rest in regional financial centers that actively engage in international banking.

INTERNATIONAL SERVICES OF U.S. BANKS

Continued growth of the international economy in the postwar decades has contributed to an ever-increasing demand for international financial services. Responding to this demand, U.S. banks have focused not only upon developing an extensive network of international banking facilities but also upon expanding the different types of international services offered and increasing the volume of these services. U.S. banks offer some of these services directly, while others are offered indirectly through subsidiaries and affiliates operating abroad. In the latter instance, as indicated earlier, the wider scope of activities permitted local banks abroad has induced U.S. banks to acquire equity interests in foreign banks and other financial institutions, and to offer a variety of ancillary services to meet the needs of their multinational clientele.

Of the international services that U.S. banks offer directly, some are an extension of those they provide in the domestic market (such as transfer of funds and acceptance of deposits), while others are unique to international banking (such as purchase and sale of foreign exchange, and letter of credit financing). Because of the variety of services that U.S. banks extend to their customers, discussion here will be limited to the more traditional ones. These include transfer of funds, financing international trade, collections, purchase and sale of foreign exchange, and international loans.

Transfer of Funds

One of the basic services offered by banks engaging in international banking is the transfer of funds between parties residing or traveling in different countries. This transfer can take place in any of three ways: airmail remittance, wire, or foreign drafts. A customer wishing to transfer funds via air mail to a party in another country would pay the bank, in cash or by a check drawn on his account, the stated amount plus a fee covering the expenses of the transaction. The bank then would send an airmail letter to its correspondent bank in the country where the beneficiary resides, specifying the amount of payment, the name and address of the beneficiary, the name of the sender, and authorized signatures. Upon receipt of these instructions, the foreign bank would verify the authenticity of the signatures and contact the beneficiary. After payment of the funds (in local currency), the account of the instructing bank would be charged for the amount of the payment.

If speed is important, the transfer may take place by means of a wire (via SWIFT) or telephone. The process will be the same, except that the message is wired or telephoned to the correspondent bank. The authenticity of the instruction is verified by code or test key arrangement. Clearly, the code or key issued would be prearranged and would change at intervals for purposes of security.

Unlike the airmail and wire remittances, which are bank-to-bank instructions, a foreign draft is a negotiable instrument drawn by a bank on its foreign correspondent bank. A draft is issued when a client wants to have an actual instrument to mail to the beneficiary abroad. In such a case it is customary for the issuing bank to send its foreign correspondent a nonnegotiable copy of the draft, or a letter of advice that includes all the necessary details, as a protection against fraud.

In earlier decades one of the widely known and used means of transferring funds abroad was the traveler's checks, a negotiable instrument of worldwide acceptability. Though few banks issued these checks, virtually every bank maintained a large inventory to accommodate the needs of its traveling customers. Traveler's checks came to be accepted by tourists as a safe and easy instrument for the transfer of funds from one country to another.

In recent years electronic advances have made possible the use of the Internet to transfer money from a U. S. bank account to any of the 500,000 Western Union agent locations worldwide, with next day service. Similarly, a transfer may be effected by sending monies from overseas into a U.S. bank account via Western Union.

Foreign Deposit-Taking and Lending

Internationally, as domestically, the major function of banks is to intermediate--that is, to obtain deposits and to make loans. In performing this traditional function, banks always strive to acquire deposits at a minimal cost and to lend these funds out to relatively low risk customers. The objective, of course, is to obtain a reasonable spread. Lending policies pertaining to major domestic corporate customers are usually determined at the bank's home office. This is less frequently the case when the bank is dealing with international loans. In such instances more reliance is placed on the foreign branch or vehicle located abroad.

As in domestic activity, the largest source of income from international operations is lending. Most active in international lending are usually the banks that maintain branches abroad or other types of vehicles that ensure a presence in foreign markets. Banks with no physical presence abroad generally limit themselves to lending funds or giving credit to their domestic customers, thereby helping to finance international trade by making possible both the production of goods for export and the import of goods for domestic use. In the latter case these shipments are financed through bankers' acceptances, drawn under letters of credit. Unlike domestic trade, where shipments are usually made on an open account basis and bank financing of accounts receivable is a generally accepted practice, in foreign trade this is hardly practical for an exporter because of the problems that it entails. Specifically, it calls for credit-checking across international boundaries to ensure the creditworthiness of the foreign buyer; and once the sale is made, the exporter has no negotiable instrument evidencing the obligation of the foreign buyer. To circumvent these and other problems, the banker's acceptance mechanism has been developed. Under this arrangement the importer's bank will substitute its own credit standing for that of its customer, accepting a time draft for the price of the goods. Upon maturity of this draft, the customer pays the bank in full. This procedure works as a short-term loan, with the difference that no funds are actually advanced. In place of interest, the bank charges its customer a fee for the use of the bank's credit standing.

Foreign-trade financing is but one type of international lending, and obviously the one with the longest history. In recent decades the international activity of U.S. banks has expanded beyond the subsidiaries and affiliates of domestic corporations to include foreign companies and governments, including developing nations.

Foreign loans may be broadly classified into three distinct types: loans or placements to foreign banks or foreign branches of U.S. banks (interbank lending), loans to governments and official institutions, and loans to businesses. The latter category exhibits significant variation: loans to foreign companies, partnerships, and proprietorships; loans to corporations or their foreign branches, subsidiaries, or affiliates with parent company guarantee or other form of support; project loans for developing natural resources; and other types. For large scale and/or high risk credits, a number of banks may join together to extend, usually on common terms, a syndicated loan. New and specialized patterns continue to emerge, of course, but the above general categories still apply. A detailed discussion of these loan categories is undertaken in later chapters.

Collections

Collection, the presenting of an item for payment, is essentially the same internationally as domestically. The major difference is the absence of an international clearinghouse for checks and other negotiable items drawn on the banks of one country and deposited in the banks of another. Correspondent relationships are therefore established between commercial banks that also serve as agents, collecting negotiable items for exporters.

These collections may be either *clean* (without documents attached) or *documentary* (with documents attached). Clean items are usually checks, traveler's checks, and money orders, which, drawn on banks in the currency of one country, are exchanged for local currency in another country. American tourists abroad using traveler's checks to pay for services received or goods purchased, represent an example of clean collections. Recipients of these checks turn them over to their local banks for settlement. These foreign banks collect by sending the clean items, usually by airmail, to their correspondent American banks, either for immediate credit or as a collection, with the amount of the item to be credited only after payment is made by the maker's bank. Clean items are thus presented for collection in exactly the same manner internationally as they are domestically.

More complicated and, at this time, more important to international trade are documentary collections. The basis of such a collection is that banks act only as agents, and must exercise care to protect the collection documents from any loss or damage. The customer gives the bank precise instructions pertaining to presentation of the collection for payment, the party that will pay the fees, the method for transferring payment, and the steps to be taken if the collection is not made. Any deviation from the explicit instructions of the foreign bank and any action initiated by the collecting bank are at the risk of the latter.

The principal international clearing center in the United States is New York. In the mid-1960s a committee composed from the New York Clearing House banks was given the task of designing a system, acquiring the equipment, obtaining subscribers, and putting in place a computerized communications network to handle the clearing of interbank money transfers and to facilitate the clearing of Eurodollar transactions. The result was the Clearing House Interbank Payments System (CHIPS), which, introduced in April 1970, has been since the conduit for settlement of more than 90 percent of the world's foreign exchange business and the leading settlement mechanism for Eurodollar markets and other international trade transactions, such as letter of credit payments, collections, and bank-to-bank reimbursements. CHIPS provides settlement within the same day in federal funds (deposit balances held with Federal Reserve banks).

CHIPS must be distinguished from SWIFT, a global communications system that transmits financial messages, payment orders, foreign exchange confirmations, and securities deliveries to nearly 7,000 financial institutions on the network, located in 190 countries. Headquartered in Belgium, SWIFT is owned by a cooperative venture, the Society for Worldwide Interbank Financial Telecommunications.

Foreign Exchange

One activity conducted by a bank's international department that has no domestic parallel is foreign-exchange trading. No matter what the nature of an international business transaction, as long as it involves foreign payment, it will entail the exchange of one currency for another. There is no one physical, central marketplace for this kind of transaction (equivalent, for example, to the New York Stock Exchange for bonds and stocks). Rather, there is an electronically linked network of banks and foreign-exchange brokers and dealers who are located in the principal financial centers of the world and whose function is to bring together buyers and sellers of foreign exchange. The foreign-exchange market is thus very informal, with no official setting of rates or trading rules, and is generally guided by a code of ethics that has evolved over time.

Most U.S. commercial banks engaging in international banking consider foreign exchange as one of the services they provide to customers, but they do not regard it as central to their product mix. These banks participate in the *retail* portion of the market. They do not maintain inventory positions in foreign currencies but rely on their correspondent banks who are active in this market to execute their orders.

A number of internationally active U.S. banks trade currencies on a continuing basis with the largest banks headquartered abroad; they are participants in the *wholesale* or *interbank foreign-exchange* market. These banks are *market makers* in the currencies in which they specialize; that is, they are prepared to buy and sell these currencies with other banks at any time. To effect foreign-exchange trading, U.S. banks hold dollar balances and foreign-currency-denominated deposits with banks abroad. At the same time, foreign banks maintain offices in the United States to manage the accounts of their foreign clients (businesses and governmental agencies). Trading is generally done by telephone, telex, or the SWIFT system that electronically links all brokers and traders. Terminals display up-to-the-minute information concerning buy and sell orders, which, carried on an anonymous basis, are visible to all market participants and may be executed anywhere in the world at the press of a few keys in the keyboard. Before the local financial market opens for business, traders communicate with their counterparts in other parts of the world where trading is already in progress. The information received, combined with their own technical analysis, give traders a better feel for market direction and developing trends, and prepares them for subsequent market trading activity. Since thousands of transactions are executed each day, a bank's working balances in foreign currencies are inevitably affected. To even out temporary surpluses and shortages, traders must continuously buy and sell various currencies to adjust the bank's position in individual currencies. This is all the more important because prices in the market are sensitive and can change quickly.

Although transactions in the interbank market are effected directly between banks, a sizable number are conducted through foreign-exchange brokers. Brokers maintain instant access to dealers worldwide; this enables them to locate quickly an opposite party with whom a client can enter into a transaction while earning a commission for their efforts. Besides dealer and nondealer banks, broker services are used by businesses and governments. Brokers thus contribute to the efficient operations of the foreign-exchange market.

With the foreign-exchange market spanning the globe, the prices and currencies traded can change in the course of the day. Changes in foreign-exchange rates affect market participants throughout the world. Because these changes can be sudden, significant losses can be realized. Dealer banks have a risk exposure when they hold foreign-currency positions. Such exposure can be managed by imposing dollar limits on positions in a certain currency, on regions of the world, or on particular customers. Alternatively, a bank may use hedging techniques to control its exposure.

Exchange-rate risk is inherent in all international commercial and financial transactions. As long as rates fluctuate, even within a narrow range, risk is involved for those who expect to convert one currency to another. Whether it is a multinational corporation, an institutional investor, or an exporter, taking on foreign-exchange risk can undermine its viability as a going concern. For an American exporter, for example, who sells goods abroad for payment in a foreign currency, a drop in the value of the foreign currency will reduce profits or cause losses, thereby undermining his ability to compete effectively in international markets. Hedging in the foreign-exchange market reduces the exchange rate risk. The exporter can cover his position through a forward, futures, or options contract, whatever best suits his needs. Commercial banks earn fee income from arranging for such coverage.

FUTURE PROSPECTS

The increasingly diverse and complex financial needs of the global marketplace will require internationally active banks to develop distinct financial products in order to gain or maintain market share. Whether because of competitive pressures, more knowledgeable and demanding clients, and technological advances, service proliferation will become a dominant trend that will reshape commercial banking and the financial services industry. As a result, new sources of revenue--such as fees--will elbow the more traditional revenue sources (e.g., interest income from loans).

Market opportunities will no doubt be accompanied with important challenges for the international bankers. The financial crisis highlighted important deficiencies in the operation and risk management of many banks as well as gaps in the regulatory environment. Such deficiencies facilitated the rapid transmission of jolts across the global financial system though internationally active banks. As regulators address the future of the global financial system, they will focus more sharply on the dangers, the measurement and tracking of systemic risk. The new regulatory environment will constrain fast paced growth and consequent vulnerability of business models by requiring internationally active banks to hold stronger capital and liquidity buffers and balance sheets that are more resilient to funding shocks.

6 INTERNATIONAL INVESTMENT BANKING

ORIGINS AND DEVELOPMENT

Investment banking has traditionally referred to the raising of capital (be it debt or equity) through the issuance of securities. Outgrowth of the financial activities of West European merchant bankers, investment banking has evolved over time to include a full range of financial services. Its transformation to its present day form may be attributed to a number of forces including deregulation, new regulation, globalization, and advances in technology.

In the closing decades of the last century, several countries around the world enacted measures to deregulate their capital markets. In the United Kingdom liberalization of its capital market was initiated through enactment of landmark legislation, the Financial Services Act of 1986, which sought to deregulate financial services and establish an institutional framework for the securities market. London's "Bing Bang" was followed by similar moves in several European countries, including Switzerland, Germany and France. As the drive to establish a single market (1992) and introduce a single currency (1999) gained momentum, European Union (EU) directives fostered liberalization measures to accommodate greater competition. As a result all EU member countries experienced some form of financial market deregulation and streamlining of operating procedures which encouraged higher levels of capital market activity and benefitted investment banks.

The lead of European countries to liberalize their capital markets was followed by other members of the world community in which significant stock exchanges existed. Thus, in the 1990s and early 2000s capital liberalization measures were adopted by such countries as Australia, Canada, New Zealand, Korea, and ultimately Japan, where the regulatory framework for banks and investment banks was more rigid.

In the United States the Financial Services Modernization Act of 1999--also known as the Gramm-Leach-Bliley (GLB) Act (Exhibit 4.3)--dismantled the firewalls that separated commercial and investment banking under the Depression-era Glass Steagall Act. The immediate effect of the enactment of the GLB has been the creation of a new regulatory framework by permitting commercial banks, investment banks, and insurance companies to affiliate with each other under a FHC structure. The convergence of a vast array of financial services under such a structure has led to the reference of an institution like Citigroup as a financial supermarket. In Europe the traditional reference to a corresponding structure is that of the *universal model,* a fully integrated financial institution that may extend to its customers the full gamut of financial services under one roof. Unlike the U.S. and the Japanese systems that separated commercial and investment banking from the 1930s and 1940s respectively, many European countries have had no effective regulatory barriers to a comprehensive coverage of financial services which enabled European banks to become rapidly universal. Examples of leading universal banks in Europe are Germany's Deutsche Bank, France's Banque Nationale de Paris (BNP) Paribas, Britain's HSBC, Netherlands' International Netherlands Group (ING), and Switzerland's Credit Suisse (CS) and Union Bank of Switzerland (UBS).

Enactment of new regulation has sought to bolster public confidence in capital markets in a period of financial adversity. Such was the case, for example, in the United States in the early 2000s when corporate scandals (e.g., Enron and WorldCom) undermined investor confidence in Wall Street and corporate America. These scandals led Congress to legislate the Sarbanes-Oxley Act of 2002 to introduce sanctions against failures in corporate governance (disciplinary or remedial sanctions on publicly held companies for unethical behavior, such as overstatement of earnings, insider trading, and self-serving executives). Other major provisions of the act deal with the oversight of the accounting profession, improved financial disclosures, and the conflict of interest of research analysts to promote issues of investment banking clients. The burst of the real estate bubble and the ensuing financial crisis (2008) is another example where financial adversity had a profound effect on the financial services industry. Of the five largest investment banking houses at the onset of 2008, none of them continued to operate as investment bank by year-end. In the course of the year Lehman Brothers failed; Bear Stearns and Merrill Lynch insolvency concerns prompted their acquisition by the financial holding companies of J.P. Morgan Chase and Bank of America, respectively; and Goldman Sachs and Morgan Stanley requested and received approval to become bank holding companies. In addition to the change in the structure of the industry, the crisis prompted Congress to provide a comprehensive regulation of financial markets and a stricter supervisory framework through enactment of the Dodd-Frank Act of 2010 (Exhibit 4.3). Consolidation of regulatory oversight and consumer protection reforms were an integral part of this law.

Globalization of financial markets dates from the early 1990s as a result of two major developments--(a) the collapse of the Soviet Union and the demand of its former member countries for capital to build market economies, and (b) the need of less developed countries to establish modern, efficient marketplaces. As capital gravitated to the freest markets, it exerted pressure on other countries to adopt market liberalization measures thereby contributing to the emergence of a truly global money and capital market. To better serve the financial needs of their international clients, firms like Morgan Stanley and J.P. Morgan have operations in many countries around the world and particularly in those with sizeable capital market activities.

Advances in technology have accelerated the globalization of financial transactions. Advent of satellites, computers and other automated systems have tied together financial centers around the world, propelling cross-border financial transactions and a stream of information around-the-clock. The Internet and computer networks have transformed the investment banking business in many ways. Exchanges have moved heavily into electronic trading contributing to increased efficiency and accuracy. Investors have a twenty-four-hours-a-day access to research, data and valuation models, and conduct their bond and stock trading online. Technology has enabled the allocation of shares of initial public offerings (IPO) through online auctions (e.g., Google), and transformed security trading by shortening investors settlement date (the time required for payment of funds and delivery of securities). Information technology has increased the capability of investment banks to design and price complex contracts and derivatives, monitor and analyze risks, engage in computerized trading (programs that track market activity), and enhance their competitive edge through real-time information on the firm's worldwide operations.

ORGANIZATION, SCOPE AND SIZE OF OPERATIONS

As a result of the U.S. financial crisis and the changed state of investment banking, the firms in the industry may be classified into diverse groupings on the basis of such criteria as legal organization, scope, size of operations, and geographic markets served. As shown in Exhibit 6.1, investment banks have gone through three legal organizational structures--partnership model, universal bank/FHC ownership, and publicly-held company. In the early days of investment banking, availability of adequate capital to fund operations prompted many of these companies to be organized as partnerships. The partnership structure made the owners the managers of the company and held them both morally and fiscally accountable for the performance of the bank. Over time, many of the early partnerships became an integral part of a universal bank or a FHC structure. In the latter case, the acquisition turns the investment bank into a member of a group of companies accountable to a parent institution (e.g., Bear Stearns and Merrill Lynch acquisition by J.P. Morgan Chase and Bank of America, respectively). Exhibit 6.1 identifies some of the major investment banks that went public and had their shares listed on major U.S. exchanges. As is the case with all publicly-held corporations, ownership is dispersed among shareholders who are represented by the board of directors in setting up goals and formulating policies, and in designating managers to run company operations. A key drawback of the model, known as the agency problem, is that directors and managers may have interests that are different from those of shareholders (e.g., outcry of compensation packages to executives and other employees at firms that were rescued by a taxpayer bailout in the immediate post-crisis period).

In terms of scope of services, investment banks may be distinguished into two basic types--full service and boutique banks. Exhibit 6.2 identifies the names of the top ten institutions in each category. With the exception of a few foreign institutions, the overwhelming majority are U.S. investment banks suggesting their dominance of

Exhibit 6.1 Legal Organizational Structure and Scope of Services

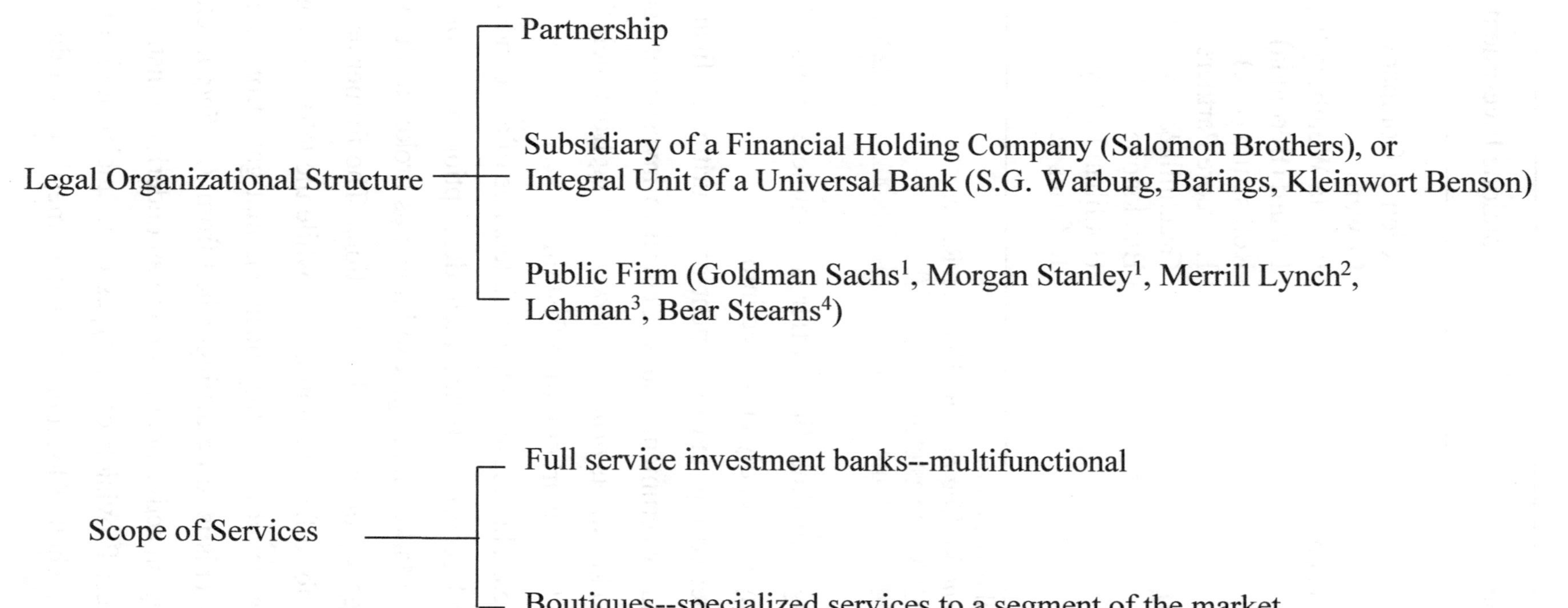

[1]Converted to a BHC (September 2008)
[2]Acquired by Bank of America Corp. (September 2008)
[3]Failed (September 2008)
[4]Acquired by J.P. Morgan Chase (March 2008)
Source: Developed by the author.

Exhibit 6.2 Ten Largest Global Investment Banks

Full-Service Investment Banks	Boutique Investment Banks
J.P. Morgan Chase	Allen & Company
Goldman Sachs	Cowen
Bank of America Merrill Lynch	Perella Weinberg Partners
Morgan Stanley	Lazard (Bermuda)
Citigroup	Rothschild (UK)
Deutsche Bank (Germany)	Evercore Partners
Credit Suisse (Switzerland)	Greenhill & Co.
Barclays Capital (UK)	Blackstone
Wells Fargo	Houlihan Lokey
UBS (Switzerland)	Jefferies & Co.

Note: Ranking based on global revenues in 2015.
Source: 2015 Global Investment Banking Review, Thomson Reuters.
http://www.valuewalk.com/2016/01/investment-banking-2015/
https://www.wallstreetprep.com/knowledge/investment-banks-list/boutique-investment-banks/

global investment banking. Full-line firms offer a complete menu of investment banking services which may be broadly classified into

- Origination, underwriting and placement of securities in financial markets for corporate and government issues. Central to investment banking, these activities are also known as *primary market making* from their focus on new issues that come to the market for the first time.
- Securities services: These refer to the maintenance of a secondary market on previously issued securities hence their description as *secondary market making* services. Market making, also known as broker-dealer services, can involve either agency or principal transactions. The former are executed on behalf of clients for a fee or commission, while the latter are carried out for the firm's own account (inventory positions that gain from a movement in security prices). This is to be distinguished from *Trading,* a related activity that entails taking an active net position in an underlying instrument/asset.
- Advisory services: Provision of all types of financial advice to companies and governments whether local or national, domestic or foreign.

- Other services: A supplemental category that covers income from all other sources (supplementary revenue-producing business), such as investment management for client firms, foreign currency trading, leasing, bridge financing, financial engineering (devising new and innovative financial products, e.g., derivatives), and *merchant banking*--investing the firm's own capital as well as funds raised from outside investors.

The largest firms in the industry are full service investment banks that attend both to their government and corporate clients (via securities underwriting) as well as to their retail customers (by acting as broker-dealers). Bank of America (through its acquisition of Merrill Lynch), Morgan Stanley, and J. P. Morgan (through its various acquisitions including Bearn Stearns) are typical, large, full-service providers.

Boutique investment banks, on the hand, specialize in a particular segment of the market, such as origination, underwriting and distribution of new issues of securities (commercial side of the business) or purchase, sale, and brokerage of existing securities (retail side of the business). Some boutiques specialize in advisory services, with specific focus a certain niche of this market (e.g., strategic planning, and bankruptcy workouts). They may cater their services to all corporate clients or select market participants, such as middle market companies, firms in a certain industry (e.g., information service companies), or in a specific sector (e.g., financial institutions). A boutique's specialization may be the result of different considerations, such as industry connections, the ongoing importance of a relationship, and in-house skills and talents. Lazard and Greenhill are examples of boutique houses; Lazard is a financial advisory and asset management firm, while Greenhill's core lines of business are advisory work on M&A and restructuring, and merchant banking services.

In terms of size of operations, commercial banks or financial holding companies account for the largest of the full service investment banks and are commonly identified as *bulge bracket* firms. This term reflects the larger and bolder print of those firms' names on a public offering announcement of a new issue (known as tombstone) and on the front page of a Securities Exchange Commission (SEC) registration statement (prospectus). The bulge bracket includes such firms as Citigroup, J. P. Morgan Chase, Bank of America, Goldman Sachs, and Deutsche

Bank. Institutions not in the bulge bracket make up the *major bracket* (second tier investment banks), followed by the *submajors* (third tier investments banks), and the *regionals* (smaller institutions tied to a geographical location). Occasionally, between the major (second tier) and the submajor (third tier) brackets there may be an extra tier a *mezzanine bracket* (small firms that have a special relationship with the issuer or the lead manager).

Still another classification of investment banks is by geographic markets served (or scale of operations). The largest of the U.S. full service investment banks (commercial banks and financial holding companies) maintain a prominent presence in the domestic and all major capital markets around the globe, deriving a significant portion of their revenues from overseas operations. A second tier are the full service firms with a national scope of operations--that is, extensive presence and active involvement in the domestic market. A third tier are the investment banks that maintain a limited branch network in major cities to attend to the needs of their main institutional clients. A fourth tier are regional securities firms with operations focused to a specific area or region, such as California or New York. A residual tier includes the rest of the firms in this industry that offer a different mix of services. This tier includes such firms as specialized discount brokers (e.g., Charles Schwab), specialized electronic trading securities firms (e.g., E-trade), venture capital and private equity firms, research boutiques, and floor specialists.

With Wall Street the primary hub for this industry, the largest of the U.S. firms alongside their many foreign counterparts have a presence in the City of New York. Some of the more important non-U.S. institutions with a New York City presence include such universal banks as Deutsche Bank, Credit Suisse, Barclays, HSBC, BNP Paribas and Mizuho (Japan's Mizuho Financial Group or MHFG). All the investment banking players present in New York compete on nearly every continent by having operations in key financial centers around the world. Especially prominent is the presence of these institutions in London where virtually all of the world's leading financial institutions have a physical presence.

As globalization and technological advances transformed investment banking into a twenty-four-hour-a-day business, they also contributed to the global eminence of U.S. financial markets. Growth in the flow of funds across borders has propelled

U.S. financial markets to the largest and most active worldwide. A high demand for U.S. securities has prompted sizeable amounts of foreign funds to be invested in domestic issues. This has been especially true in periods of overseas turmoil when investors worldwide seek a safe haven for their funds. In such periods dollar-denominated instruments, and U.S. Treasury securities in particular, become a dominant asset in foreign portfolios.

CORE ACTIVITY AREAS

As stated earlier, full service investment banks engage in a range of transactions that cover the following key activity areas: primary market making, secondary market making, trading, advisory services, and other services. Exhibit 6.3 provides an overview of these activity areas. Although each one of these is promoted and offered to clients independently, they may be extended simultaneously as the case may be (e.g., arranging for the issue of debt or equity securities to finance a merger or an acquisition).

Primary Market Making

This activity area is so named because the primary market is the first market in which new securities are issued. Whether the new securities are of the government and its political subdivisions, or corporations, the activities of investment banks in the origination, underwriting and distribution of these issues are vital for the functioning of the primary market. The divergent roles of investment banks in these areas are highlighted in Exhibit 6.3.

Origination and Underwriting

The role of a full service investment bank in the underwriting process varies depending upon whether the securities issued are placed with public or private investors. In a public offering the securities may be underwritten on a firm commitment or a best effort basis, while in a private offering the investment bank places the securities with one or a few institutional investors.

Firm commitment is so named because of the underwriter's commitment (guarantee) to purchase at a fixed price all of the securities offered for sale by the

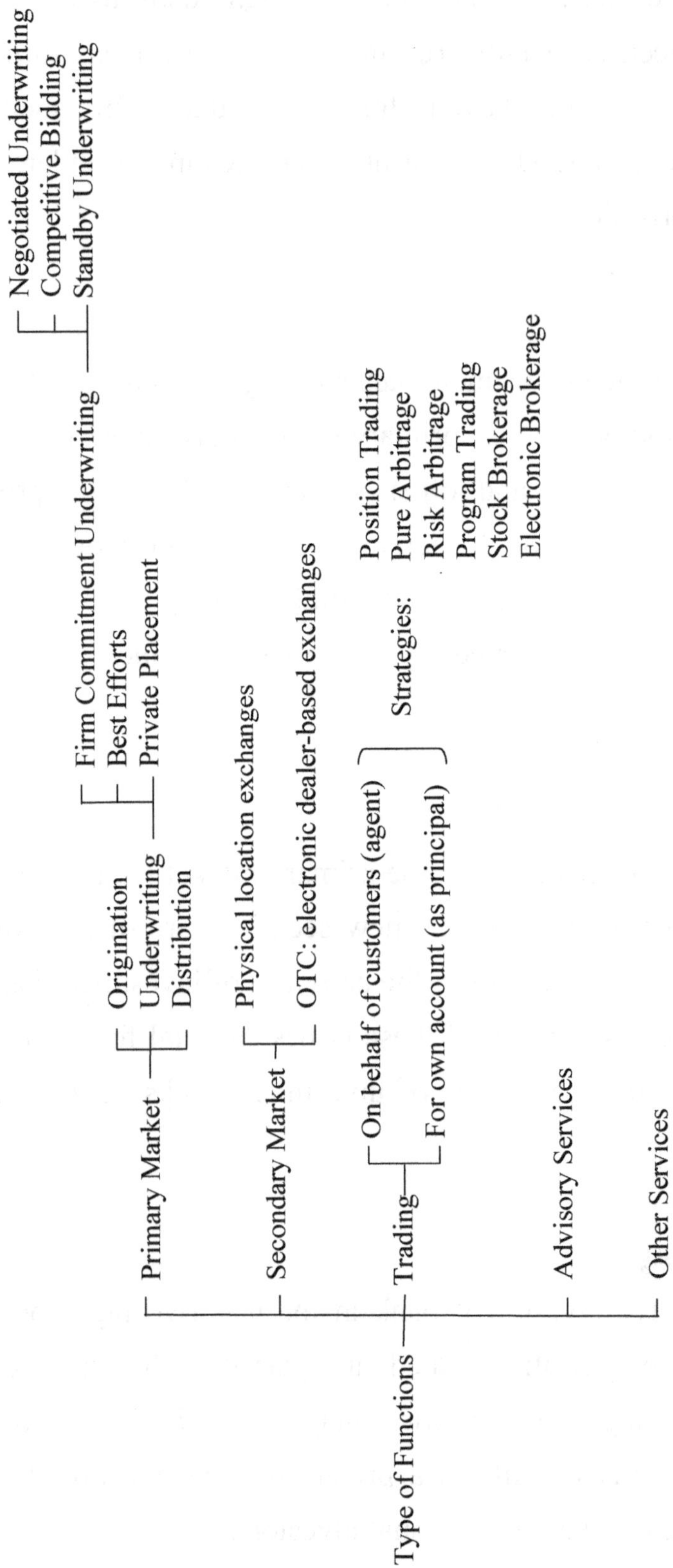

Exhibit 6.3 Functions of Full Service Investment Banks

Type of Functions (cont.)

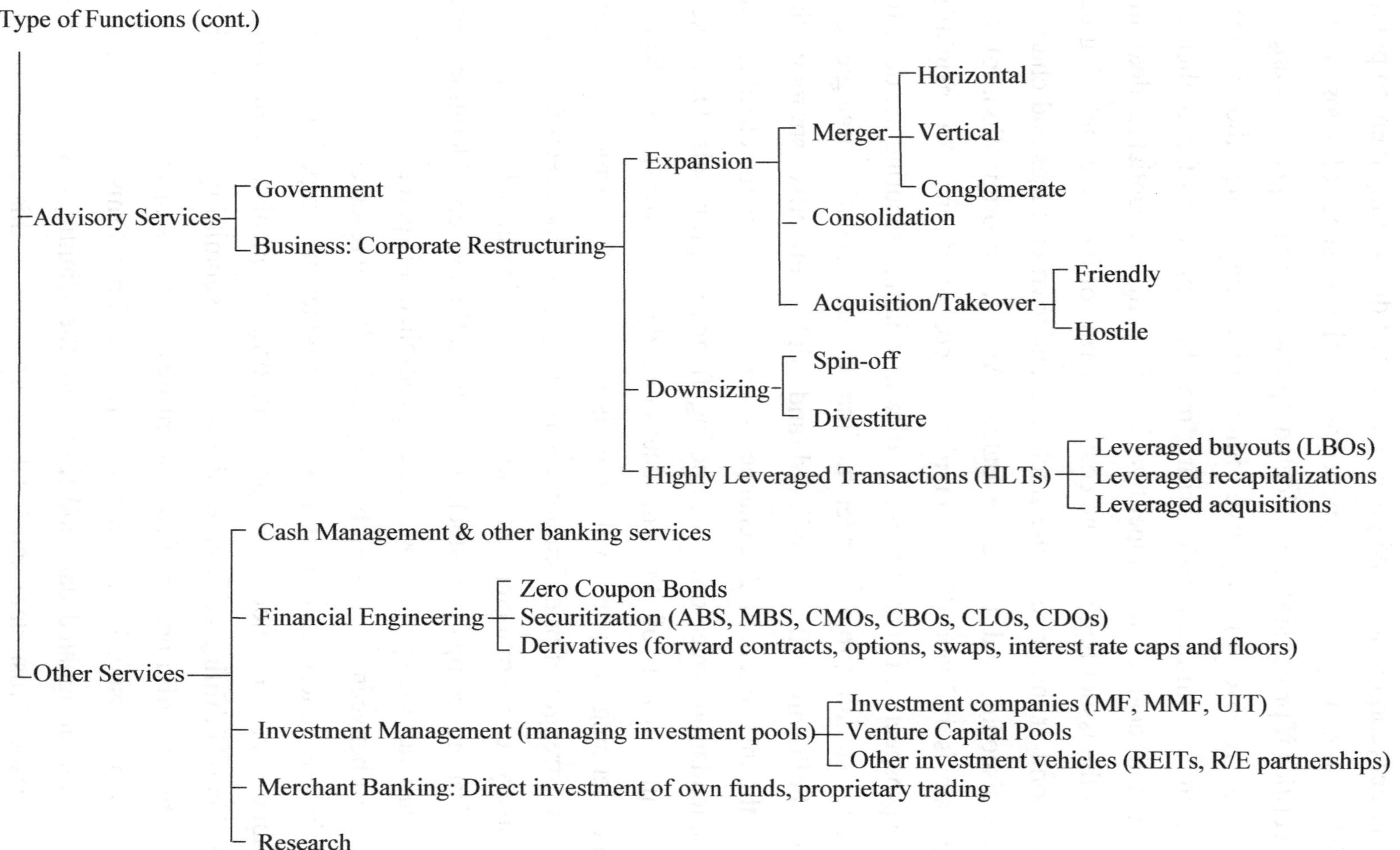

Source: Developed by the author

issuer. Essentially the investment bank acts as a principal purchasing the securities outright from the issuer (corporations and government) and distributing them to public investors. The risk assumed by the investment bank is the prospect of a loss in the resale of these securities if prices suffer a sudden drop due to an unexpected change in interest rates or a release of negative information impacting the issuer's creditworthiness. Firm commitment underwriting may be a product of two alternate processes--a negotiated deal or a competitive bidding. In a negotiated deal the investment bank and the issuer negotiate the cost and terms of the issue including the interest rate of the bond or the price of the stock, the underwriter's fees and charges, the original issue discount, and the issue date. Award, or origination, of the underwriting mandate is influenced by a number of considerations. An insightful presentation to the prospective client carries significant weight in securing the deal. Its design and crafting should project understanding of the client's strategic and operational plans. Following often a tailored and highly effective strategy, the presentation offers the investment bank a chance to demonstrate why the client should choose its recommendations over other competing financing proposals. Other key considerations in the award of the mandate include the investment bank's underwriting and lending rapport with the issuer (past securities offerings underwritten and the strength of prior lending relationships), its track record and peer ranking in the industry, core competencies, and sector specific client list. Aggressive upgrading of the issuing company's stock was an additional consideration until enactment of the Sarbanes Oxley Act 2002 which prohibited this practice by labeling it a conflict of interest between investment banking and sell-side research.

Firm commitment underwriting may also be a product of competitive bidding (sale through public auction). Under this approach, origination of an underwriting mandate is a function of fulfilling auction requirements and submitting a winning bid. An advertisement, by way of a notice of sale, identifies the terms of the auction and the characteristics of the issue. Interested investment banking firms are invited to submit their bids at the designated date and time with the winning bid awarded the right to market the issue. Most state and local governments in this country require their bonds to be issued through the competitive bidding approach (notice of sale is posted in a trade publication, such as the Bond Buyer). The same approach is used in the sale of the dominant portion of U.S. government debt, which represents the highest quality of marketable securities available from a credit standpoint. Issued to finance the national debt and other federal government expenditures, all four types of U.S. Treasury securities (Treasury bills, Treasury notes, Treasury bonds, and Treasury Inflation Protected Securities) are sold through regularly scheduled auctions. A select number of full service investment banks (21), designated as "primary dealers," submit electronically their competitive bids for particular quantities of specific denominations. Given the nature of the auction (Dutch auction), all winning bidders are awarded securities at the price that the entire offering can be sold (noncompetitive tenders of individuals and small investors up to $5 million each are awarded securities at the accepted bid).

As underwriters, investment banks (primary dealers) purchase the vast majority of the U.S. Treasury securities sold at auctions. This same practice is followed by many foreign governments abroad. Specifically, some foreign governments (e.g., Belgium, India, Japan, Singapore, Spain and the United Kingdom) sell their securities only to primary dealers; others have included additional institutions to this group. As the U.S. Treasury issues all its new securities in book-entry form, technological advances have increased the speed and efficiency of trading transactions be it with other dealers, financial institutions, and other investors. Transactions in the United States are cleared and settled among primary dealers and other active market participants primarily through the Government Securities Clearing Corporation (GSCC). The GSCC compares and nets member trades, thereby reducing the number of transactions through the Federal Reserve's Fedwire.

With the U.S. primary dealers maintaining a worldwide network, new issues of U.S. government debt can be distributed widely. For example, Daiwa Securities and Mizuho Securities distribute new U.S. debt to Japanese buyers, while BNP Paribas, Barclays, Deutsche Bank, and Royal Bank of Scotland Securities distribute the debt to European buyers. Conversely, these institutions facilitate the issue and distribution in U.S. markets of the dollar-denominated debt of foreign governments and their political subdivisions (e.g., Republic of Italy and the City of Naples). "Sovereign debt," as this debt has been traditionally referred to, has been also issued and traded in other major global currencies including the British pound, the euro, the Swiss franc, and the Japanese yen.

Firm commitment is also extended in standby underwriting agreements used in conjunction with *preemptive rights*. A public offering still practiced in the United Kingdom and some countries in continental Europe and Asia, preemptive rights grant shareholders the right to purchase new shares of the company, within a prescribed period, before they are offered to outsiders. In this country, the corporate laws of select states, or some corporate charters, give existing shareholders this right to maintain their proportional ownership in the company. With the offering price set slightly below the market price, existing shareholders may exercise their rights (purchase the allotted new shares) or sell them. The issuing company arranges for a standby underwriter to purchase--on a firm commitment basis--any unsubscribed shares for resale to the public. Use of preemptive rights has been on the decline in the United States as companies have sought to broaden their shareholder bases to include new investors.

Best efforts underwriting is an arrangement whereby the investment banking firm agrees to do its best to sell the securities but does not guarantee the price and hence bears no risk, which rests with the issuer. Essentially the investment bank functions as a distribution agent trying to sell the securities at the issuer's originally set price, with any unsold securities returned to the issuer. In return for its services the investment bank earns a fee.

Private placement provides for the private sale of the securities. Acting as an agent for a fee the investment bank would identify one or more large institutional buyers (e.g., insurance companies, and pension funds) to purchase the entire issue of bonds or stocks, as the case may be. As large investors are presumed to have the resources and expertise to analyze risk, privately placed issues do not have to register with the SEC and meet the requirements for publicly traded securities. Further, as these securities are often of less known issuers (e.g., of mid-sized municipalities, and small and medium enterprises), they are among the most illiquid securities which only the very largest institutional investors are able to buy and hold. The greater risk of these issues has led to more restrictive provisions to protect lenders--privately placed bonds pay a higher rate of interest than publicly offered bonds, while stocks are placed at a lower price than the publicly offered stocks. A 1990 amendment of SEC Rule 144A has allowed the trading of privately placed securities among qualified institutional buyers (QIBs). The improved liquidity of these issues has contributed to the rapid growth of the market and the expansion of investment banking activity to include firm commitment underwriting for privately placed debt.

Underwriting of Corporate Issues. The divergent underwriting modes described above apply also on corporate debt and equity issues. Although both types are designed to enable corporations to match their funding requirements to investor needs, there is significant variation in characteristics between, and within each of, them. Corporate debt, issued both in this country and in markets around the world, is made up of three major instruments--commercial paper, medium term notes and corporate bonds. The commercial paper (CP) is an unsecured promissory note ranging in maturity from 1 to 270 days, issued by prime-rated companies to meet cash needs (e.g., working capital requirements). While a usually unsecured debt, some CP has been secured by specific financial assets (e.g., mortgages) with the cash flow of those assets paying off the debt on maturity. Two key characteristics that propelled the CP to one of the major money market instruments are its short term maturity which exempts it from SEC's registration requirements, and its lower cost of financing compared to bank borrowing. Commercial papers are sold to investors either directly by the issuer's own sales force, or indirectly by an investment bank through firm commitment underwriting. Medium term notes are intermediate debt instruments issued typically in small amounts on a continuous basis, over a two-year period. Because of the ongoing nature of their sale, note offerings are typically registered with the SEC (Rule #415 *shelf registration*). The investment banking firms active in this market place corporate notes on a best efforts basis.

Bonds are the most common form of debt issued by corporations to support their long term financing needs. Although a dominant capital market instrument, corporate bonds themselves typify the differentiation in characteristics. For example, the distinguishing characteristic of an issue may be based on such a consideration as recording of investor's identification information by the issuer (registered as opposed to bearer bonds); maturity of the issue being a single date or a series of dates (term versus serial bonds); availability of a pledged asset as collateral (secured versus unsecured bonds); priority in debt service (debentures versus subordinated debentures); right to exchange one issue for another, or to purchase another security of issuing firm (convertible bonds versus bonds with warrants); requirement to sell issue back to issuer (callable bonds). Alternatively, the differentiation may refer to the coupon (zero coupon, fixed, or floating rate), the frequency of its payment, or the length of maturity. Compared to the U.S. Treasury, for example, whose bonds may have a maturity of up to 30 years, Walt Disney Company's "sleeping beauties" were issued (July 21, 1993) with a maturity of 100 years, followed by Coca Cola's 100-year bonds (July 22, 1993), Norfolk Southern's 100 year-bonds (August 23, 2010) and Safra Republic Holdings' 1,000-year bonds (October 8, 1997). Investment banking firms underwrite and distribute corporate bonds in primary markets in the same manner identified earlier, e.g., firm commitment, best efforts and private placement.

Unlike governments that rely solely on debt issues to meet their funding requirements, corporations have the alternate option to raise capital through equity. Equity, or corporate stock, is a long term source of financing for businesses and represents ownership rights in a firm. Of the two types of corporate stock--common and preferred--most public corporations prefer to issue only common stock. As a result, this instrument has grown to a widely held financial asset among major investor groups. Most new issues of stocks are sold in the primary market through the same underwriting processes used for bonds--firm commitment, best efforts, and private placement.

Underwriting of State and Local Government Debt. Issued by different levels of state and local government (state, county, city, school districts and special districts) this debt provides for the funding of budgetary deficits and long-term capital outlays (e.g., construction of transportation systems, schools and public utilities). With the bulk of financing of a long-term nature, these issues are known as municipal bonds or "munis." They are also referred to as tax-exempts because the interest paid to investors is exempt from federal income taxes (most states exempt their own issues from state income taxes as well). As a result they are of appeal to investors who are subject to a high marginal tax bracket. Municipal bonds are of two types, general obligation bonds, backed by the full faith and credit of the issuing government, and revenue bonds backed only by the revenue stream generated by the project being financed (e.g., airports, public housing, bridges and highways). If the project's cash flow is not sufficient to service the debt, the issue will go into default and the investors' only hope would be a possible resumption of payments in the future. As a result, revenue bonds are generally riskier than general obligation bonds. The underwriting process for municipal bonds may take any of the three forms discussed earlier--firm commitment, best efforts, and private placement.

Global Markets Underwriting Activity. Economic conditions play a decisive role on the state of financial markets and the overall underwriting activity. In the 1990s, good U.S. prospects for economic growth induced a heavy inflow of foreign capital in this country; as a result, U.S. financial markets boomed with a consequent effect on underwriting activity. The economic downturn that followed at the end of that decade ushered a drop in financial values and in the volume of new issues brought to the markets. Recovery was short-lived. The financial crisis of 2008 and its subsequent spread worldwide was a major setback for financial markets that affected accordingly the issue and sale of new securities. As markets rebound in the early teens, underwriting activity surged past pre-crisis highs and so did the volume of new issues. Thus, between 2011 and 2014 the underwriting and issue of new debt and equity securities in global markets rose from $5.57 trillion to $6.63 trillion, a 19 percent increase over the four year span. Exhibit 6.4 shows that in 2015 global debt and equity underwriting eased to $6.17 trillion, a decrease of 7 percent from that of the previous year. The top ten investment banks alone accounted for $3.31 trillion or 53.7 percent of the total underwriting activity, suggesting their dominance of the industry. J. P. Morgan Chase held the lead in terms of deals completed and advisory fees earned.

Exhibit 6.5 shows that debt, in the form of syndicated loans and capital market issues, was the primary source of financing worldwide with a total of $9.35 trillion underwritten by investment banks in 2015. Global capital market issues alone accounted for $5.30 trillion, or 57 percent of total debt, and consisted of different types of bonds (e.g., asset-backed, investment grade corporates, and high yield

Exhibit 6.4 Top Underwriters of Global Debt, Equity and Equity-Related Issues
Ranked by Value of Proceeds, 2015
(in billions of dollars)

Rank	Bookrunner	Proceeds	Number of Deals	Imputed Share	Advisor Fees
1	J. P. Morgan	$461.9	1,808	9.3%	$2.986
2	Bank of America Merrill Lynch	392.4	1,574	8.1	2.517
3	Citigroup	388.2	1,587	8.2	2.205
4	Barclays	380.8	1,424	7.3	1.659
5	Morgan Stanley	326.2	1,576	8.1	2.531
6	Deutsche Bank	325.6	1,436	7.4	1.720
7	Goldman Sachs & Co.	325.6	1,155	6.0	2.405
8	HSBC Holdings PLC	261.3	1,230	6.3	.885
9	Credit Suisse	246.8	1,072	5.5	1.652
10	Wells Fargo & Co.	204.8	1,124	5.8	1.157
Top Ten Total		**3,313.6**			**19.716**
Industry Total		**$6,170.0**	**19,382**		**$38.400**

Source: *Debt Capital Markets Review*, Thomson Reuters, 2015.
http://share.thomsonreuters.com/general/PR/DCM-4Q15-(E).pdf

Exhibit 6.5 Top-Ranked Underwriter in Each Market, 2015
(in billions of dollars)

Type of Issue	Industry Total	Bookrunner	Proceeds
Global debt, equity and equity-related	$6,170.0	J. P. Morgan	$461.9
Global debt and syndicated loans	9,352.6	J. P. Morgan	704.1
Global debt	5,299.9	J. P. Morgan	395.0
Global asset-backed securities	344.1	Citigroup	39.6
Global mortgage-backed securities	447.8	Credit Suisse	54.9
Global investment grade corporate debt	2,641.4	J. P. Morgan	208.0
Global high yield debt	347.2	J. P. Morgan	34.5
All international emerging market bonds	339.1	HSBC Holdings PLC	36.5

Source: Debt Capital Markets Review, Thomson Reuters, 2015.
http://share.thomsonreuters.com/general/PR/DCM-4Q15-(E).pdf

bonds). As seen in this Exhibit, J. P. Morgan Chase was the top-ranked underwriter in five of the eight different global capital market issues cited.

Distribution

Distribution pertains to the selling of newly issued securities to investors. These may represent a first-time issue of shares by a private company going public or a new offering by a firm that has shares already trading in the secondary market. The former is known as an IPO while the latter as a "seasoned offering" or a "follow-on." Unlike a first time issue which requires the investment bank to address several steps of the process, including choice of the market where the new issue will trade, in a seasoned offering the process is faster because some of the same steps are already in place including the market that the firm's prior debt or equity issue trades.

For a first-time issue the distribution phase depends upon the agreed form of underwriting--private placement or public offering. In a private placement the investment bank acts as an agent for a fee, with the distribution of the issue focused on a segment of the market, the large, sophisticated investors or QIBs. By contrast, in a public offering, be it best efforts or firm commitment, the focus of the distribution is the public at large. In a best-efforts public offer, the firm acts as an agent and receives a fee based on the success of its selling effort. In a firm commitment underwriting the investment bank acts as a principal taking outright ownership of the securities to be offered to the public. As the risk of loss in the public sale of the issue is high so is the return to compensate for this risk. Negotiated between the investment bank and the issuer, the underwriting spread (difference between the guaranteed price paid to the issuer and the higher resale price to public investors) represents the bank's compensation for the risk and expenses associated with the sale of the issue.

The investment bank that receives the mandate for the issue of a new security is known as the "lead manager," or "bookrunner" (runs, or is in charge of, the book of securities sold). On very large issues, two or more banks may be negotiating directly with the issuing company, in which case they would be the originating houses, lead banks or joint bookrunners. A **syndicate** is formed by inviting other investment banks to participate in the selling group. All members of the syndicate are entitled to the underwriting spread based on the following allocation schedule: the manager's fee goes to the managing underwriter for his role in putting the deal together; the underwriting or syndicate allowance covers the underwrting syndicate's miscellaneous expenses (e.g., advertising, legal, and other costs); and the selling concession paid to all syndicate participants according to the amount of securities they accept to sell. The lead bank's reputation contributes to its market credibility and command of confidence by both the issuer and participating institutions.

Being the lead manager of a new public offering requires the investment bank to have conducted a thorough investigation of the issuing company whose securities they sell. To limit potential liability under securities law, the investment bank must confirm all material facts in regards to the issuer, such as its financial records, production operations, marketing, articles of incorporation, and bylaws. "Due diligence," as this comprehensive investigation is known, must extend to include all legal and accounting information deemed material to the transaction and the company. Due diligence also plays a critical role in ensuring that the registration statement required by the law is a high-quality disclosure and marketing document. Prepared by the issuer and the underwriter and filed with the SEC prior to the public offering of the new issue, the registration statement must include information about the company's business, the background of management, the risk factors of investing into the company, and the basic provisions and features of the new issue. The intent of the law is to ensure that the registration statement complies with disclosure requirements; that is, that it includes all the pertinent information that will enable investors to make informed investment decisions. The SEC takes a minimum of 20 days to review the registration statement and request additional information or changes. The period between the filing of the registration and its effective date has been referred to as the waiting, quiet, or cooling-off, period.

The registration statement is made up of two component parts, with the first part called a prospectus. While the statement is under SEC review, the issuer and the investment bank distribute, as a separate booklet, a preliminary version of the prospectus (known as red herring from the red lettering of the caption in the cover page) to solicit indications of investor interest, but no actual sales. It has been customary during this period for company executives and investment bankers to go on roadshows to make presentations to promote the sale of the new issue. The roadshows also enable underwriters gain insights into investors' interests, which assists in determining the final price and size of the issue. In recent years, as a result of technological advances, face-to-face roadshows have been replaced by internet roadshows that enable investors to view presentations electronically.

Another type of publication allowed during the cooling-off period is the tombstone, an announcement only, and not an offer to sell nor a solicitation to buy. The tombstone advertisement that appears in domestic or international financial periodicals and newspapers announces the particulars of the issue--it identifies the issuer, the price and size of the issue, and the name of the bookrunner or lead manager, a bulge bracket investment bank. It also includes the names of invited participants, investment banks in the major or submajor brackets, listed according to the degree of their participation (e.g., co-managers, and participants). The number of invited banks spreads the risk associated with the sale of the issue. It also results in a larger pool of potential investors, increasing the probability of a successful sale and widening the scope of the investor base.

Once the SEC is satisfied with the registration statement it registers the issue at which point sales to the public may commence under a best efforts or a firm commitment underwriting. The "final prospectus" is promptly delivered to investors and is the official, complete disclosure of all facts relating to the issue including the final size and price of the public offering. Indications of interest may be converted to purchase orders, at the buyers' discretion. On occasion some IPOs may be poorly received or, at the other extreme, may exhibit large price runups. For example, if during an IPO of common stock, the distribution cannot be completed because of a lower than anticipated demand, the underwriter may intervene to stabilize the security by bidding for it in the open market at a price not to exceed the offering price. The SEC considers stabilization transactions as necessary for preventing or retarding a decline in the market price of a security to facilitate an offering. Although essentially a price support, if an underwriter does not engage in such activity, investors may cancel their indication of interest or renege on their orders (prior to the transaction's settlement date), precipitating a cascade. On the other hand, if there is a large price run-up because of higher than anticipated demand, the underwriter may sell additional shares up to 15 percent of the offer size, within 30 calendar days after the offering (green shoe or over-allotment option).

Secondary Market Making

Once a security is issued it needs to be traded among investors without the issuing companies' involvement. For the investment banks that act as primary government securities dealers and/or underwriters of municipal and corporate issues, secondary market making is an extension of their primary market activities. The firms active in this market may function as an agent (e.g., a stockbroker or a dealer) earning a fee or a bid-ask spread from a transaction, or as a principal gaining from a price movement in their inventory position. Whatever the function and the type of issue, secondary market making can involve transactions in a physical location exchange (national or regional) or the over-the counter market. In the case of government debt, the secondary market for U.S. Treasury securities is the over-the-counter (OTC) market where participants trade with one another on a bilateral basis (although these securities are officially registered at the New York Stock Exchange, their trading activity in this market is negligible). Most of the trading activity in the OTC market is centered in the 21 primary government security dealers who act as market makers for the securities purchased at auctions. Their customers include non-primary dealers, other financial institutions (such as banks, insurance companies, pension funds, and mutual funds), nonfinancial institutions, and individuals. In the process of making markets, dealers buy and sell Treasury securities for their own account at their quoted bid and ask prices and earn a spread. Primary dealers also trade directly between themselves using interdealer brokers as intermediaries to preserve their anonymity.

The trading of U.S. Treasury securities spans the globe. Major trading in these issues starts each morning in Tokyo, moves west to London, and passes on to New York before it begins again the next day in Tokyo. Although the volume of trading ebbs and flows across three distinct geographic locations, the transaction process is the same. The same securities are traded by the same dealers through the same interdealer brokers with the same brokerage fees. Trades agreed upon during overseas hours typically settle as New York trades do--one business day later through the GSCC. While the volume of activity at each major trading center varies across days,

New York accounts for the vast majority of daily trading. This is to be expected since Treasury securities are obligations of the U.S. government held widely by U.S. financial institutions, individuals, state and local governments, and the Federal Reserve System, which participates actively in the market as part of its implementation of monetary policy. Further, with any macroeconomic reports and policy changes of relevance to these securities announced during New York trading hours, their consequent effect is reflected in the daily volume of trading.

The secondary market for municipal bonds is also the OTC market. The prime-credit issues of large, well known state and local government units enjoy a national market. The great majority of municipal securities, however, trade only on a regional or a local basis. The investment banks or securities firms that trade in various municipal issues and the inventories they carry are advertised in a daily publication the Blue List. As a market maker these firms stand ready to buy or sell these issues at their posted bid and offer quotations and earn a spread. However, secondary market trades are relatively infrequent because of lack of information on bond issuers, as well as the special provisions (such as covenants) that are contained into bond contracts. This is especially the case for the issues of smaller government units where information pertaining to their credit worthiness is more costly to obtain and evaluate, although partly offset by the ratings of bond rating agencies.

Corporate bonds trade in two secondary markets--physical location exchanges and the OTC market. In the former instance, the New York Stock Exchange (NYSE) is the main exchange for the trading of corporate bonds. Transactions may be completed through the NYSE's all-electronic trading system Arca (previously ArcaEx, an abbreviation for Archipelago Exchange acquired in 2005) which includes the bonds of all listed companies and their subsidiaries and offers investors prompt access to transparent information on pricing and trading. However significant the trading in exchange markets may be it trails in importance the volume of transactions in the OTC market where full service investment banks (e.g., Morgan Stanley Smith Barney and UBS Paine Webber) are major traders. In fact some of the trading firms make both primary and secondary markets in corporate bonds and enable the participation of individual investors in these markets. The size of the secondary market is so large as to accommodate major trades, including when these involve bonds listed on an exchange (e.g., the NYSE bond market). As a result prices for large transactions in the secondary market are viewed as more reliable estimates to those reported on the exchanges. Unlike the safety and liquidity appeal of U.S. Treasury securities, corporate debt exhibits significant variation in quality, ranging from issues of the highest credit standing to the most speculative and risky. In addition to credit risk, the secondary market trading of corporate issues can entail a significant degree of liquidity risk.

The packaging and sale of corporate bonds collateralized by other assets such as mortgages, car loans, and credit card receivables gave rise to the development of asset backed securities (ABS) rated on their own merit, independently of the issuing company. A securitized asset is a "derivative security" in that its value is based on the value of the underlying asset. An explosion in the issue of new securitized instruments since the 1970s led to the unprecedented growth of the derivative securities markets. Investment banks have been major market makers in derivative securities and ended up taking sizeable losses when the prices of the underlying assets moved significantly against them with the burst of the housing bubble. The drop in the value of subprime mortgages, and the (derivative) securities backed by such mortgages, caused bankruptcy or acquisition of major investment banks (e.g., Lehman Brothers, Bear Stearns, and Merrill Lynch), global losses of $1 trillion by 2009, and the near collapse of the world's financial system.

Corporate equities, too, trade both in physical location exchanges and the OTC market. The NYSE and the National Association of Securities Dealers Automated Quotation (NASDAQ) system are respective examples of these markets. In the case of the NYSE, individual stocks are assigned to independent firms other than investment banks/underwriters. Known as "specialists," they have the obligation to provide an orderly market--to act as a market maker by buying or selling the stock to stabilize its order flow and price. The role of the specialist is especially important in periods of financial adversity when there is a large imbalance between buy and sell orders. Retail and institutional investors wishing to transact in stocks may contact their broker firm which transmits the order to its exchange floor representative to execute by conducting the trade with the stock's designated market maker.

Stocks that are not listed in exchanges trade in the OTC market. The

NASDAQ, an electronic exchange and one of the world's largest, provides continuous trading for very active stocks. Whether or not the original underwriter, market makers stand ready to buy or sell particular issues at their quoted bid and ask prices and earn a spread. For investors wishing to transact in OTC stocks, their broker firm would contact the dealer offering the best price, for the particular security, to execute the order. Alternatively, investors may bypass the broker firm by using the Internet to trade directly with the security dealer. Online trading by individuals and professional traders has become one of the fastest growing areas for financial services firms.

The 1980s witnessed the development of a secondary market for the trading of the debt of developing countries. Also known as emerging markets debt it owes its origin to the spiraling price of oil in the 1970s and the consequent inability of several countries to service their debts to major banks around the world. In time much of the outstanding debt was converted into securities, known as Brady bonds after U.S. Treasury Secretary Nicholas Brady who sponsored the plan of debt restructuring (1989). Collateralized by specially issued U.S. Treasury 30-year zero-coupon bonds held in escrow at the Federal Reserve, Brady bonds were funded by the debtor countries through a combination of sources--IMF, World Bank and the countries' own foreign currency reserves. At year-end 1999, the outstanding face value of Brady bonds was $130 billion, with U.S. dollar issues representing approximately 90 percent of this amount. Brady bonds accounted then for the primary segment of the emerging market debt instruments. Several of the full service investment banks (e.g., J. P. Morgan Chase, Morgan Stanley, Citigroup, Credit Suisse, and ING) were active dealers in this market. Exhibit 6.6 identifies some of the largest issues of sovereign debt by emerging markets in recent years. As seen in this Exhibit, Saudi Arabia held the lead with its first-ever sale of $17.5 billion global bonds in 2016.

Restructured in recent years, the secondary market for emerging markets debt is made up of the following three components: sovereign debt issues, the largest of the three segments, denominated in a major currency (e.g., U.S. dollars or euros) and rated according to the issuer's political and economic risks; performing sovereign loans, original or restructured, that are current in their debt service to creditors or debt holders; and nonperforming sovereign loans that trade at deep discounts.

Exhibit 6.6 The Largest Sales of Sovereign Debt by Emerging Markets
(in billions of dollars)

Issuer	Year	Value
Saudi Arabia	2016	$17.5
Argentina	2016	16.5
Qatar	2016	9.0
Qatar	2009	7.0
Russia	2012	7.0
Russia	2013	7.0
China*	2007	6.1
China	2005	6.0
Mexico	1996	6.0
Russia	2010	5.5
Mexico	1996	5.4

*China Ministry of Railways.
Source: The Wall Street Journal, October 19, 2016. Reprinted by permission of Dow Jones & Company, Inc. via the Copyright Clearance Center. http://www.wsj.com/articles/saudi-arabia-to-offer-international-investors-17-5-billion-in-bonds-1476876478

Trading

Investment banks and securities firms are among the most active traders in the secondary market conducting transactions on behalf of customers (as an agent) or for their own account (as a principal). Closely related to market making, trading entails taking an active net position in a financial asset in the context of any one of alternate trading strategies, such as position trading, pure arbitrage, risk arbitrage, program trading, stock brokerage, and electronic brokerage.

Position trading is a strategy that focuses on holding a position in specific securities for a few weeks or months in anticipation of a favorable price movement. Unlike day traders that try to gain from very short term price fluctuations, position traders look to profit from longer-term trends. Buying assets that have not started to trend is a research-intensive endeavor and the core of a position trading strategy (buying assets that have started to trend is less research-intensive and hence preferred by some position traders). Trends often begin with the breakout of the price from the range or other chart pattern that it was confined; once the price breaks out of the pattern it can often trend for some time. After the initial research is complete, and the position trader decided on how to trade the asset (long or short), there is little left to be done. Since minor price fluctuations are not a concern, the position is monitored until the speed and/or size of price movement confirms the trend and enables the trader to capture the profit.

Pure arbitrage is a trading strategy that aims to profit from imbalances in the price of the same (or equivalent) securities in different markets. For example, by simultaneously buying in a lower-priced market and selling in a higher-priced market, a resourceful arbitrager can profit from any disparity in prices between these markets. With price inefficiencies quite small, it takes large positions to realize substantial profits. Today many of these intermarket arbitrage opportunities do not exist as a result of technological advances. Real time access to market data and increased transparency are now shared more widely; with every trader having the same information at the same time, profit opportunities have declined precipitously.

Risk arbitrage attempts to produce profits from anticipated events or special situations that arise in security markets from time to time. Event-driven arbitrage may involve such special situations as corporate restructurings, and changes in economic policy that impact interest rates. An example of this strategy would be taking a long or short position in anticipation of a merger or acquisition announcement, or a press release by the Federal Reserve on interest rates. If the merger or acquisition deal fails to go through, or the change in interest rates does not materialize, the arbitrager would sustain a loss. The high loss potential on the downside compared to the small gain prospect on the upside underscores the term risk in the title of this strategy.

Program trading is defined by the NYSE as a trading strategy that uses computer programs to initiate the simultaneous purchase and sale of a portfolio of at least 15 different stocks valued at more than $1 million. A computer-driven type of pure arbitrage program trading owes its growth to the development of electronic communications networks. As access to electronic exchanges became easier and faster, orders from the trader's computer entered directly into the market's computer system and were executed automatically. The proliferation of hedge funds and the large volume trades of institutional investors have helped drive the growth of program trading. Program trading seeks to gain from differences in the price of related financial instruments between markets. Index arbitrage is one such type of program trading that attempts to profit from discrepancies between the cash market price of an index (e.g., Standard and Poor's 500) and the futures market price for that index. With computers' monitoring of prices in the cash and futures markets continuously, program trades are executed if index prices fall or rise to a certain level.

Stock brokerage refers to the trading activities of brokerage firms and broker-dealers for the account of their retail and institutional clients. Trade orders are executed through an organized exchange or over the counter, as the case may be, in return for a fee or commission. Securities that are bought from clients or other companies in the capacity of dealer (for the firm's own account), may be sold to clients or other companies, acting again in the capacity of dealer, or they may become a part of the firm's own security holdings. Full-service brokerage firms (e.g., Merrill Lynch, Morgan Stanley, and Wells Fargo) provide clients a large variety of services including research and advice, portfolio management, tax or estate planning, and wealth management services. Of course, all these services come at a price--commissions are much higher compared to discount brokerage firms which offer no personalized investor support and execute trades for a small fee.

Electronic brokerage, available through major brokerage firms, enables frequent and active investors direct access to securities markets via the Internet. An online trading platform functions as a hub for trade transactions and provides, in addition, tools to track and monitor securities, portfolios and indices, as well as research tools, real-time streaming quotes and up-to-date news releases, all of which are necessary to trade profitably. Clients use online platforms to trade directly with organized exchanges and market makers bypassing traditional brokers. Electronic trading carried out by users from any location are rapidly replacing the conventional modes of floor trading and telephone-based trading. Transactions are executed in a fraction of a second and their confirmations are instantly displayed on the trader's computer screen. Online trading's growing popularity is attributable to the speed and ease of the online order entry, and to the low transaction cost. Some firms have platform or software fees which may be waived for trades up to a specific volume per calendar month. These benefits have been of significant appeal to retail investors.

Although retail electronic trading in the United States is on the rise, its volume is dwarfed by institutional, inter-dealer and exchange trading. By contrast retail trading in emerging markets, and Asia in particular, constitutes a major portion of the overall trading volume.

Advisory Services

Full service investment banks offer a wide range of advisory services to their government and business clients on a global basis. This variation in service offerings diversifies the sources of fee-based income and contributes to greater earnings stability. Within the realm of these services, corporate advice is preeminent because of the scope and profitability of the constituent lines of business. The demand for corporate restructuring services is a case in point. The changing market environment produced by technological advances and globalization has fostered the demand for restructuring services as the U.S. industry sought to become more competitive in global markets. Corporate restructuring may involve such services as changing the organization, product mix, ownership, and overall operations of a company to make it more efficient and profitable. Financial restructuring (e.g., asset/liability management) or bankruptcy workouts may be a concomitant advisory service. Investment banks can help expand or shrink a company by assessing its key business dimensions and objectives.

Although the ultimate objective of corporate expansion is to maximize shareholder wealth, it may be motivated by such considerations as synergies, market share, geographic or product-line diversification, survival in a changing environment, and tax considerations. Expansion may be attained through different venues, such as mergers, acquisitions, and consolidations. While an acquisition entails, from a legal point of view, ownership or control of another company's assets or equity, a merger involves the complete takeover (absorption) of one company by another. Taken together, M&A are a core advisory service and source of income for full service and specialized investment banking firms. To offer advice and assistance in finding a merger partner, the investment bank must consider which of the strategic options would be a best fit for the client's business operations and objectives--a horizontal merger, with a target firm in the same line of business; a vertical merger, with a target firm in a different stage of production in the same product line; a conglomerate merger, with a target firm in an unrelated business. The strategic recommendation must be complemented with a tactical suggestion of the proposed price and terms of agreement to ensure the successful negotiation of the deal. When the board of the target company approves the transaction the process is known as a friendly takeover. By contrast when it objects to it, and the acquiring firm proceeds despite the opposition, the process is known as a hostile takeover. Although the vast majority of M&A are friendly, investment banks may assist a firm to prevent, or defend itself against, being a merger target through poison pill provisions that would render a hostile takeover as costly as to deter it. Exhibit 6.7 shows that in 2015 a total of 31,213 M&A deals were completed worldwide, valued at $3.16 trillion. Of the top ten investment banks portrayed, Goldman Sachs was the lead financial advisor, with 365 deals valued at $1.08 trillion, which resulted in advisory fees of $2.80 billion.

Another expansion venue is consolidation whereby two or more firms in the same industry combine to form a new business entity with each of the combining firms giving up its corporate identity. Consolidation may be the result of a merger of equals where the companies involved agree that joining together is in the best interest of both. Japanese banks went through such consolidations (e.g., Mizuho Financial Group, and Sumitomo Mitsui Financial Group) in the 1990s and 2000s to survive deregulation and global competition.

Shrinking of a corporation, on the other hand, may come through a "spin-off" or a divestment. A spin-off is the creation of an independent company through sale of an existing line of business or a company division. Some of the reasons behind a spin-off include the lack of a competitive offer for the purchase of company assets or the need to allow for a high-growth division to command, once separated from the parent company, higher valuation multiples. Shareholders of the parent company receive equivalent shares in the new company in order to compensate for the loss of equity in their original investment. Divestment, too, can sever a part of a business by means of sale of certain assets. Some of the motives for divestiture include the need to undo a merger or acquisition, focus on the core part of the business, raise additional funds, eliminate an underperforming division, secure regulatory approval for a proposed merger, and initiate closure or bankruptcy.

Exhibit 6.7 Top Ten Firms in Mergers and Acquisitions Ranked by Value of Deals Completed Worldwide, 2015
(in billions of dollars)

Rank	Financial Advisor	Value of Deals	Market Share	Number of Deals	Imputed Advisor Fees
1	Goldman Sachs	$1,085.5	34.3%	365	$2.802
2	J. P. Morgan	731.6	23.2	285	1.810
3	Morgan Stanley	627.5	19.9	342	1.926
4	Bank of America Merrill Lynch	625.9	19.8	225	1.306
5	Citigroup	532.4	16.8	234	1.006
6	Lazard	477.6	15.1	226	.893
7	Deutsche Bank	364.3	11.5	203	.734
8	Credit Suisse	352.9	11.2	199	.882
9	Barclays	321.1	10.2	175	.802
10	UBS	267.0	8.5	145	.509
Industry Total		**$3,160.8**	**100.0**	**31,213**	**$29.387**

Note: With investment banks extending financial and legal advisory services to both the acquirer and the target companies, they receive full credit for the same deal. As a result details do not add to totals.
Source: *Mergers & Acquisitions Review*, Thomson Reuters, 2015.
http://share.thomsonreuters.com/general/PR/MA-4Q15-(E).pdf

A massive wave of mergers, acquisitions, spin-offs, and buyouts in the 1980s turned corporate restructuring into a growth area of investment banking services. As it involved extensive use of borrowing to finance these transactions regulators labeled them "highly leveraged transactions" (HLTs). HLTs arose from three types of transactions:

- Leveraged buyouts (LBOs) where corporate raiders would buy a target company and take it private with a minimum amount of equity and a large amount of debt that was paid down through the sale of specific company assets. If the company was turned around and earnings improved, investors would sell it or take it public to gain from its increased value; if investors miss-forecast prospects and paid too much, the target company would go bankrupt
- Leveraged recapitalizations where a company takes on significant additional debt to pay a large cash dividends to shareholders or to buy back its own shares. This strategy causes a change in the company's capital structure.
- Leveraged acquisitions where a cash purchase of a another related company produces an increase in the buyer's debt structure

Other Services

Supplementary revenue producing business includes an assortment of activities that range from bank related services to financial engineering, investment management, and merchant banking.

Cash management represents an early attempt of investment banks to make inroads into commercial banking. Launched by Merrill Lynch in the late 1970s, "cash management accounts" (CMAs) were a close substitute to bank deposit accounts with balances invested in money market mutual funds. A major appeal of these accounts was that they earned yields that reflected prevailing money market rates at a time when interest rates on bank deposits were restrained by government regulation (legal interest rate ceilings). Equally important, CMAs offered check-writing capabilities and a credit card. Adopted soon, under various names, by other investment banks and securities firms CMA accounts grew rapidly. Passage of the GLB Act recognized

CMAs as deposit accounts and hence subject to insurance by Federal Deposit Insurance Corporation (FDIC). Further, it enabled investment banks to expand the scope of their activities to include such banking products and services as loans (e.g., project financing financing, bridge financing, and loans to small businesses), debit and credit cards, and ATM services. These activities have been supplemented by foreign currency trading, wealth management, leasing, custody and escrow, and clearance and settlement.

Financial engineering is a major source of revenue-producing business and refers to the development of derivative instruments--namely, derivative securities and derivative contracts. Although derivative securities were developed earlier on with the packaging and sale of ABS, structured finance teams at investment banks contributed to the growth of the market by structuring such instruments as collateralized mortgage obligations (CMOs), where cash flows from mortgages were redistributed over a series of tranches; collateralized bond obligations (CBOs), debt issues backed by high-yield bonds; collateralized loan obligations (CLOs), debt issues backed by commercial loans; and collateralized debt obligations (CDOs), debt issues backed by speculative-grade bonds (junk bonds) or risky bank loans. Of these securities the last one was the most damaging to financial institutions and the world's markets during the financial crisis as it was backed by subprime debt.

Derivative contracts is an alternate product suite in financial engineering. Active participants in the OTC market, investment banks enable clients to manage various risks on the balance sheet through use of such off-balance-sheet instruments as forwards, options, swaps, and interest rate caps and floors. A forward contract entails the exchange of a non-standardized asset for cash at an agreed future date and price. Investment banks and broker-dealers are prime traders of forward contracts in the world's major currencies. Negotiated directly and hence custom-made, these contracts enable corporate treasurers and investors to protect their investments and earning streams against adverse swings in currency rates. Growth of the forward market has prompted the advent of an active secondary market in some forward contracts with traders posting their buy and sell prices over computer networks. A direct outcome has been the increased standardization of forward contracts and the enhanced liquidity of the secondary market. An option is an alternate contract to manage risk (e.g., in foreign exchange). It gives the purchaser (buyer) the right, but not the obligation, to buy or sell, a given amount of foreign exchange at a fixed price per unit for a specified time period. A number of investment banks offer custom-tailored options (e.g., on transactions of $1 million or more) on all major trading currencies for any period up to one year, and in some cases, two or three years.

Swap, a primary derivative contract traded by investment banks, includes a number of generic types: interest rate swap, currency swap, and credit default swap each of which enables firms to better manage interest rate, foreign exchange and credit risks respectively. Interest rate swaps, the largest component of the swap market, allow financial institutions with a mismatch in their asset/liability maturity profiles to hedge against interest rate risk exposure. Currency swaps enable firms with a mismatch in the currencies of their assets and liabilities to hedge against currency risk exposure. Credit default swaps allow financial institutions to hedge against exposure to loss from a credit event (e.g., default or missed payment) by transferring the risk across to a counterparty (credit default swap seller). One such counterparty was Lehman Brothers which found itself unable, during the financial crisis of 2008, to honor billions of dollars of promised payments on the insured contracts it had written. Following the crisis, calls for a sweeping overhaul of the U.S. financial regulatory system were formalized in the Dodd-Frank Act. Key provisions of this law reshape the investment banking industry by introducing stricter oversight and supervision of investment banks. The law also addresses the derivatives markets by mandating regulators to undertake rulemaking authority to increase the transparency and reduce the systemic risk of these markets. Recognizing the important role that derivatives play in capital markets the law calls for a new trading and clearing infrastructure by requiring all trading to be conducted through exchanges and their clearing through a registered clearing organization. In the case of credit swaps it provides for the international standardization of contracts to prevent legal disputes in ambiguous cases.

Interest rate caps and floors help financial institutions hedge interest rate risk. Purchase of a cap (similar to buying a call option on interest rates) protects against a rise in interest rates above the cap rate, while purchase of a floor (like buying a put option on interest rates) protects against a drop in interest rates below the floor rate. In either case the seller of the cap, or the floor, will compensate the buyer for any losses in return for an up-front premium. A collar is a simultaneous position in a cap and a floor that allows an institution to cover the cost of financing of the one transaction by the other (e.g., buying a cap and selling a floor).

Investment management is another source of revenue producing business and refers to the management of funds for various investment vehicles. Recent decades have experienced the growth of an array of financial institutions that pool the financial resources of individuals and businesses and invest them with the objective of generating superior returns. A typical example of such institutions are investment companies (open-end or mutual funds, closed-end funds, and unit investment trusts--all engaged in the business of investing in securities), real estate partnerships (formed to invest in real estate), and venture capital pools (organized to fund startups and early stage firms with attractive growth prospects). Development of these firms, both at home and abroad, required professional expertise and led to the consequent demand for investment management services. For investment banking houses, entry into this market offered the prospect of such benefits as increased menu of products and services, synergy to the underwriting business, expanded brokerage services (e.g., to hedge funds), and a stable stream of income. Swayed by these considerations nearly all U.S. investment banks assumed investment management operations during the 1990s. In time these operations surged to become an integral part of the investment banking business.

Merchant banking pertains to the commitment of a bank's own, and externally-raised, capital to direct investments to attain very high, albeit riskier, returns. Use of traders to fulfill this objective led to the emergence of proprietary trading that spread over diverse markets, used varied strategies, and employed different financial instruments and risk management techniques that were independent of client positions and needs. In due time proprietary trading accounted for a significant portion of annual profits at many investment banking houses. With the onset of the financial crisis and the call for comprehensive regulation of financial markets, growth of proprietary trading came to a halt. Key regulations of the Dodd-Frank Act, originally proposed by former Federal Reserve Chairman Paul Volcker, restricted investment banks from making speculative investments that do not benefit their customers. The "Volker rule," as these regulations are known, introduce a ban on proprietary trading, arguing that such speculative activity played a contributing role in the financial crisis. Although the rule's original provisions have been revised and their implementation delayed, investment banking houses have since shed their proprietary-trading desks, and ceased other activities that would run afoul of the rule's restrictions.

Research is an inconspicuous yet important function; although not a direct source of revenue, it underlies many of the activities of investment banks. Research is conducted both for internal and external use and may cover a range of topics, such as macroeconomic forecasts (e.g., of economic activity, foreign exchange rates, and interest rates), commodity markets outlook, investment opportunities and portfolio strategy, and company reviews and industry prospects. Internally, the research output assists traders in trading, and the sales force in their interaction with clients. Externally, investment advice to clients (e.g., institutional investors and high-net-worth individuals) may prompt them to execute trades through the bank's sales and trading division and generate revenue for the firm. Nonetheless, the benefits of research are especially evident in advisory services and the formulation of strategy.

TRENDS AND CHALLENGES

As the mid-teens unfold, large U.S. financial-services conglomerates have grown to become the financial supermarkets of the world with an expanded menu of services and large complex cross-border transactions. Their strong international presence and leadership positions on a broad array of investment banking products have enabled them to dominate global investment banking. Of the ten largest full-service global investment banks, the top five are U.S. institutions (J.P. Morgan Chase, Goldman Sachs, Bank of America Merrill Lynch, Morgan Stanley, Citigroup), followed by four European (Deutsche, Credit Suisse, Barclays Capital, UBS), and an interposing U.S. institution (Wells Fargo).

Global competition and rapid innovation through technological advances, are among the defining characteristics of the current reality, which has the potential to reshape global investment banking industry in a number of ways. Global competition is requiring investment banks to reassess their business and operating models to optimize use of capital and maximize after tax income, while adhering to regulations. This restructuring challenge covers three core domains--business activities, product mix and client mix. In business activities it calls for investment banks to explore streamlining opportunities on a geographical basis--e.g., instead of having broker-dealer licenses in multiple areas (including low-volume markets), it may be more efficient to have a license in a single area or select jurisdictions. Same perspective would be used for other activities such as securities trading, securities financing, securities warehousing, derivatives management, and cash management. In assessing product mix, investment banks would need to ensure efficient use of scarce capital by focusing on products and business lines that generate competitive returns on equity, while phasing out less profitable ones. In client mix, the same considerations would emphasize the targeting of profitable client segments at the expense of relationships that have a high cost of service. Rationalization of business and operating models across markets contribute to a more efficient use of capital, reduced costs and increased profitability. Recent moves of global investment banks emphasize the relevance of these themes. For example, an update to Barclays' group strategy of late (2014) recognized current restructuring challenges, including plans to reallocate capital to growing lines of business. Similarly, Deutsche Bank moved to terminate its presence in Russia (2015) as part of an ongoing review of its global investment banking footprint. Credit Suisse merged its fixed income and equities divisions in the Asia Pacific market as part of an overhaul of its global strategic direction (2016).

Technological advances have already changed and will continue to change the capabilities of investment banks across processes and functions. Software and information technology (IT) systems are enabling investment banks to improve services to clients, design and price complex contracts, monitor and manage risks, and increase overall efficiency and control through real time information of operations worldwide. Given the competitive advantages associated with IT, investment banks are challenged to innovate, by launching new products and services, and to lay the foundation for the next phase of digital strategy by adopting new programming languages, databases, messaging platforms, operating systems and hardware technologies.

Although the drive to digitize is prompted largely by the growing competition and the global digital revolution that sweeps across all aspects of daily life, it represents a major industry challenge. This is highlighted by the Deutsche Bank experience which outsourced the IT infrastructure of its wholesale banking division to Hewlett-Packard in a 10 year multibillion-dollar deal (2015), while retaining International Business Machines for its retail banking arm. The strategic goal behind this move was both to cut costs and expedite the launching process for new products and services.

The digital challenge has been especially critical for the brokerage line of business--a traditionally core area of investment banking. U.S. deregulation of the brokerage business and the consequent abolition of fixed commission rates (1975) in favor of negotiated ones has contributed to a long-term downward trend in commissions that was magnified by the widespread use of Internet trading. Faced with growing self-service trading and shrinking commissions across the globe, investment banks have been reevaluating their involvement in the brokerage business. Some institutions (e.g., Nomura and Standard Chartered) have already downsized their trading activities by implementing job cutbacks, while others (UBS and Credit Suisse) have exited from parts of this business altogether.

The above trends and challenges are representative of the forces that are currently reshaping the investment banking industry. Instead of being addressed as threats, they should be viewed as opportunities to refocus resources, streamline strategies, and create a new competitive edge. Advances in digital technology increase the cost efficiency of business and operating models in reaching out a wider market audience at a faster pace than previously possible. These advances also create prospects for innovation that would appeal to the digital generation (millennials), enable customers to interact on their own terms, enhance the efficiency of trade executions, drive automation, and encourage customer loyalty. The digital challenge marks the beginning of a new stage for investment banks and the financial services industry in general.

7 FOREIGN EXCHANGE MARKET

Foreign transactions, whether they involve the purchase or sale of goods and services or capital flows, create the need for the exchange of currencies of the various countries. This need is met by the foreign exchange (FX) market. The price at which the currency of one country (e.g., Japanese yen ¥) is exchanged for the currency of another (e.g., the U.S. dollar $) in the FX markets is known as the *foreign exchange rate*. With exchange rates subject to change, currency transactions are exposed to the *exchange rate or currency risk*.

CURRENCY REGIMES AND GROWTH OF THE FX MARKET

Up until the early 1970s, the currency regime of the global community was that of fixed exchange rates--currency values were fixed in relationship to other major currencies. Exchange rate stability translated into firm international prices and low business risk for traders and investors in the present and the immediate future. Rapid growth in international trade and capital mobility soon gave way to widely diverging national economic policies and inflation rates which precipitated the system's demise and its replacement by an eclectic combination of exchange rate regimes and arrangements. As implied, the contemporary international exchange rate regime cannot be described in simple terms. If it is to be distinguished in terms of currency sovereignty, present-day regimes may be classified into countries that continue to use their own national currency as the sole legal tender, those which as members of a currency union have introduced and share the same legal tender (e.g., European euro), and those that have adopted the currency of another country (e.g., the U.S. dollar). If currency valuation is the key consideration, present-day regimes may be distinguished into two extreme groups depending upon whether exchange rates are set by market forces or official action. In the former instance countries may be sub-grouped into those whose currency values are market-driven without government intervention (*free floating*), and those whose currency values are product of occasional intervention (*floating or floating with intervention*). On the other side of the spectrum are countries whose exchange rates are set by official action--that is, countries that peg their rates for short, or long, periods to a particular currency, a basket of currencies, or an index. A good number of countries subscribe to some system between the two extremes.

The advances in technology and globalization experienced in recent decades contributed to a surge in international trade and investments and propelled FX markets to become among the largest of all financial markets. An April 2016 BIS survey estimated the global trading in the foreign exchange markets to avarage $5.1 trillion per day (compared to a $5.4 trillion average in April 2013). Unlike physical location exchanges, the FX market is a communications network market--an informal, over-the-counter market made up of trading centers around the world. The widespread use of computers has contributed to the increased automation of the market with three major firms--Reuters, Telerate, and Bloomberg--the leading suppliers of trading systems and exchange rate information. Increased automation has enabled FX deals to be executed at any hour of the day. The FX market is often described as a 24-hour market with trading activity beginning each morning in Sydney and Tokyo, moving as the day progresses to Hong Kong and Singapore, then to Bahrain, the main European centers (Frankfurt, Zurich, and London), New York, and ending with the West Coast financial centers, at which time Tokyo is about to open up. BIS survey data for 2013 indicate that London remains the largest center of FX market activity (over 40% of daily currency trading), followed by New York (19%), Singapore (6%), Tokyo (6%), and other centers of lesser activity. The United Kingdom and the United States accounted jointly for nearly 60% of all daily trading.

MARKET PARTICIPANTS

The operation of the FX market is reflective of the divergent functions of its participants --commercial bank and nonbank dealers, business firms and individuals, central banks, speculators and arbitragers, and foreign exchange brokers.

Bank and Nonbank Dealers

Just as in the domestic payments system, banks are at the center of the international payments system being the channels through which money transactions flow, and claims are settled, across national boundaries. Although many U.S. banks handle foreign-exchange transactions, only the very largest of them, together with nonbank foreign exchange dealers (e.g., investment banks, and other financial institutions), operate in the interbank or wholesale market. The Federal Reserve estimates this group to number about 200 financial institutions. Collectively they are a major component of a select group of institutions worldwide that are active market makers. Additionally these institutions are also active in the retail market servicing the needs of their clients, including other commercial banks. The major players in this market trade a limited number of currencies, buying and selling them as warranted by market conditions. Each foreign currency is quoted in two prices. These prices, or foreign-exchange rates, are frequently referred to as "double barreled." One quotation represents the "bid" (purchasing) price of the foreign currency, the other--which is slightly higher--the "offer" or "ask" (selling) price. Banks and nonbank dealers profit from the difference (spread) between the bid and ask prices.

The currencies that banks select to function as “market makers” are those in which they maintain an inventory position. These are held in the form of deposits in foreign branches or correspondent banks. As might be expected, these inventories fluctuate. They are augmented as U.S. banks purchase credit instruments (drafts) denominated in foreign currencies from their customers. These instruments, once cleared abroad, are credited to their accounts in foreign banks. Their inventories decline when they sell credit instruments payable in foreign monies to their customers. Banks maintain large foreign currency inventories in the currencies that are in greatest demand, such as the pound sterling, the euro, the Swiss franc, and the Japanese yen.

As currency values fluctuate constantly in response to market conditions, FX trading inevitably involves taking on risk--e.g., the currency purchased may decline in value before it can be resold. For this reason most bank traders only hold positions for a few minutes before they cash out. Holding on to a position until later in that day (or even the next), perhaps in anticipation of favorable news, is speculative and may result into big profits or big losses. The wholesale market enables traders to balance their positions in foreign currencies, depending upon their daily trading activity in these currencies. Based upon the daily volume of each kind of currency bought and sold, banks may experience shortages or overages in their inventories of individual currencies. To adjust their positions in particular currencies, banks use independent foreign-exchange brokers. These brokers, by operating among banks, play an important role in the negotiation of trades in the interbank market. For a fee they put a bank with a shortage in a specific foreign currency in contact with one experiencing a surplus. The brokers preserve the anonymity of the transacting parties until the deal is closed, to prevent any influence of their names upon price quotations.

Use of an independent broker is but one method of temporarily adjusting a bank's shortage in a particular currency. Other methods include borrowing from a foreign correspondent bank appropriate amounts of the currency in shortage; using a "swap" arrangement with a foreign correspondent, whereby you borrow the needed currency for a limited time in exchange for lending your own currency for the same time; and purchasing the needed amounts from a foreign correspondent, or through it, and paying accordingly in another currency. The basic characteristic of all these methods of adjusting shortages is that foreign-currency inventory is replenished through bookkeeping entries that transfer deposits denominated in various currencies from one holder to another. No money leaves the country of its origin; only the ownership of deposit balances changes.

Business Firms and Individuals

Businesses and individuals are a vital part of the FX market. Multinational enterprises make extensive use of the market to pursue two distinct management objectives, hedging and speculation. Corporate treasurers use hedging to protect company investments and earnings streams from adverse swings in currency rates. Alternatively, they may take open positions in the expectation of profit. Other important participants in the market include tourists, importers and exporters, and portfolio managers of financial institutions, such as pension funds, insurance companies, and investment companies (e.g., mutual funds and hedge funds). Hedge funds are especially active in this market as they seek high rates of return for their (wealthy) individual and other investors. Some of the more aggressively managed funds borrow vast amounts of money to take massive positions in the expectation of foreign currency swings.

Central Banks and Treasuries

Central banks and treasuries play a key role in the FX market as they seek to build or expend their country's foreign reserves as well as to impact the price at which their own currency is traded. Market intervention by governments and central bank authorities has been typical during the era when the fixed exchange rate system prevailed. Under this regime, if the country's currency declined (depreciated) in value because of an excess supply on world markets, the government would then either devalue it or have the central bank expend official reserves to support it (sell official foreign exchange reserves to acquire it and shore it up). By the same token, if as a result of an increased demand on world markets the country's currency rose (appreciated) in value, the central bank sought to slow down its surge by pursuing the opposite course of action--accumulate additional foreign exchange reserves by using its domestic currency for payment. Although many countries have adopted floating exchange rate regimes long ago, the governments and central banking authorities of many of them still concede, privately and publicly, what value their currency should hold. Thus different degrees of market intervention still persist as a means of moving a currency's value in a direction that serves best national policy interests. As the motive of intervention is to influence the value of the currency rather than earn a profit, central banks and treasuries are often loss takers--a distinct posture that sets them apart from all other market participants. A frequently cited case is that of the central banks of Britain and Germany that spent approximately £50 billion in an ill-fated intervention to support the sterling (September 1992). Gorge Soros, a prominent American hedge fund manager, made profits of $1 billion by betting against the pound. Other banks and dealers made large profits as well from the sterling crisis.

Speculators and Arbitragers

Speculators and arbitragers operate for their own interests and pursue distinct trading strategies with the aim to realize a profit. A speculator seeks to profit from changes in the exchange rate, e.g., appreciation or depreciation in the value of the foreign currency. An arbitrager will seek to take advantage of pricing inefficiencies for the same currency in different markets; that is, to make a risk-free profit from the price mismatch in related markets.

In addition to the profits which banks and nonbank dealers realize from the spread between the bid and ask prices on foreign currency, they also profit from their proprietary trading activities in FX markets. Traders employed by banks and nonbank dealers conduct a sizable amount of arbitrage and speculation for their institutional employers. For example, if a trader at a major bank believes that a foreign currency will appreciate in value, he or she will buy it up and hold it to profit from its expected increase in value. With currency values fluctuating constantly, and trades usually in huge denominations, a very small increase in value would make a significant contribution to the bank's own bottom line. For many of the largest banks in the United States currency trading profits may account on average between 10% and 20% of their annual net income.

TYPES OF TRANSACTIONS

There are three types of foreign exchange transactions: spot, forward and swaps. A *spot* transaction involves the immediate exchange of a currency at the current (or spot) exchange rate. In the interbank market a spot transaction settles in two business days (in the North American market, settlement or "value date" is the next business day). On value date, dollar denominated transactions worldwide are settled electronically through the New York based Clearing House Interbank Payments System (CHIPS). The BIS survey in April 2016 estimated spot transactions to amount to $1.7 trillion or 33.3% of the $5.1 trillion in average daily global turnover in the foreign exchange market.

A *forward* transaction is the delivery of a stated amount of one currency for a stated amount of another currency at a specified future date and a specified exchange rate. Although the exchange rate is set at the time of the agreement, payment and delivery are not due until maturity. Forward contracts are typically written for value dates of one, two, three, six, and twelve month periods, but in practice they can be arranged for any given length of time. An example would be an agreement to exchange dollars for yen at a given (forward) exchange rate six months into the future. Of the $5.1 trillion in average daily trading volume in the foreign exchange market in April 2016, $3.4 trillion (66.8%) involved forward and swap transactions, Forward contracts are a key hedging tool against foreign exchange risk. Contract prices are determined by bid and ask quotes derived from observable data. As such the forward rate does not represent an estimate of the future spot rate but a product of computation of three variables--the current spot rate and the ratio of interest rates for issues of same risk and maturity in the two pertinent currencies. Thus the forward rate would deviate from the spot rate in response to the interest rate differential between the related foreign exchange markets.

A *swap* involves the simultaneous purchase and sale of a specified amount of foreign exchange for two different value dates, with the same counterparty. Executed as a single transaction, it does not entail any unexpected risk for the dealer and may comprise both a spot and forward contract (spot against forward swap), or two forward contracts (forward-forward swap). In the former case the dealer would purchase a currency spot and simultaneously sell it back to the same counterparty at an agreed-upon price at a specified future date, while in the latter the purchase would take place at a specified future date. An example of the latter transaction (forward-forward swap) from a seller's perspective would be a dealer's sale of Swiss francs Sfr1,000,000 forward for dollars for delivery in, say, four months at Sfr1.5000/$ and simultaneously purchase of this amount forward for delivery in six months at Sfr1.4950/$. The April 2016 BIS survey estimated the daily turnover of swaps at $2.4 trillion (in large part as a result of increased trading transactions in Yen).

EXCHANGE RATE QUOTATIONS

Designated by traditional currency symbols or codes, exchange rate quotations between two currencies may be stated in two ways: European or American terms.

With the U.S. dollar used globally in commercial and financial transactions, it has been a market practice to quote the number of units of a foreign currency in terms of one dollar. This practice has been known as *European terms.* The reverse approach, expressing the number of U.S. dollars per unit of foreign currency, is known as *American terms.* In practice, all currencies are quoted in European terms except for the British pound and the euro which are quoted in American terms. Two other frequently used terms in reference to the listing of exchange rates are direct and indirect quotations. *Direct quote* refers to the number of domestic (home) currency units that can be exchanged for one unit of the foreign currency, while an *indirect quote* expresses the opposite, the number of the foreign currency units exchanged for one unit of the domestic currency. An example of select spot rate quotations is provided in Exhibit 7.1. These rates are reciprocals of each other.

Exhibit 7.1 Select Exchange Rate Quotations

Currency	Symbol	Code	Direct (USD equivalent)	Indirect (Currency per USD)
Brazilian real	R$	BRL	0.2509	3.9836
British pound	£	GBP	1.454	0.691
Euro	€	EUR	0.8945	1.1184
Japanese yen	¥	JPY	0.0088	114.1284
Mexican peso	$	MXN	0.053	18.8781
Swiss franc	Fr	CHF	1.0145	0.9856

Note: Numerical differences between direct and indirect are due to rounding.
Source: Yahoo Finance February 12, 2016. http://finance.yahoo.com/currency-converter

Because of the dominance of the U.S. dollar in international transactions, exchange of money between other currencies led traders to first convert the money into U.S. dollars and then convert it into the desired currency. Cross currency trades allow traders to bypass this step and save the client from having to absorb the cost associated with the initial conversion into U.S. dollars. Cross currency exchange rates for major countries may be found in financial publications and websites, such as the

Bloomberg and Yahoo sites. Exhibit 7.2 identifies key currency cross rates for select countries from still another source, The Wall Street Journal.

For countries whose cross rates are not included in these listings or their currencies are inactively traded, rates may be established in terms of a third currency. For example a Thai importer who considers a transaction with an Egyptian firm and payment in Egyptian pounds may determine the cross rate by identifying the common quotation of both currencies against the U.S. dollar. If the exchange rate of Thai Baht to the U.S. dollar is THB35.654/$ and of the Egyptian pound to the U.S. dollar is EGP7.828/$, the cross rate--calculated by dividing the two quotes--will identify the number of Thai Baht per Egyptian pound

(THB35.654/$) / (EGP7.828/$) = THB4.5546/EGP

The cross rate could also be established as the reciprocal (Egyptian pounds per Baht):

(EGP7.828/$) / (THB35.654/$) = EGP0.2195/THB

An important use of cross rates is to check on opportunities for profit from sequential trading between markets, or intermarket arbitrage.

Intermarket Arbitrage

Intermarket arbitrage is the process of converting one currency into another, then to another and, finally, back to the original currency in the expectation of risk free profit. As an example, consider the following exchange rate quotations:

J.P. Morgan Chase quotes U.S. dollars per pound sterling	USD1.6939/GBP
HSBC quotes euros per pound sterling	EUR1.4600/GBP
BNP Paribas quotes euros per U.S. dollar	EUR0.8631/USD

The cross rate between HSBC and BNP Paribas is:

(EUR1.4600/GBP) / (EUR0.8631/USD) = USD1.6915/GBP

Exhibit 7.2 Key Currency Cross Rates

Countries	Dollar	Euro	Pound	S Franc	Peso	Yen	CdnDlr
Canada	1.3853	1.5592	2.0092	1.4176	0.0733	0.0122	----
Japan	113.2530	127.4719	164.2621	115.8954	5.9887	----	81.7564
Mexico	18.9110	21.2853	27.4285	19.3522	----	0.1670	13.6517
Switzerland	0.9772	1.0999	1.4173	----	0.0517	0.0086	0.7054
U.K.	0.6895	0.7760	----	0.7056	0.0365	0.0061	0.4977
Euro	0.8885	----	1.2886	0.9092	0.0470	0.0078	0.6414
U.S.	----	1.1256	1.4504	1.0233	0.0529	0.0088	0.7219

Source: The Wall Street Journal, February 12, 2016
http://www.wsj.com/mdc/public/page/2_3023-keyrates.html

This cross rate, relative to the higher quote of J.P. Morgan Chase, reveals an opportunity to profit from arbitrage. A BNP Paribas market trader, with an initial amount of EUR1,000,000, can capture this profit by pursuing the following sequence of transactions: he can sell the Euros spot to HSBC for pounds, sell the acquired pounds to J.P. Morgan Chase for U.S. dollars, and then sell the dollars to BNP for Euros. These transactions, known as *triangular arbitrage,* are depicted in Exhibit 7.3.

Exhibit 7.3 Triangular Arbitrage by a Trader

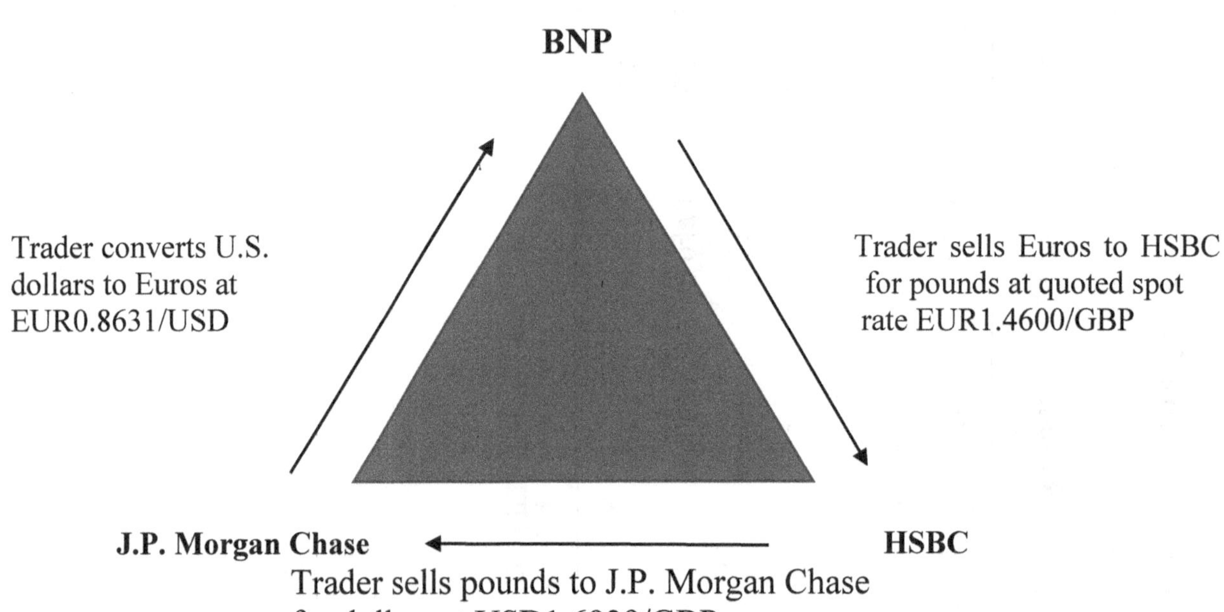

Sequence of simultaneous transactions:
Sell euros for pounds: 1,000,000/1.4600 = 684,931.50 pounds
Sell pounds for dollars: 684,931.50 x 1.6939 = 1,160,205.40 dollars
Sell dollars for euros: $1,160,205.40 x 0.8631 = 1,001,373.20 euros
End profit: EUR1,373.20 (EUR1,001,373.20 – EUR1,000,000); this profit amount is before transaction costs and taxes.

The exchange rate disparity that underlies the above arbitrage will continue until market forces will make the J. P. Morgan Chase quotation to equal the cross rate. At that point the profit opportunity will disappear and exchange rate equilibrium would be restored.

Covered Interest Arbitrage

The relationship between spot and forward exchange rates and interest rates is known as interest rate parity. According to this theory, markets are in a state of equilibrium when the differential in national interest rates for securities of similar risk and maturity is offset by the difference between the spot and forward exchange rates. As this equilibrium state is not constant, any deviation gives rise to yet another type of riskless profit opportunity. Recognized quickly by arbitragers it will prompt them to take advantage of it by investing in whichever currency brings the higher return on a covered basis. This transaction is known as *covered interest arbitrage (CIA)*--"covered" because it entails simultaneous trade in the spot and forward markets to lock in riskless profit.

Any foreign exchange trader at the arbitrage division of a major international bank, may conduct a CIA transaction for funds that the bank holds. Consider, for example, a U.S. trader with $1,000,000 in short term funds deciding whether to invest these funds in a U.S. six-month government-issued note earning 8.00 percent per annum compared to a Canadian-issued note of the same quality and maturity earning 6.00 percent per annum. If the spot exchange rate for Canadian dollars is C$1.60/$ and the six-month forward exchange rate is C$1.56/$, the trader's schematic options are identified in Exhibit 7.4.

Exhibit 7.4 Covered Interest Arbitrage

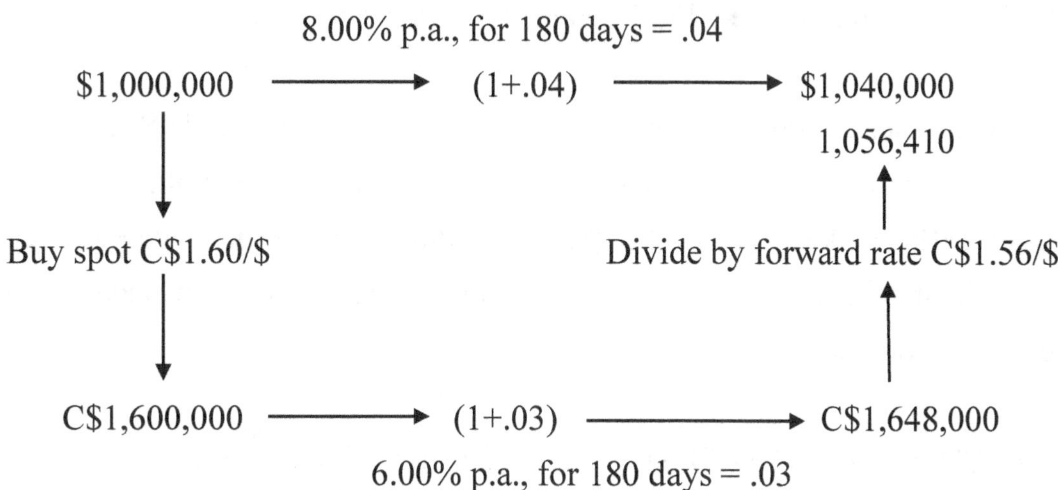

As depicted in this Exhibit, the Canadian investment would generate a more attractive return ($56,410 or 5.64%) than the U.S. alternative ($40,000 or 4.00%) for the period under consideration. However, with conditions in the exchange markets monitored widely the profit opportunity may not last long. The U.S. trader would need to act expeditiously to lock in the higher return by executing the following concurrent transactions:

-Buy Canadian dollars at the going spot rate ($1,000,000 x C$1.60/$= C$1,600,000) to invest in the six-month Canadian note.
-Sell simultaneously the expected six-month investment proceeds (C$1,648,000) forward for U.S. dollars at the 180 day forward rate (C$1,648,000 / C$1.56 = $1,056,410).

Considering the opportunity cost of investing funds at 8.00 percent per annum (or 4.00%) for 180 days, with principal and interest totaling $1,040,000, the CIA end profit is $16,410 ($1,056,410 –$1,040,000).

MEASURING CHANGE IN SPOT AND FORWARD RATES

Changes in spot rates over time may be measured through use of specific formulas. If the changes are denoted in indirect quotes (foreign currency price of a unit of the domestic or home currency) the formula to determine the percentage change (% Δ) in the foreign currency is

% Δ = [(Beginning rate – Ending rate) / (Ending rate)] x 100

For example, consider the value of your home currency, the U.S. dollar, in Thailand. If in the course of the last two years the value of the U.S. dollar changed from Thai Baht THB29.00/$ to THB32.57/$, use of the above formula would reveal a 10.96% drop in the value of the Baht against the dollar (notice the negative result of the computation).

[(THB29.00/$– THB32.57/$) / (THB32.57/$)] x 100 = -10.96%

If the expressed change is denoted in direct quotes (domestic or home currency price for a unit of foreign currency), the above-cited formula would be adjusted as follows:

% Δ = [(Ending rate – Beginning rate) / (Beginning rate)] x 100

The reciprocal numbers of the example used above would produce the same result--a drop in the U.S. value of the Baht:

[(USD0.03070/THB – USD0.03448/THB) / (USD0.03448/THB) x 100 = -10.96%

Unlike spot rates that provide a complete quote, forward rates (bid and ask) cite only the last digits of a currency quotation. These digits are known as *pips*, or points away from the spot rate (bid and ask). For major currencies, such as the euro, pound sterling and the yen, forward bid and ask quotations may run from the next business day out to several years. Forward rates for contracts maturing less than two years are known as *cash rates*, longer than two years *swap rates* (use of this term exemplifies the essence of the transaction which involves borrowing of one currency by lending equivalent amounts of another).

Forward rate quotations may also be expressed as a percentage deviation from the spot rate on an annual basis. This deviation may result into a forward premium or discount relative to the spot rate. In the case of indirect quotes the formula for determining the percent-per-annum (360/n) forward premium or discount is

Spot–Forward/Forward) x (360/n) x 100

For example, if the spot rate for Canadian dollars is C$1.3819/$ and the 90-day forward is C$1.3680/$, the outcome would be:

(1.3819–1.3680)/1.3680) x (360/90) x 100= +4.06%

If direct quotes are used, the above-cited formula would be adjusted as follows:

(Forward–Spot/Spot) x (360/n) x 100

The reciprocal rates produce an identical result

(0.73099–0.72364/0.72364) x (360/90) x 100= +4.06%

The positive sign and identical result of these computations imply that the Canadian dollar is selling forward at a premium of 4.06 percent against the dollar (it costs 4.06% more dollars to buy a Canadian dollar at the 90-day forward rate).

FOREIGN EXCHANGE RISK

For a financial institution that is an active participant in the FX market, exposure to risk results from its aggregate position (investments) in a given currency--its holdings of assets and liabilities that are denominated in that currency and held in its portfolio, and its trading activity in that currency through spot transactions and dealings in financial derivatives, such as forward, future and option contracts. Thus to determine an institution's overall exposure, both currency positions must be taken into account to establish its net exposure in that currency. The formula that measures net exposure may be summed up as follows:

Net exposure = (FX assets – FX liabilities) + (FX bought – FX sold)
= Net FX assets + Net FX bought = Net position

If an institution can balance out the formula components individually (assets=liabilities, and bought=sold), or combined (asset-liability holdings=currency trading), to result to a zero net position, the institution has no FX exposure. A more likely outcome would be an imbalanced position: a positive net position would denote that the institution is *net long* in that currency (holds or bought more of a currency than it owes or sold), or a negative net position which would imply that it is *net short* (owes/sold more than it holds/bought). In the former instance the institution stands to profit from an appreciation in the value of the foreign currency, but sustain losses in the opposite scenario. In the latter case, the institution would profit if the foreign currency depreciates in value, but suffer losses if it does not. The U.S. Treasury Bulletin statistics on the FX holdings of the major market participants in September 2015, highlight this difference in net exposure position. For example, as seen in Exhibit 7.5 below, the overall exposure of U.S. market participants in Japanese yen was a positive net, or long, position while in Euros it was a negative net, or net short, position.

Exhibit 7.5 Yen and Euro Holdings of Large FX Market Participants (Monthly Report, September 2015)

Currency of Denomination	Assets	Liabilities	FX Bought	FX Sold	Net Position
Japanese yen (billions of ¥)	148,727	134,765	659,135	669,026	4,071
Euros (millions of €)	2,044,063	2,001,516	8,396,952	8,593,199	-153,700

Source: *Treasury Bulletin*, December 2015, pp. 57-69. https://www.fiscal.treasury.gov

Whatever the net exposure in a given currency, a financial institution's position in the FX market is representative of diverse trading activities, such as to facilitate customers' carry on of international trade transactions, or the conduct of foreign investments in real and financial assets. Alternatively, they may portray a hedging strategy to control against risk, or they may well be an *open* (or speculative) *position* in anticipation of a movement in exchange rates. Clearly the last of these activities, the open or speculative position, has the potential for losses if exchange rates move against the financial institution's position. Such has been, for example, the case of Deutsche Bank, Citigroup and Barclays when they lost a total of $400 million following the Swiss Central Bank removal of its cap off the franc in January 2015. There have been other precedents in the past as well. Sizable exchange rate volatility in 1974 caused important losses for banks in England and Switzerland, and contributed to the closing of the Franklin National Bank of New York and the collapse of Bankhaus Herstatt in West Germany. The day German regulators closed the bank,

Herstatt had $620 million of uncompleted trades which caused U.S. banks to sustain losses close to $200 million. In the 1990s major losses were sustained with the failure of Drexel Burnham Lambert, the closure of the Bank of Credit and Commerce International (BCCI) and the collapse of Barings Brothers.

Banks' increased concern of the settlement risk (payment of cash or delivery of assets prior to receipt of cash or assets) prompted the creation in 2002 of the Continuous Linked Settlement (CLS) system to provide clearinghouse services to its participants. The CLS settles 55% of foreign exchange transactions in 17 different currencies. Its record of single-day gross-value settlement was $10.3 trillion in 2008. Its membership includes 9000 institutions with many global banks among them.

Individuals, businesses and investors manage their foreign exchange exposure by hedging through such financial derivatives as forward, futures and options contracts. Businesses, including importers and exporters, generally prefer to hedge through forward contracts because they are tailored as to the desired amount and maturity and require no daily margin calls (additional deposits) for the contracts to be marked to market. Forward exchange contracts are briskly traded wherever spot currency markets exist. These are found in the major international money markets, such as Amsterdam, Brussels, New York, Paris, Zurich, and London. These markets all trade in the world's major currencies; forward trading in currencies of less important countries is sporadic. For highly unstable currencies, forward contracts are costly because of the degree of risk involved.

Individuals find foreign currency futures contracts useful because they do not usually have access to forward contracts. A key attribute of futures contracts is that they are standardized and as a result their trading is done in organized exchanges instead of being negotiated directly with banks. These contracts are also of appeal to speculators because they are rarely delivered; settlement normally takes place through an offsetting position. Foreign currency futures contracts are of two basic types, long hedges and short hedges. A long hedge protects a buyer from increases in the price of the currency he must eventually acquire; a short hedge protects the seller from decreases in the price of the currency he will receive payment.

Foreign-currency futures contracts are traded on the International Monetary

Market (IMM), a division of the Chicago Mercantile Exchange. On the IMM contracts are available for such currencies as pounds sterling, Canadian dollars, Japanese yen, Mexican pesos, Euros, and Swiss francs. Foreign-currency options contracts on cash instruments are traded in the Philadelphia Options Exchange. The IMM trades options on foreign currency futures contracts.

8 INTERNATIONAL RETAIL AND PRIVATE BANKING

Corporate lending services have long been a traditional domain and a major source of earnings growth for commercial banks. However, deregulation of the financial services industry in recent decades has broadened the market to include many nonbank competitors such as insurance companies, investment banking firms, and finance companies. Moreover, many creditworthy borrowers can now borrow directly from financial markets by issuing commercial paper or long term bonds. Commercial paper is inexpensive to issue and can be placed privately by investment banks with relative ease. Long term bonds provide an expedient source for funding corporate activity. Increased market acceptance of high-yield debt issues for corporate purposes, rather than for acquisitions or buyouts, has rendered junk bonds (rated below BBB) a suitable source of funding for small or new businesses. In U.S. markets competitive pressures are even more intense because of the activities of tax-exempt organizations such as credit unions and the Farm Credit System.

Increased competition and aggressive pricing has exerted significant pressure on profit margins, and this pressure has induced many commercial banks to expand their product and service offerings in order to generate additional fee income. Thus many institutions have expanded the scope of their operations to include retail and private banking services, both of which share similar qualities that are attractive to commercial lenders: a firm client base, reduced earnings volatility, and lower capital adequacy requirements to support operations.[1]

[1]Since the 1998 Basel Agreement, banks have had to maintain higher levels of capital in order to support their lending operations. These capital adequacy requirements have made non-lending transactions more attractive.

Serving the banking needs of individuals, even wealthy individuals, has not been one of international banking's exciting sectors. Nonetheless, retail and private banking share the virtue of boosting fee-based income which compensates for the decline in traditional corporate lending services.

INTERNATIONAL RETAIL SERVICES

Retail banking provides banking services for individuals. These include taking deposits, making loans for homes, cars and other purchases, and offering credit card services, transaction services, and even insurance and investment management services for individual clients. Although retail banking has long been valued for its ability to lend low-cost deposits at high rates to generate high yields and net interest income, branch banking was one of the last areas within banking to globalize.

Significant retail banking in Latin America began in the 1990s and continued through the turn of the century. Political stability and economic growth enabled Latin America to experience an extended period of economic prosperity, except for the brief halt that came as a result of the global financial crisis (2008). The favorable economic environment produced a marked drop in poverty rates, expanded the middle class and caused a surge in the demand for insurance products, consumer loans, and credit cards. Loan growth has been running at 20 percent per annum compared to 6-8 percent in developed countries. Stiffer bankruptcy laws and stronger banking supervision has made it safer to lend in the lucrative low-income market. The marked improvement in the well- being and quality of life of Latin Americans has made community banks an attractive takeover target.

The region is also benefitting from the growing momentum of mobile technology that serves the needs of the 5.3 billion people of the world who live on the fringes of the traditional financial system. In one noteworthy effort Movistar, a subsidiary of Spain's Telefonica, and Master Card have launched a joint mobile banking service in 12 Latin American countries.

Development of homegrown multinationals, often referred to as "multilatinas," has added momentum to the regionalization of retail banking operations. Whether prompted by acquisition of a rival or independent considerations, the cross border move has included such financial institutions as Banco do Brasil, Itau (Brazil), Aval, Sura and Bancolombia (Colombia). The multilatinas dynamic has been notable not only for the swelling number of its participants but also for its revitalization of the region's integration aspirations. Although Latin America has been experimenting with a multiplicity of sub-regional, regional and pan-regional integration schemes, this dynamic is exerting important influence toward convergence of regulatory standards across markets.

Regionalization of retail banking operations is also taking place in Asia, where the middle class is growing by an average of more than 100 million people a year and is expected to account for more than half of the world's total population by 2020. The market's growth momentum has attracted the interest of international lenders and contributed to a boom in retail services, e.g., credit cards and installment loans for cars, motorcycles and home appliances. Consumer credit in the region (excluding Japan) rose 67 percent in the past five years, compared to only 10 percent in the United States during the same period.

Although regionalization of retail banking services has grown considerably since the 1990s, full globalization of retail banking may nonetheless prove quite arduous. While banks have been successful in globalizing their wholesale operations, they have encountered significant difficulty competing with local banks for the business of individual customers. This is partly because, whereas corporate and investment banking is comparatively uniform from country to country, retail banking products, customs and regulations can vary substantially across borders and regions.[2] As a result, new entrants often find it difficult to compete with established local banks. This, for example, has been the case in the European Union (EU) which, although thriving as a single market, has no powerful regional players.

However, one major exception to local resistance has been Citigroup, which has succeeded in creating a global brand name in retail and private banking. Its Global

[2]Local regulations sometimes impede the ability of multinational providers to enter new markets. For example, because of important variation in law, and customer needs and preferences, the process of extending a mortgage loan varies widely across emerging markets.

Consumer Bank (GCB) serves more than 100 million customers in the fastest growing cities around the world. Operating approximately 3,000 branches in more than 100 top cities, GCB, offers branded cards, retail services, retail banking and commercial banking in Asia; Europe, the Middle East and Africa (EMEA); Latin America; and North America. In 2015, the business held $301 billion in deposits, had $391 billion in average assets and included $281.3 billion in average loans.

Moreover, Citi is the world's largest credit card issuer, with more than 138 million accounts, $363.9 billion in annual purchase sales and $133.2 billion in average receivables across the Citi Branded Cards and Citi Retail Services. Citibank offers the full range of consumer banking services, including checking and savings, loans, wealth management advice and small business services to clients around the globe.[3]

Twenty-first century technology now offers new ways for multinationals to compete in local markets. In addition to providing access to individual customers, internet banking (also known as *direct banking* and *online banking*) provides economies of scale and low transaction costs. On the other hand, internet banking does pose some risks. In particular, as internet banking has proliferated, so have internet banking scams in which business that are not legally chartered by state or federal governments, and whose deposits are not insured, pose as legitimate banks online, leaving their clients vulnerable. Moreover, internet banking requires large upfront investments in technology. Nonetheless, internet banking offers customers greater convenience and lower fees, while bankers benefit from lower costs and greater access to local markets across international borders. This has been especially true in Europe where the introduction of the euro has greatly simplified processing transactions across borders.

INTERNATIONAL PRIVATE BANKING

Sources of Personal Wealth

Private banking deals with the provision of wealth management services to high net worth individuals. Originating in Europe, it focused on advising about and performing all financial and banking services for wealthy families and royal houses.

[3]http://www.citigroup.com/citi/about/consumer_businesses.html

Over time private banking has developed into an exclusive niche of banking activity. Wealth is a purely economic measure; it often results from the extension of goods and services along with capital income that has been earned on accumulated assets over time (interest, dividends, and capital gains). Although knowledge of the sources of clients' wealth is required in the United States and abroad to enforce anti-money laundering and terrorism financing (AML) regulations,[4] it is also useful in order to address client needs more effectively.

The sources of clients' wealth, typically fall into one or more of five categories: *family wealth*, *corporate wealth*, *entrepreneurial wealth*, *political wealth*, and *criminal wealth.* Private bankers target the first three of these sources of wealth, which, by some estimates, account for some 85 to 90 percent of the total assets under management.

Family wealth is usually inherited wealth; it involves the ongoing transfer of assets from older family members to younger family members through the generations. Family wealth tends to be especially sensitive to national fiscal and economic policies, especially taxation. Worldwide, the heaviest concentrations of family wealth are in North America, Asia and Western Europe, which is the seat of conventional private banking.

Corporate wealth is typically earned by working in a high-level executive capacity within a corporation, and it takes the form of salaries, bonuses, deferred compensation, stock options, and severance payments. Corporate-derived wealth is especially important in the United States, where, by comparison to other countries, executive compensation is markedly high.

Entrepreneurial wealth derives from full or part ownership of one or more businesses or enterprises. This type of wealth tends to be accumulated over large periods of time, and often exists only in paper until the business is sold or goes public, and its intrinsic worth is translated into actual value. Europe and Asia have been

[4]"Know your customer" (KYC) requirements in this country were enforced through enactment of federal legislation--Bank Secrecy Act of 1970 as amended by the U.S. Patriot Act of 2001. These requirements prohibit banks from knowingly accepting illicit funds. In early 2016, the U.S. Treasury's Financial Crimes Enforcement Network (FinCEN) issued new regulations clarifying and strengthening requirements for financial institutions.

traditional sources of entrepreneurial wealth due to the strong concentration or family-owned or controlled companies (as opposed to the United States and Canada which are characterized by a widely dispersed ownership of publicly traded firms). However, as the result of the success of many start-up companies, especially in technology fields, entrepreneurial wealth is also becoming increasingly common in the United States.

Although political wealth is often accumulated legally, it frequently derives from payments, discounted business opportunities, and other preferential treatment made by their constituents to political office holders in exchange, explicitly or implicitly, for political favors and preferential political treatment. Illegal forms of political wealth may also result from misappropriation of public funds, bribery, extortion, misused political contributions, kickbacks, and financial holdings that are illegally linked to government contracts. Political wealth is most common in markets where transparent, rule-based legal systems and administrative infrastructures are largely absent and where democratic institutions do not flourish. Worldwide, political wealth is overly concentrated in the emerging markets of Africa, Asia, and the formerly planned economies of Eastern Europe.

Criminal wealth derives from lucrative illegal activities such as organized crime, extortion, theft, financial fraud, arms smuggling, and drug trafficking, among other illicit activities. Transferred through different financial institutions to conceal its source and ownership, criminal wealth is "laundered" before it is invested into legitimate assets. Although criminal activity is found throughout the world, it flourishes mostly where law enforcement is lax and markets are less open and transparent.

Size of Global Wealth and Determinants of its Distribution

In its annual report for 2015, The Boston Consulting Group (BCG) maintained that global financial wealth amounted to $168 trillion (Exhibit 8.1). With many equity and bond markets staying fairly flat or even falling during that year, the report attributed the bulk of global wealth more to the creation of new wealth, such as rising household income, than to the performance of existing assets.

Exhibit 8.1 Geographic Distribution of Private Financial Wealth and Forecast (in trillions of dollars)

Region	2015	2020 Estimate
Asia-Pacific	$36.6	$59.8
Eastern Europe	3.6	5.3
Japan	13.6	15.3
Latin America	4.8	7.1
Middle East and Africa	8.0	11.8
North America	60.4	76.0
Western Europe	40.8	48.7
Total	$167.8	$224.0

Source: Global Wealth 2016: Navigating the New Client Landscape, The Boston Consulting Group, Inc., Boston, 2016.

Although the 2015 record represented a 5.2 percent increase over the preceding year, the report identified a significant slowdown in the growth rates of several regions. For example, the report attributed the adverse performance of the equity and bond markets in Western Europe to uncertainty about the future of the EU and the continued low commodity prices. Slowdowns of economic growth in several developing regions were traced to political unrest, international sanctions, and general economic tension. Overall, the Asia-Pacific region continued to show the highest growth in private wealth (13% in 2015), while the lowest levels of growth were experienced in the developing markets in the Middle East and Africa (3% in 2015), where low commodity prices and political instability led to lower equity and bond markets. On the premise of a recovery in financial markets over the next five years, the report projected global wealth to total $224 trillion by 2020, a significant increase attributed to the combined effect of new wealth creation and existing assets performance.

The worldwide distribution of individual wealth is primarily determined by three factors: *per capita income*, *market distribution mechanisms*, and *government policies.* As might be expected, countries and regions with a high level of per capita income would possess greater concentrations of private wealth than lower-income countries. Market distribution mechanisms including levels of education and other sources of earning power vary widely from country to country. Consequently, significant differences exist among countries in how wealth is accumulated and distributed. Governments' views of wealth, expressed through economic, political and socio-cultural considerations and through national policies with regard to private property and taxation, affect the holdings of the wealthy and influence how and where individual wealth is amassed. Policies can change gradually or quickly, impacting accordingly the preservation of wealth.

Profile of the Private Banking Client

A main difference among competing financial institutions is how much wealth they require their private clients to possess. Often banks use classifications to distinguish among their current or potential clients, breaking them into such groups as the ultra-high net worth (e.g., over $100 million), upper high ($20-$100 million), lower high ($1-$20 million), and affluent ($250,000-$1 million). They might, for instance, limit their traditional private banking services to the top three groups, while servicing the (mass) affluent group electronically. While the cut-off point of each group is based on a set figure, banks may sometimes make exceptions for preferred clients or those who appear to offer significant future potential. Sometimes the decision is based not on the amount of the client's wealth but on how much income in fees the bank will earn.

Traditionally, private clients fall into several categories. Many are *individuals and families* with high net worth who require professional advice on structuring portfolios, planning inheritance, and forming long-term investment strategies, in addition to taking advantage of global investing and trading opportunities. Others are *entrepreneurs* who own small and medium-sized businesses and/or family controlled industry groups and are seeking advice on both business and personal financial matters. *Professionals and executives*, notably those who derive much of their wealth from stock options, often need banking services to address tax-driven compensation and asset-holding patterns, and their private banking focus is typically based on their personal assets. *Highly paid entertainers and artists* seek assistance for managing royalty and endorsement income and extracting value from intellectual property and residuals. Similarly, wealthy *sports professionals* increasingly seek professional advice for managing their finances. Finally private bankers are often consulted by *owners and/or managers of family offices* and by *intermediaries and external asset managers* seeking independent advice.

Millennials--those born roughly between 1980 and 2000--though not yet wealth management clients, represent a largely untapped potential clientele. The BCG report, which estimates that millennials already hold 10 percent of global private wealth, projects their market share to grow at an annual rate of 16 percent, and, by 2020, to account for about 16 percent of the market.[5] Tech savvy and inclined to carry out their own proactive research, millennials, according to this report, seek full transparency on both management fees and investment performance, especially in the current low-return environment, and they overwhelmingly chose pricing as their top criterion for choosing a financial institution.[6] Because of this preference, banks face significant competition from so-called Robo advisors who provide online financial advice or portfolio management based solely on software-driven mathematical algorithms with little or no human involvement. In many ways Robo advisors represent the opposite of private bankers, whose professional judgment and personal involvement are their main selling points.

Client Objectives

Unlike other segments of international finance, whose clients typically share the same goals, private banking serves clients with diverse objectives. Some of the most common objectives are *safety*, *capital preservation and/or performance*, *confidentiality*, and *high levels of service.*

Many traditional individual clients come from countries experiencing political instability and financial uncertainty, and these clients are primarily concerned with the safety of their wealth. For instance, political and economic turmoil in Latin America

[5]*Global Wealth 2016: Navigating the New Client Landscape,* The Boston Consulting Group, Inc., Boston, 2016, p. 22.
[6]Ibid., p. 23.

in recent decades has prompted many wealthy individuals to seek safety for their funds abroad. Typical cases are those of Panama, itself a tax haven, under the dictatorship of Manuel Noriega (1983-1989), Colombia in the course of its civil strife (1964-2016),[7] and more recently Venezuela under socialist regime. The political and economic conditions of these countries swell the ranks of private banking clients at many foreign banks.

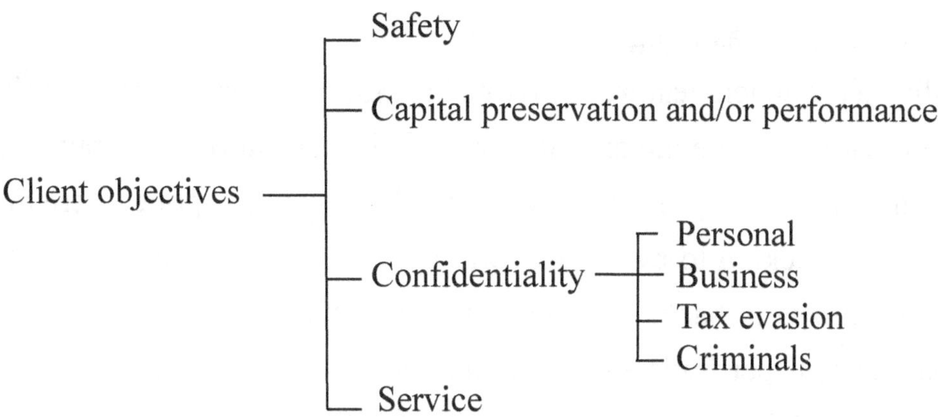

Old-money families have traditionally relied on personal contacts to choose their personal bankers. The same holds true for wealthy clients who have earned their wealth through inheritance or savings over time. Inheritors, or savers, do not usually possess tolerance for risk and may see themselves as temporary custodians of wealth, which leads them to adopt a lower-risk approach to wealth protection and preservation. These clients have tended to be much more interested in wealth preservation than in high performance. However, younger-generation clients with earned, rather than inherited, wealth usually demand a more active approach to their wealth management and are hence more performance focused. Likewise, entrepreneurs and business owners, or

[7]Colombia's 52-year civil war involved paramilitary groups, crime syndicates, left-wing guerrillas such as FARC (Revolutionary Armed Forces of Colombia), and the National Liberation Army (ELN), all fighting each other to increase their domestic influence. The prolonged strife drove many wealthy individuals to seek the security of their funds abroad. FARC used to levy a 10 percent tax on individuals and businesses with assets in excess of one million U.S. dollars. Failure to pay the levy resulted in abduction. Widespread use of this practice led 2000 to become a record year with 3,700 abductions for an average period of six months and an average ransom of $65,000.

those that became wealthy through the sale of a business, by definition, have had to take risks in order to become successful and they possess a higher risk tolerance. This type of client, having earned his or her wealth, usually demands a more active approach to wealth management and is more performance focused. Such clients frequently prefer their profits to derive more from capital appreciation than from income interest or dividends. In addition, because wealthy individuals of all ages are often subject to large tax requirements, many seek out private bankers to help them manage their money in ways that will minimize their tax obligations.

Confidentiality, a prominent feature of private banking, is valued highly by private clients. Wealthy individuals value the appeal of personal financial privacy; businesses value the safeguard of proprietary information from competitors, suppliers, creditors, and other parties; those seeking to evade the scrutiny of domestic regulatory and tax authorities hold their assets in banks outside their country; and for criminals private banking often eliminates paper trails and incriminating evidence. In all cases, clients seek safety from unwanted disclosure of financial information.

Other private banking clients also require services that are handled discretely. Due to the personal nature of most private banking, clients tend to develop loyalty to banks with whom they have had positive experiences. This loyalty offers clients confidence and reassurance, and it provides the bankers unique marketing opportunities because their customers are not as sensitive to the prices charged or the performance of their assets, and they are often more receptive to the purchase of other bank products. Thus competition for such clients centers around quality of service more than simple price-based considerations.

Private Banking Services

In order to provide comprehensive assistance to their clients, private banks frequently provide a wide array of financial services depicted in Exhibit 8.2. These include *cash management services*, *investment management*, *extension of credit and personal lending*, *business finance*, and *personal services*.

Cash management services include checking accounts, cash management accounts, money market accounts, savings accounts, CDs, commercial paper, Treasury

Exhibit 8.2 Private Banking Services

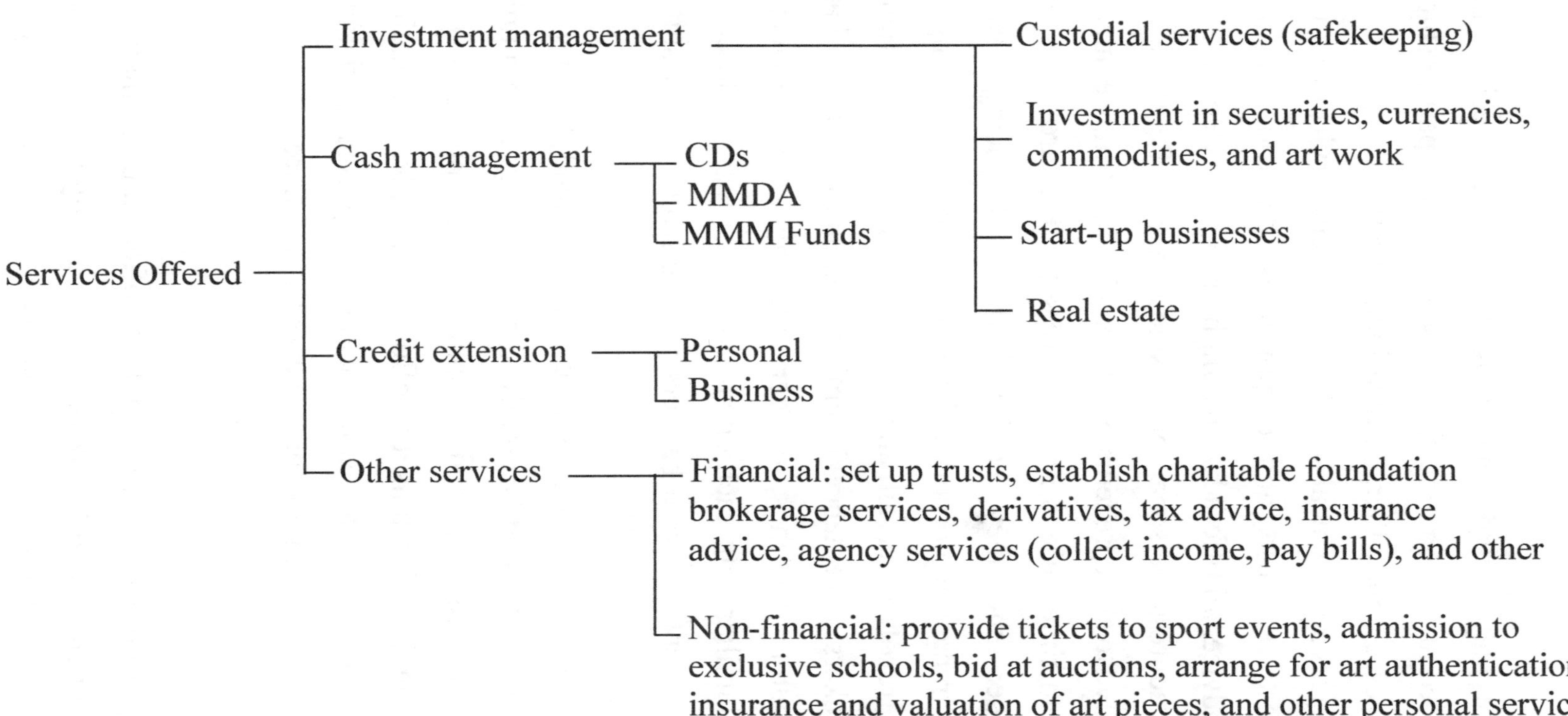

Source: Developed by the author.

bills, bankers' acceptances, and taxable and nontaxable mutual funds. Although these services are available to retail clients as well, private clients receive a higher level of service.

Investment management may include managing real estate, precious metals, currencies, emerging market equities, commodities, artwork, limited partnerships that are investing in start-up businesses, and other, conventional assets.

Brokerage and trust services are a typical set of private client services that include assistance in establishing estates, trusts and corporations, provision of ordinary brokerage services, and tax advice, all offered with a high level of service.

Credit extension may address personal or business needs. Personal lending services are especially attractive to entrepreneurs, who are often creating wealth and are not highly liquid. They sometimes use private bankers to structure deals around existing personal assets; other times they require short-term financing. Business financing entails offering a range of corporate banking services, including credit facilities (e.g., lines of credit, revolving credit, and term loans), foreign trade financing (e.g., letters of credit and bankers' acceptances), remittances, and investment banking services (e.g., underwrite public offerings, merger and acquisition services, and advisory services). Already familiar with each client's attitude toward risk, currency, maturity and liquidity requirements, private bankers are particularly well suited for servicing their banking needs.

Finally, some private banks also offer services that extend beyond purely traditional banking transactions. Performed discretely, these can range from running an equestrian facility and managing its staff and equipment to the provision of such personal services as arranging introductions to influential people, facilitating the admission of children and grandchildren to exclusive schools, providing tickets and invitations to high-profile sporting and entertainment events, and more.

Private Banking Strategies

There are two main approaches for private banks to offer value to their clients: *offering client segmentation based on product requirements* and *offering best in-class products and services.* Client segmentation requires the bank to deliver as many proprietary services as possible in order to leverage multiple in-house capabilities and thereby make the economies of operation more efficient.

On the other hand, by offering the best in-class products and services, regardless of whether or not they are produced in-house, banks can broaden the range of products available to clients and thereby better address their needs. This, in turn, can create the clients' good will, as they feel the bank is looking out for their interests. This approach relies more heavily on advisory fees and reduces or eliminates product-linked fees. Its primary appeal is that it better enables banks, to satisfy their clients by offering a wide range of trustworthy products. Bundling of products can further help banks achieve economies of scale.

Exceptional moments in clients' lives can create so-called "event windows" that produce new opportunities for bankers to offer additional products and services. For instance, a wealthy individual's receipt of a large inheritance may prompt the banker to suggest new asset-holding structures or other products and services that the bank offers. The sale or launching of a business venture can create an event window for entrepreneurs who may suddenly require an entirely new wealth management strategy, as well as advice on investment banking services, tax matters, and ownership and control concerns. Executives' event windows may stem from implementation of a compensation plan, retirement benefits, both of which may also require new wealth management strategies. Similarly, athletes, artists and entertainers sometimes achieve success that results in a vast increase in their remuneration, and they too may benefit from the advice, new strategies, and additional products that a private banker can offer.

So-called 360-degree private client service offerings are intended to attract and retain wealthy individuals by providing high levels of intimacy, trust, and discretion. Because private banking relies on a discrete and intimate relationship between a bank and a loyal, wealthy individual client, bank strategy must seek to retain clients not only through their own lifetime, but also throughout the lives of their heirs. Retaining an intergenerational relationship requires financial and succession planning and wealth management, legal and tax-effective structures, and discretionary asset management. Of course, consistently providing the high level of service that the bank promises its wealthy clients is paramount.

PART II LEGAL ISSUES AND LENDING SCOPE

9 LEGAL CONSIDERATIONS FOR INTERNATIONAL LENDING

Although the gunboat diplomacy of the nineteen and early twenty century has given way to judicial remedies, the change has not been without its challenges. Because international lending transactions involve more than one country, and thus more than one legal system, they are more complicated than purely domestic transactions. At least two systems of law must be negotiated in any international lending transaction: the law of the lender's country and that of the borrower. International transactions become even more complicated when other parties to the transaction, such as guarantors or additional lenders, are located in additional countries, or when the lender makes the loan from an office outside its home country. In those cases the number of applicable laws increases correspondingly. Principles of international law may also come into play from time to time, particularly with respect to the enforcement of judgments. (International lending issues are not unlike those in interstate lending, where U.S. state laws differ. Moreover federal law may also affect some aspects of the loan. However, while state laws are all ultimately based in English common law, and they are typically similar and sometimes identical, this is often not the case for the applicable laws between two or more nations, each of which formulated its legal codes independently of the others.)

It is important, particularly for the lender, that the financing be made as predictable and clear-cut as possible, and this is typically accomplished by structuring and documenting the transaction within a known legal framework. In particular, it is essential that a single legal system governs all of the substantive aspects of the loan and that a well-defined forum exists for resolving any disputes that may arise.

However, some legal aspects of any international financing agreement will always involve matters that cannot be changed by agreements between the parties. For instance, exchange control regulations applicable to the borrower or guarantor, and government authorizations required for the particular transaction exist beyond the scope of the private agreement between the borrower and lender. Thus the transaction and its documentation will inevitably be governed by more than one legal system. It is important, therefore, for the lender and its counsel to coordinate the particulars of each transaction with knowledgeable, well-experienced counsel in the borrower's country (see "Use of Local Counsel" below).

This chapter discusses the choice of legal framework and the choice of forum, as well as sovereign immunity and other matters related to international lending transactions. The chapter considers these subjects in the context of a U.S. lender financing a borrower located outside the United States; however, the discussion also applies to the legal relationships between a U.S. lender and any guarantor of credit located outside of the United States. The same general concerns extend to international transactions not involving U.S. entities, but the particular considerations and solutions may differ.

While the following discussion highlights certain areas in which legal advice is essential, lenders should nevertheless be aware that legal documentation does not guarantee that the credit will be repaid; it only establishes the rules of the transaction that have been agreed upon at the commencement of the loan and establishes a bargaining position for the lender if the credit goes bad. But lenders should remember that foreign laws and policies sometimes change rapidly, as may a borrower's attitude about the loan. Thus the best assurance remains the lender's sound judgment about the borrower's creditworthiness and about any need for collateral security or third-party guaranties.

CHOICE OF GOVERNING LAW FOR THE TRANSACTION

Lenders to foreign borrowers should insist upon financing governed by a predictable system of substantive law that is not readily subject to change by or for the benefit of the borrower. This is especially true if the borrower is a government or government entity. Preferably the legal framework will also be familiar to the lender. For a U.S. lender the law of the state in which the lender is located, which includes any applicable federal laws, is typically the most desirable choice. For syndicated credits the best legal system is usually that which governs the jurisdiction in which the agent or the majority of the lenders are located. In the contract between the lender and borrower the typical choice-of-law clause reads, "This Agreement shall be governed by, and construed and interpreted in accordance with, the laws of the State of X."

The local law will determine whether the parties' choice of governing law is acceptable. In most American jurisdictions the courts will respect the parties' choice of law if it is reasonably appropriate for the transaction. In such cases courts will consider where the lender's and the borrower's offices are located, where the credit is negotiated, where the documents are signed, where funds are disbursed, and where payments are to be made by the borrower.

In many countries local constitutions or statutes may require that local law govern foreign loans. In Latin America this requirement appears in the Calvo Doctrine, which was developed in the nineteenth century in response to military and diplomatic intervention on behalf of foreign investors and lenders. The Calvo Doctrine essentially maintains that a foreigner doing business in a country must agree to be governed by solely local law, and that by choosing to do business in the country, the foreigner implicitly agrees to be treated as a local resident. In other cases, borrowers, usually governmental, may refuse to accept any law other than their own as the governing legal framework for the loan. Therefore, in order to avoid uncertainty in future interpretations of the contract, the lender's local counsel in the borrower's home country and its U.S. counsel should always ensure that the choice of governing law will adequately protect the lender's interests.

In the event that a borrower rejects the governing law preferred by the lender, or the preferred legal framework is not permitted under any local law, that lender has several options. First, the borrower and lender may agree upon the law of a neutral jurisdiction, if this is permitted by the borrower's local law. In this instance the lender's counsel and local counsel must ensure that the neutral forum would, indeed, apply the agreed-upon law, and that any judgment would be enforced in the borrower's country. Counsel should also evaluate how difficult it might be to advocate for the lender within the framework of the law of the neutral jurisdiction.

On the other hand, the lender may agree to be governed by the law of the borrower's country. If most, or all, of the borrower's assets are located in the borrower's country, then this option may well be an acceptable alternative, as the lender would be able to appropriate them in the event of a favorable judgment. In cases where local courts do not apply foreign law to cases before them, but would enforce foreign judgments rendered under foreign law, the contract might specify that one law will apply to proceedings that occur outside of the borrower's country, while the borrower's local law will pertain if proceedings are brought locally. However, this option introduces the complications inherent in applying more-than-one set of laws, as well as introducing higher levels of uncertainty to the process. Finally, the documentation may simply omit any reference to the choice of governing law, in which case a forum court or tribunal will determine the proper law to be applied in case of a dispute. However, this option will introduce significant uncertainty into the resolution of disputes, something lenders should always seek to avoid as much as possible.

Regardless of which option is selected, the choice of the governing law for a transaction does not supersede relevant regulatory laws, such as applicable lending limits, local bankruptcy law, and requirements for government approval for the loan or for the obtaining and using foreign exchange.

CHOICE OF FORUM FOR THE RESOLUTION OF DISPUTES

The agreed-upon law governing the loan typically specifies the forum for resolving disputes. International lenders prefer a forum that offers impartial judges experienced in international commerce and an adequate number of courts and competent attorneys, so that any litigation may proceed expeditiously. The choice of a forum should be a nonexclusive choice--that is, the complaining party should be able to use the designated forum if it chooses, but this use should not be mandatory. The lender should retain the option of using a different forum if it appears more desirable to do so--for instance, in situations where the borrower has assets in a different jurisdiction that may disappear before the lender is able to obtain a judgment in the forum specified in the contract.

The forum may be specified directly in a provision within the contract, such as, "The parties agree that all disputes relating to this Agreement may be tried before the courts of the State of X or the courts of the United States sitting in X." Conversely, the choice of forum may be specified indirectly through the borrower's submission to the personal jurisdiction of the chosen forum (discussed below). Forum selection clauses are generally accepted if they are not unreasonable, contrary to public policy, or the result of fraud or an abuse of bargaining power. In either case the lender should consult with its counsel to confirm that the chosen forum will have subject matter jurisdiction over any dispute brought before it and that its judgments will be enforced in jurisdictions where the borrower's assets are located.

Moreover, counsel should be satisfied that the circumstances under which a *forum non conveniens* argument might be made successfully are acceptable to the lender. *Forum non conveniens* is a legal doctrine in the United States that permits courts to refuse jurisdiction over a case if another forum is available, offers effective redress, and would be more just and convenient for the parties. In federal courts a successful *forum non conveniens* motion will reassign the suit to a more appropriate federal court, if there is one with jurisdiction over the parties, or to dismissal of the suit. Similarly, in state courts a successful motion generally leads to the suit's transfer to a more appropriate state court or, if there is none, to its dismissal.

The documentation for an international loan usually requires the borrower to waive its right to raise a *forum non conveniens* objection. Although the waiver will not preclude a federal court judge or judges in some state courts from considering the *forum non conveniens* issue on the court's own motion, the waiver would be a factor to be considered in ruling on the motion. Any such waiver should also forbid the parties from initiating a *forum non conveniens* motion.

SUBJECT MATTER AND PERSONAL JURISDICTION

Before the parties make their final choice of forum, the lender's counsel should ensure that the forum courts will have jurisdiction both over the disputed subject matter and over the borrower and any other potential defendant. Subject matter jurisdiction entails the court's intrinsic power to adjudicate the disputed claims. In the United States subject matter jurisdiction, unlike personal jurisdiction, cannot be created by consent of the parties; nor may the parties agree to deprive a court of subject matter jurisdiction. Personal jurisdiction entails the court's power to deal with the litigants. It depends principally upon adequate notice to any defendant of the claim(s) asserted against it and upon the existence of a relationship between the court trying the case and the defendant that justifies the court's ruling against the defendant. The bases for personal jurisdiction over a foreign state or foreign state agency are statutorily specified (see "Sovereign Immunity" below). Personal jurisdiction over a nongovernment defendant may generally be founded on one or more of the following bases: the defendant's presence or conduct of business in the forum jurisdiction, the defendant's consent to the personal jurisdiction of the forum court, or the application of a "long-arm" statute that provides that certain contacts between a transaction or event and the forum jurisdiction will give the forum courts personal jurisdiction over the parties to the transaction or event.

Jurisdiction over a nongovernment defendant that extends to assets located in the forum jurisdiction (known as *quasi in rem* jurisdiction) may be obtained by attaching the defendant's assets located in that jurisdiction. In the case of a foreign borrower, the lender may not be certain that the borrower will be present or conducting business in the forum jurisdiction or that a long-arm statute will apply when a dispute arises. Obtaining jurisdiction by attaching the defendant's assets only works if the defendant has assets in the forum jurisdiction. Moreover, any judgment is enforceable only against those assets and not against the borrower personally. (Jurisdiction over a sovereign or sovereign entity may not be obtained by attaching its assets--see "Sovereign Immunity" below.) Consequently, a consent by the nongovernment borrower to the personal jurisdiction of the courts of the chosen forum should be included in the transaction's documentation. Such an agreement might read as follows:

> The Borrower hereby irrevocably submits to the nonexclusive jurisdiction *in personam* of any court of the State of X [the forum state] or any Federal court sitting in the State of X in any action or proceeding arising out of or relating to this Agreement.

Occasionally a borrower requests that as a matter of equal treatment of the parties the lender should also expressly submit to the personal jurisdiction of courts in the borrower's country. The lender should deny this request, which could have unfavorable tax ramifications or other consequences if the agreement were to cause the lender to be held to be doing business in the borrower's country when it would not otherwise be so held.

The consent-to jurisdiction provision usually also includes one or more methods for service of legal process on the borrower in the forum jurisdiction, including the appointment of an agent in that jurisdiction to receive process on behalf of the borrower. For instance, the submission-to-jurisdiction might read:

> The Borrower hereby irrevocably appoints A, with offices on the date hereof at (address in State X), and its successors ("Process Agent") as its agent to receive on its behalf and on behalf of its property service of all legal process that may be served in any such action or proceeding. Such service may be made by mailing or delivering a copy of such process to the Borrower in care of the Process Agent at the Process Agent's address provided herein or such other address as the Process Agent shall designate in writing to the Lender, and the Borrower hereby irrevocably authorizes and directs the Process Agent to accept such service on its behalf. As an alternative method of service, the Borrower also irrevocably consents to the service of any and all legal process in any such action or proceeding by the mailing via certified mail of copies of such process to the Borrower at its address set forth on the signature page hereof or at such other address as shall be designated by the Borrower in writing to the Lender. Nothing herein shall affect the right to service of process in any jurisdiction in any other manner permitted by law.

Any person or entity may serve as an agent, but the lender should ensure that the agent it chooses can properly fulfill its duties. Borrowers, particularly governments and government agencies, sometimes seek to use their consul or a diplomatic officer in the forum jurisdiction as the agent to receive process. However, although this request is often honored, it introduces new risk to the lender because the consul or other officer may be able to avoid proper service of process by invoking diplomatic immunity. If the consul is named as the agent for service of process, the contract should specifically allow for service on the consul by mail, because the consul would be unable to effectively avoid service without stopping the delivery of all mail to the consulate. Corporate service organizations provide this service for a relatively small fee in most major cities in the United States.

In some cases, especially in countries covered by the Calvo Doctrine, the borrower's local law may forbid it from submitting to the jurisdiction of foreign courts. In such cases the lender may provide for disputes to be settled by arbitration. However, silence on the question of jurisdiction may be preferable to arbitrations since arbitrators often prefer to "split the difference" between disputants, which is typically an unsatisfactory resolution for lenders trying to collect an unpaid debt. Moreover, arbitrators are not necessarily bound by rules of evidence that apply to courts; borrowers may have limited rights to appeal the arbitrator's decision, and enforcement of the arbitral award may be uncertain. The choice of the jurisdiction may sometimes alleviate these concerns. For instance, in England questions of law may be taken to the courts for decision during an arbitration. And the contract may specify the rules that an arbitrator must follow. Nonetheless, arbitration inevitably involves uncertainty, and the lender may prefer to remain silent on the matter of jurisdiction instead.

SOVEREIGN IMMUNITY

Sovereign immunity is the doctrine under which, "as a consequence of the absolute independence of every sovereign authority, and of the international comity which induces every sovereign State to respect the independence and dignity of every other State," the courts of one sovereign nation surrender jurisdiction over another sovereign nation. The theory of absolute sovereign immunity asserts that a sovereign cannot be made to answer in the courts of another sovereign without its consent. However, the U.S. State Department rejected this theory in 1952, adopting in its place the theory of restrictive sovereign immunity that distinguishes between a nation's public and sovereign acts and its private and commercial acts. Worldwide, there is no uniform practice pertaining to sovereign immunity, but in recent years the trend has been to adopt the restrictive theory over the absolute theory. Governments have become increasingly involved in economic matters, and a corresponding need for private parties conducting business with governments and government entities to appeal to courts to settle disputes has arisen. The restrictive theory is now codified by statute in both the United States and the United Kingdom.

The U.S. Foreign Sovereign Immunities Act of 1976 (FSIA) gives state and federal courts in the United States exclusive jurisdiction over the matter of sovereignty in any given case brought before them. FSIA does not change the applicable law of liability that applies in any case; nor does it address diplomatic or consular immunity or the responsibilities of the various entities of a foreign state. FISA only establishes the standards for sovereign immunity to be decided by state and federal courts and the means by which process may be served on a nonimmune sovereign. However, any applicable international treaty to which the United States is a party takes precedence over the FSIA in case of any conflict between them. Moreover, FSIA distinguishes between immunity from jurisdiction and immunity from attachment, arrest, and execution. It establishes different rules in each case and even more restrictive rules in the case of attachment before judgment than in the case of post-judgment attachment.

While state courts retain whatever subject matter jurisdiction their particular state laws give them over cases involving sovereigns, FSIA expressly gives U.S. district courts subject matter jurisdiction over any nonjury civil action against a foreign state, including its political subdivisions, agencies, or instrumentalities, and corporations owned by foreign governments those states are not entitled to immunity under FSIA or any applicable international agreement. The federal district courts also have jurisdiction over all civil actions involving $10,000 or more between citizens of a U.S. state and citizens or subjects of a foreign state, or between a foreign state as plaintiff and citizens of one or more U.S. states. A foreign state defendant may transfer suits begun by plaintiffs in state courts to a federal district court. If the action is brought against a foreign state or political subdivision thereof (but not an agency or instrumentality), the district court for the District of Columbia is a proper forum.

FSIA presumes that a foreign state is immune from the personal jurisdiction of federal and state courts unless one of the statutory exceptions to immunity provided in the FSIA exists.

1. The foreign state waived its immunity expressly or implicitly (and a waiver may not be withdrawn except in accordance with its own terms).
2. The suit is based upon a commercial activity of the foreign state conducted in the United States, an act performed in the United States in conjunction with the foreign state's commercial activity elsewhere, or an act outside of the United States in conjunction with commercial activity of the foreign state outside of the United States, which act has a direct effect in the United States.
3. The action is a suit in admiralty to enforce a maritime lien against the foreign state's vessel or cargo; the lien is based upon the foreign state's commercial activity, and notice of the suit is given as provided in the statute.

Other exceptions relate to expropriations, U.S. property acquired by inheritance or gift, U.S. real property, certain torts, and counterclaims with respect to which the foreign state would not be immune were the claim brought in a separate action and certain other counterclaims.

In prescribing how service of process may be made, FISA distinguishes between foreign states and their political subdivisions, and agencies and instrumentalities of foreign states. An "agency or instrumentality of a foreign state" is defined as any entity that is a separate legal person; an organ of a foreign state or a political subdivision of a foreign state, or an organ of which the majority is owned by the foreign state or political subdivision; or a corporation not incorporated in or having its principal place of business in any state of the United States, any of its territories, the District of Columbia or Puerto Rico, nor created under the laws of any third country. Service of process upon a foreign state or a political subdivision of a foreign state may be made by any of four methods:

1. By any means agreed upon between the plaintiff and the foreign state or political subdivision
2. If no such agreement exists, in accordance with an applicable international convention
3. If service cannot be made by the first two methods, by having the court clerk send the process and a notice of suit (in a form prescribed by the U.S. secretary of state), together with translations of those documents

into the foreign state's official language, to the head of the ministry of foreign affairs of the foreign state
4 If service cannot be made by any of the above means, by sending the process, notice of suit, and translations to the U.S. secretary of state for transmittal to the foreign state through diplomatic channels.

Service of process upon an agency or instrumentality of a foreign state may be made in any of three ways:

1. In accordance with any arrangements agreed upon between the plaintiff and the agency or instrumentality
2. If no such arrangements exist, by delivery of the process to an officer, a managing or general agent, or any other authorized agent, or in accordance with an applicable international convention
3. By a means reasonably calculated to give actual notice of the suit and as directed by an authority of the foreign state, or by mail requiring a signed receipt, or as directed by the court.

FSIA does not permit attachment of sovereign property as a means of obtaining *quasi in rem* jurisdiction.

In the area of the immunity from attachment, arrest, and execution that is to be accorded property of a foreign state, FISA also presumes that a foreign state's property is immune from any attachment, arrest, or execution. However, property of a foreign state used for a commercial activity in the United States is not immune from attachment in aid of execution or from execution upon a judgment if:

1. The foreign state waived its immunity expressly or implicitly (again, no withdrawal of a waiver is permitted except in accordance with the waiver's own terms)
2. The property is or was used for the commercial activity on which the claim is based.

Other exceptions involve expropriation, inherited property or property received by gift, real property located in the United States, and insurance covering tort liability. In addition, U.S. property of an agency or instrumentality of a foreign state engaged in commercial activity in the United States is not immune from attachment in aid of execution or from execution on a judgment if the agency or instrumentality has waived such immunity, or if the judgment relates to claims from which the agency or instrumentality is not immune (that is, arising out of commercial activities having a connection with the United States, expropriation, torts, or maritime liens), regardless of whether the property is or is not used in the activity upon which the claim is based.

The court must in all cases allow a reasonable time for the defendant to satisfy any judgment before a permitted attachment or execution is carried out, except that an attachment may be made to assure the availability of assets if the defendant foreign state has expressly waived its immunity from attachment prior to judgment.

Express and specific waivers of immunity are necessary to create two other exceptions to the general rule of immunity from attachment, arrest, and execution. The property of a foreign central bank or monetary authority held for its own account is immune from attachment in the absence of an express waiver of such immunity by the bank or authority of its parent government. Military property of a foreign state of a foreign state is always immune from attachment and execution

Under the U.S. International Organization Immunities Act, international organizations designated by presidential executive order are entitled to the same immunity from suit and judicial process granted to foreign governments unless they expressly waive such immunity. The status of international organizations not covered by the International Organization Immunities Act and of foreign regimes not officially recognized by the United States (Taiwan, for example) is unclear.

"Commercial activity" is defined by the FSIA as either a regular course of commercial conduct or a particular commercial transaction or act. The courts must determine whether an activity is commercial by examining its nature rather than its purpose. Existing case law does not clearly distinguish between commercial and noncommercial activities. Therefore, in order at least to prevent the borrower from claiming otherwise in court, it is a good practice for the lender to include in the documentation a statement by the borrower that the particular transaction is a commercial transaction.

Lenders' concern with restricting borrowers' possible claims to sovereign immunity has led to sophisticated waivers of immunity in the documentation of international transactions with sovereigns or sovereign entities. Such a waiver might read as follows:

> To the extent that the Borrower or any of its property has or hereafter becomes entitled to any immunity, whether on the grounds of sovereignty or otherwise, from the jurisdiction of any court, from any legal process (whether through service or notice), from attachment prior to the entry of judgment, from attachment in aid of execution, from arrest or from execution upon a judgment in any jurisdiction, the Borrower hereby irrevocably waives such immunity for itself and its property (including property held for its own account) in respect of its obligations under this Agreement to the fullest extent permitted by applicable laws in any jurisdiction where any action or proceeding arising out of or relating to this Agreement may be brought.

The waiver should expressly cover both immunity from jurisdiction and immunity from attachment in aid of execution, and execution, because an express waiver of one may not implicitly waive the other. Moreover, only an explicit waiver can waive central bank assets. It also should expressly waive immunity from attachment prior to judgment, because implicit waivers of that immunity are ineffective. A lender should ensure that the person or entity signing the waiver has the necessary authority to bind all relevant government entities and/or the government.

Finally, lenders should always remain beware that if a borrower does not have assets in the forum jurisdiction or a third country that will enforce the lender's judgment, the borrower may be able to avoid paying the judgment, irrespective of any sovereign immunity, if the lender cannot enforce it in the borrower's own country.

ENFORCEMENT OF JUDGMENTS

If the jurisdiction in which the lender wants to enforce its judgment will not recognize a judgment rendered by a foreign court or under a foreign law, the lender will gain nothing by insisting that suits be tried in the foreign court and/or under the foreign law. Some countries are simply not receptive to foreign judgments; others will enforce a foreign judgment unless it violates principles applied by the local courts to foreign judgments. Considerations include the finality of the foreign judgment; whether notice of the suit to the defendant borrower was given in a sufficient manner under local law; whether the contract was valid under local law; whether the foreign court's choice of law was appropriate; and whether the judgment in any way violates local or international law (including the local concepts of due process and fairness) or contradicts local public policy. The enforcement of foreign judgments may also be the subject of international treaties, and counsel should consider whether any treaty applies to a particular case (the United States is not a party to any such treaty except with respect to the enforcement of arbitral awards). Local courts will rarely enforce foreclosures or other foreign judgments against local real property because real property, by its very nature, is considered to be subject to the local authority exclusively.

In the United States the recognition and enforcement of foreign judgments are typically matters of common law rather than statutes; many states have adopted the Uniform Foreign Money-Judgments Recognition Act, which was written to codify the existing common law, and no statutes dealing with enforcement of foreign judgments exist on the federal level.

In countries that rely on civil law, a foreign judgment is enforced by *exequatur,* which is a writ enabling execution of the foreign judgment within the local jurisdiction. The *exequatur* proceeding is adversarial: the plaintiff-judgment holder must present proof of the foreign judgment. If the court refuses to issue the writ, the plaintiff may then bring an action *de novo* in the local courts.

An ancillary issue in the enforcement of judgements is the currency in which the judgment will be given. Any variation from the currency in which the credit transaction is denominated creates an exchange risk for the lender. In U.S. federal courts and typically in state courts judgments must be expressed in U.S. dollars. For damages in a foreign currency, the rate of exchange used to calculate the dollar equivalent in court judgments may be the rate in effect on the date of default or on the date of judgment, depending on the court and the facts of the particular case. In some countries a judgment may be given in a foreign currency; enforcement of the judgment within the country, however, may be legally required or permitted to be in the local currency. In such instances the amount of local currency required to satisfy the foreign currency judgment must be determined, something that introduces additional risk to the lender.

To reduce these exchange risks, the documentation should explicitly state that recoveries by the lender, whether pursuant to a judgment or otherwise, will discharge the debt only to the extent that the lender receives payment in the currency in which the debt is denominated. The following is a typical provision:

> If for the purpose of obtaining or enforcing judgment in any court it is necessary to convert a sum due hereunder in United States dollars into another currency (the "Second Currency"), the rate of exchange that shall be applied shall be that at which, in accordance with its normal banking procedures, the Lender could purchase United States dollars with the Secondary Currency on the business day preceding that on which final judgment is given. If payment of any sum due hereunder is made to or received by the Lender, whether by judgment (and notwithstanding the rate of exchange actually applied in giving such judgment) or otherwise, in a Second Currency, the obligations of the Borrower hereunder shall be discharged only in the net amount of United States dollars that the Lender in accordance with its normal bank procedures is able lawfully to purchase with such amount of Second Currency. If the Lender is not able to purchase sufficient United States dollars with such amount of Second Currency to discharge the United States dollar obligations to the Lender, the Borrower's obligations to the Lender shall not be discharged to the extent of such difference, and any such undischarged amount will be due as a separate debt and shall not be affected by payment of or judgment being obtained for any other sums due under or in respect of this Agreement. If the Lender is able to purchase an amount in United States dollars in excess of the amount necessary to discharge such United States dollar obligations, the Lender shall promptly remit such excess to the Borrower.

Such provisions are largely untested in courts; therefore their effectiveness in protecting the lender from exchange risks remains uncertain, especially if a court thinks the lender is taking unfair advantage of the borrower in some manner.

TAXES

As early as possible, the lender should investigate with its counsel and local counsel whether taxing authorities in the borrower's country will tax payments of interest, fees, commissions, and other amounts. Any withholding that cannot be recouped promptly or otherwise compensated will reduce the lender's return on the loan; consequently the lender must decide whether it will bear all or part of that cost or pass it on to the borrower. If withholding taxes exist, tax treaties between the borrower's country and the lender's country may reduce the rates. Such rate reductions may, however, require the lender to submit a withholding exemption certificate in the borrower's country.

If the lender does not intend to bear the cost of withholding taxes and there is no tax treaty that eliminates the withholding, then the preferred solution is to require the borrower to "gross up" for the withheld taxes--that is, the borrower is required to pay an additional amount so the lender will receive the net amount it would have received had there been no withholding. The additional amount may be identified as just that, or it may be described as an increase in the interest rate. Local counsel should consider whether the additional payment will count as additional interest for the purposes of local usury laws, exchange control rules, and so on.

If the borrower pays withholding taxes the tax payments made on the lender's behalf may be regarded as additional income to the lender, income that may be subject to further withholding in the borrower's country. The "gross up" payments may also be treated as additional income to the lender in its own country. To offset that additional income, U.S. lenders can claim a credit for the foreign tax paid against its U.S. income taxes.

An experienced borrower that agrees to increase the cost of its financing by accepting a gross-up provision will often request that the lender share any tax benefits the lender accrues by paying foreign taxes. However, these benefits are subject to limitations based on the amount of the lender's income, the percentage of its income that comes from foreign sources, and the effects of other credits, loss carry-forwards, and loss carry-backs. Consequently, the amount of benefit attributable to any single foreign tax credit is often difficult, if not impossible, to calculate. Also, if a lender has more foreign tax credits than it can utilize, it faces the potential problem of having agreed to share more benefits than it actually receives. Accordingly, many lenders resist sharing benefits, or, if they must share, insist upon a fixed percentage or another formula basis and require the borrower to return any shared benefits if the claimed benefits do not materialize.

Some countries do not permit lenders to require the borrower to gross up for the withholding. In such cases the lender may be able to reprice the credit and absorb the taxes, so long as the increased price does not then violate usury laws or other laws or regulations affecting the credit. If the lender does agree to absorb the local taxes, any increase in the rate will affect the lender adversely; hence the lender should consider providing for prepayment or renegotiation of the terms of the credit if the local taxes are increased. In some cases it may also be possible to reduce local tax assessments by taking advantage of special provisions in the borrower's country, such as special tax exemptions for loans used for specifically designated purposes.

Many jurisdictions also impose stamp, registration, or other taxes on documents related to credit transactions. In most instances the borrower pays these taxes. Whenever possible, lenders should insist that the borrower pay these taxes at the beginning of a transaction even though the tax may not be incurred until later. This is to avoid having the lender assume responsibility for the tax payment if the borrower defaults.

LENDING LIMITS

Banks in the United States and in some other countries must adhere to statutory or regulatory lending limits that prevent overexposure to the credit risk of any individual borrower. These limits are generally written in terms of a fixed percentage of a bank's capital funds. In the United States the most common limit is 15 percent of the bank's capital and surplus. Exceptions usually involve instances where there is collateral securing the loan and loans to governments.

Banks must often determine whether loans to a government entity must be aggregated with loans to the government itself. The question often arises with loans to socialist and mixed economies where the government owns otherwise apparently separate entities. The U.S. comptroller of the currency requires U.S. banks to perform a "means" test to ensure that the borrower has resources or revenues of its own sufficient to service its debt obligations, as well as a "purpose" test to ensure that the loan is for a purpose consistent with the borrower's general business. If the borrower fails to meet either test, then the loan is counted against the lending limit applicable to the parent government. Edge Act corporations must aggregate their loans to a foreign government with all loans to that government's departments or agencies that derive their funds principally from general tax revenues. The rules governing state banks vary from state to state.

Loans to corporations and their subsidiaries are also subject to aggregation. The applicable rules vary among the regulatory authorities. For example, the comptroller of the currency requires national banks to aggregate loans to a corporation with loans to all subsidiaries in which it maintains a majority interest; but if the parent corporation is not borrowing, loans to the subsidiaries do not usually need to be combined. On the other hand, the state of New York does not require state banks to combine loans to a subsidiary corporation with loans to its parent corporation unless the loan to the subsidiary is made for the benefit of the parent. Likewise, the requirements for leases of personal property, letters of credit, and contingent obligations, including standby letters of credit, vary from jurisdiction to jurisdiction.

USE OF LOCAL COUNSEL

It is extremely important for lenders to avail themselves of local counsel in the borrower's country, especially for structuring and documenting transactions so they are enforceable in the borrower's jurisdiction. In addition to being present to meet with any government authorities whose approval is required and to advise the lender and its counsel with respect to topics previously discussed in this chapter, local counsel may advise the lender about such matters as local priorities for one class of creditors over another (i.e. local lenders over foreign lenders and lenders whose documents have been notarized or over lenders with unformalized documents), requirements for approval by or registration of the transaction with regulatory authorities, requirements for further approval if the transaction is altered after it is entered into, and for whether the lender itself must register or be licensed in the borrower's country in order to make or enforce the loan to the borrower. Local counsel is also desirable in jurisdictions where any collateral security is located because the lender's rights in such collateral would almost invariably have to be enforced in the local courts and under local law.

Local counsel should render an opinion on such basic considerations as the existence of the borrower; its ability to enter into and carry out the transaction; the legality, validity, and enforceability of the documentation; the government authorizations required for the borrower to enter into and carry out the transaction; the legality of the transaction within the local jurisdiction; the binding effect of governing law specified in the documents; the borrower's submission to the jurisdiction of the chosen forum for litigation and any waiver of immunity; and whether the documentation is in proper form to be enforced in the borrower's country.

APPENDIX 9A

EXAMPLE OF A DISPUTE IN INTERNATIONAL BANKING

Argentine Republic files legal case against the United States in the International Court of Justice at The Hague, Netherlands, August 7, 2014. See Press Release www.icj-cij.org/presscom/files/4/18354.pdf

INTERNATIONAL COURT OF JUSTICE

Peace Palace, Carnegieplein 2, 2517 KJ The Hague, Netherlands
Tel.: +31 (0)70 302 2323 Fax: +31 (0)70 364 9928
Website: www.icj-cij.org

Press Release

Unofficial

No. 2014/25
7 August 2014

The Argentine Republic seeks to institute proceedings against the United States of America before the International Court of Justice. It requests US to accept the Court's jurisdiction.

THE HAGUE, 7 August 2014. The Argentine Republic filed today in the Registry of the International Court of Justice a document, dated 7 August 2014, entitled "Application instituting proceedings" against the United States of America, regarding a "Dispute concerning judicial decisions of the United States of America relating to the restructuring of the Argentine sovereign debt".

The Argentine Republic contends that the United States of America has committed violations of Argentine sovereignty and immunities and other related violations as a result of judicial decisions adopted by US tribunals concerning the restructuring of the Argentine public debt.

The Argentine Republic "seeks to found the jurisdiction of the Court on the basis of Article 38, paragraph 5, of the Rules of Court". Under that Article:

> "When the applicant State proposes to found the jurisdiction of the Court upon a consent thereto yet to be given or manifested by the State against which such application is made, the application shall be transmitted to that State. It shall not however be entered in the General List, nor any action be taken in the proceedings, unless and until the State against which such application is made consents to the Court's jurisdiction for the purposes of the case."

In accordance with Article 38, paragraph 5, of the Rules of Court, the Application by the Argentine Republic has been transmitted to the US Government. However, no action will be taken in the proceedings unless and until the United States of America consents to the Court's jurisdiction in the case.

The International Court of Justice (ICJ) is the principal judicial organ of the United Nations. It was established by the United Nations Charter in June 1945 and began its activities in April 1946. The seat of the Court is at the Peace Palace in The Hague (Netherlands). Of the six principal organs of the United Nations, it is the only one not located in New York. The Court has a twofold role: first, to settle, in accordance with international law, legal disputes submitted to it by States (its judgments have binding force and are without appeal for the parties concerned); and, second, to give advisory opinions on legal questions referred to it by duly authorized United Nations organs and agencies of the system. The Court is composed of 15 judges elected for a nine-year term by the General Assembly and the Security Council of the United Nations. Independent of the United Nations Secretariat, it is assisted by a Registry, its own international secretariat, whose activities are both judicial and diplomatic, as well as administrative. The official languages of the Court are French and English. Also known as the "World Court", it is the only court of a universal character with general jurisdiction.

The ICJ, a court open only to States for contentious proceedings, and to certain organs and institutions of the United Nations system for advisory proceedings, should not be confused with the other — mostly criminal — judicial institutions based in The Hague and adjacent areas, such as the International Criminal Tribunal for the former Yugoslavia (ICTY, an ad hoc court created by the Security Council), the International Criminal Court (ICC, the first permanent international criminal court, established by treaty, which does not belong to the United Nations system), the Special Tribunal for Lebanon (STL, an independent judicial body composed of Lebanese and international judges, which is not a United Nations tribunal and does not form part of the Lebanese judicial system), or the Permanent Court of Arbitration (PCA, an independent institution which assists in the establishment of arbitral tribunals and facilitates their work, in accordance with the Hague Convention of 1899).

___

Information Department:

Mr. Andrey Poskakukhin, First Secretary of the Court, Head of Department (+31 (0)70 302 2336)
Mr. Boris Heim, Information Officer (+31 (0)70 302 2337)
Ms Joanne Moore, Associate Information Officer (+31 (0)70 302 2394)
Ms Genoveva Madurga, Administrative Assistant (+31 (0)70 302 2396)

10 CREDIT ANALYSIS OF FOREIGN LOANS

Credit analysis is the process through which a lender determines a borrower's ability and willingness to repay a loan in accordance with the terms of a loan contract. As in all lending, determining the creditworthiness of the borrower is important, but with foreign borrowers there is an additional dimension: evaluating the country and foreign exchange risks associated with the credit.

The method of analyzing a credit proposal is basically standard in most commercial banks. What is less standard, however, is the person who performs the credit analysis. At one extreme it is the international banker who must gather and analyze all relevant information about the loan applicant. This approach is highly effective where loan officers are specialists in specific industries. At the other extreme the credit analysis may be performed by credit departments, which usually are staffed by junior officers or trainees.

Just as in domestic lending, the functions of the credit department are to assemble, record, and analyze credit information, with the objective of ascertaining the degree of risk associated with each loan request and determining the amount of credit that the bank can prudently extend in each case. Once the analysis has been completed, it is addressed to the banker in charge of the specific account. In some banks the credit department may be authorized to make recommendations regarding the loan application; in others it may not.

With the analysis completed, a decision must be reached on the loan request. This stage, too, is subject to important variation among banks engaged in international lending. In some banks the banker handling the specific account is responsible for presenting the credit request to a loan committee. In other banks decision makers are the loan officers, who have authority to lend up to a certain amount. This authority is called a discretionary lending limit. In such instances, banks frequently require the signatures of at least two officers to approve the credit. Where this approach is used, the signatures of two senior officers may be sufficient to commit the hank. In still other banks a combination of these extremes may prevail--that is, low lending limits by loan officers with a credit committee functioning as the senior authority.

Where a bank has foreign branches, these branches are usually given a local lending limit, with authority delegated to the branch manager to implement this limit. There are exceptions, notably European, Canadian, and Japanese banks, which usually require all lending decisions to be made at the head office.

Banks denote the maximum level of exposure desired in any one country through "country limits," and "sublimits" on loans to specific sectors--e.g., the government of that country, private corporations, or banks. Country limits and sublimits are usually reviewed on an annual basis, or more often if world events so necessitate. Prudence dictates that the loan portfolio be diversified among different creditworthy borrowers and among countries considered to be of equal creditworthiness or risk.

FACTORS TO BE CONSIDERED IN CREDIT ANALYSIS

The objective of credit analysis is to evaluate the degree of risk involved in a requested loan and the amount of credit that can be prudently extended to a borrower. To answer these questions, the officer engaged in foreign credit analysis will analyze and evaluate the factors commonly referred to as the five Cs of credit: character, capacity, capital, collateral and conditions. Since the loan request originates from a foreign borrower, the analyst must also review the country and foreign exchange risks associated with the loan request. Both of these considerations are discussed in other chapters, so this section will focus on the basic factors of credit analysis: character, capacity, capital, collateral, and conditions.

Character

The term "character," as used in lending, implies not just willingness to pay debts but also a strong desire to settle contractual obligations in accordance with the terms of the contract. When the borrower is an individual, for example, character is largely a function of that person's moral qualities, personal habits, style of living, business and personal associates, and general standing in the business and social communities. When lending a country, character is a function of such factors as stability of the government, its philosophy and policies, its relations with other countries and major trading partners, and other considerations. When the borrower is a company, character is a function of management integrity, reputation, and standing in the business and financial communities. In the final analysis, of course, the reputation, integrity, and standing of a company's management are primarily a reflection of the character of the individuals responsible for the formulation and execution of company policies. Whether the borrower is an individual, a country, or a business, the previous record for meeting financial obligations plays a determining role in evaluating the borrower for credit purposes. This points to the importance of having an experienced loan officer on the scene.

Capacity

Capacity has both a legal and an economic connotation. From a legal perspective, lenders are interested to know whether the party requesting the loan can legally obligate itself to borrow contractually. The lender should retain legal counsel in the country of the borrower to make this determination. Specifically, where the borrower is an official entity, the lending bank should determine whether this entity has authority to borrow or must obtain prior approval from a supervisory authority. Furthermore, the bank should determine whether this entity is eligible to borrow abroad for the purpose intended and under the terms proposed. Determining the borrowing authority of an official entity raises a number of practical issues for the lending bank, most important of which involves assessing the specific unit in the government hierarchy responsible under law or policy in the event of nonpayment, and the extent of its responsibility. These considerations should not be disregarded, as is often the case by assuming that the government nature of the would-be borrower necessarily assures the quality of the loan.

In lending to a partnership, the loan officer should ascertain that the signing partner has legal authority (that is, a power of attorney from the other partners) to obligate the partnership. Similarly, in lending to a private corporation, it is advisable to examine the corporate charter and bylaws to determine who has the authority to borrow for the corporation. In the absence of any explicit statement, a bank may accept a corporate resolution that, signed by the board of directors, identifies the person who has authority to negotiate for the company and sign the loan contract.

In considering a corporation's loan request, it is also important to analyze the outstanding loans already made to the corporation, in order to assure that any new loan is not restricted or prohibited by covenants in a previously made loan. A similar analysis is made of loans to private banks with the additional investigation that the proposed loan is within the banking regulations of the country.

From an economic perspective, capacity implies ability to meet loan payments as they come due. A bank loan may be repaid from a variety of sources--earnings generated from operations, sale of assets, and borrowing from another lender. Of these sources, the least acceptable to a bank is clearly the last one, not only because it encourages the borrower to switch loans from one bank to another but also because of the degree of risk involved: the borrower's position may subsequently deteriorate, rendering it virtually impossible to locate another lender. Nonetheless, banks look closely at a borrower's overall availability of credit lines and line rotation ability. Many banks request 30-60-day line cleanups to test performance. Often borrowers cannot pay back all their obligations from cash flow, and must refinance from other lines of credit. Neither do U.S. banks generally favor being repaid from the proceeds of the sale of assets pledged. Such method of repayment is costly and time consuming, and adversely affects a bank's public image. This leaves one source of debt repayment: income. Income, being an effective measure of financial performance, has generally been accepted as a good indication of a borrower's current and potential ability to meet loan payments as they come due.

When the borrower is an individual, ability to generate income depends in part on business experience, education, good judgment, ambition, maturity or age, and shrewdness. For a corporation, however, its power to generate income depends upon such factors as the quality of goods or services sold, cost and availability of raw materials and labor, market competition, profit sensitivity to cycles, effectiveness of advertising, and company location. In recent years, however, it has been increasingly recognized by banks that the single most important income-generating factor for a company is the quality of its management. Good management is based primarily on the talent and ability of the individuals responsible for running the company. The success or failure of a company depends to a large extent on the abilities of those who manage it. Time and again studies have concluded that inexperience and incompetence, neglect, and fraud are among the chief causes of business failures. Thus, management should inspire sufficient confidence as to its ability to adapt to changing conditions, replace inefficient practices with more efficient ones, take advantage of opportunities as they arise, and ensure that company products enjoy a strong customer base because of their price and/or quality.

Evaluation of a company's capacity will rely to a great extent upon its financial statements, and particularly on the balance sheet and income statement. International bankers place different emphasis upon each of these statements. Many foreign bankers rely heavily on balance sheet items because they are basically oriented toward short-term lending. This orientation is primarily due to tradition and undeveloped capital markets in their home countries. In many European countries, for example, a usual form of lending has been through short-term notes or overdrafts, many of which are of an evergreen nature, thereby functioning as term loans. In Latin America discounting of promissory notes has been a common practice of bank financing. In Japan a dominant form of lending has been the time loan, extended on a three-month basis with automatic rollover. Secured by a mortgage or other type of collateral, a time loan has been granted for financing capital expenditures.

U.S. banks emphasize both statements, depending upon the maturity of the loan. Thus, when negotiating short-term loans, U.S. bankers place more emphasis on balance sheet items, while in negotiating longer maturity loans greater emphasis is placed upon income statements. Indeed, for medium-term loans U.S. banks look into a company's income statement to determine its ability to generate sufficient income from operations to meet potential loan repayments. The analytical tool used in this respect is the cash flow, which in its simplest definition is the sum of net income plus noncash charges (principally depreciation) minus noncash income. The essence of cash-flow lending is that it enables a bank to analyze a company's financial projections and, if they are acceptable, develop a repayment schedule that reflects its ability to generate cash. Cash-flow lending constitutes a credit technique that U.S. banks introduced in the domestic credit markets immediately after World War II[1] and have applied to foreign lending as well.

When the party requesting the loan is a foreign government, the lending officer's task again will be to determine the borrower's ability to create income. However, in this case the sovereign nature of the borrower limits the effectiveness of cash flow as predictor of ability to service potential debt. Specifically, a corporation may go bankrupt and cease to exist, but technically a country, or its central bank does not (it may reinvent itself, however, such as has been the case of the former republic of Czechoslovakia now made up of the Czech Republic and Slovakia). Another limitation on using the corporate cash-flow analogy on loans to governments is that a government borrower can always generate the necessary local funds to service a local-currency-denominated debt (that is, through issuance of government securities or the printing of monies). Though such funding may add to the inflationary pressures on the domestic economy, it nevertheless enables a sovereign borrower to meet its debt-servicing requirement.

Even if the loan is denominated in foreign currency, a government would be in a position to generate the necessary foreign exchange to meet debt servicing, should it choose to do so. Clearly, political expedience plays an important role in this respect. Debt servicing can be effected through policies that would be conducive to maintenance of a sustainable balance between payments to and from other countries, on current and capital accounts combined. In this respect it may be observed that in addition to monetary and fiscal policy, a government has at its disposal a variety of measures to influence its balance of payments and hence enhance its foreign debt servicing ability. Some of the measures used to date, albeit with differing degree of

[1]Cash flow lending owes its origin to the "anticipated income" theory of liquidity, developed in 1949 by Herbert Prochnow. The theory emphasized that banks, in making intermediate term and long-term loans to consumers and business firms, should rely on the anticipated income of the borrower and its coverage of debt service requirements. To this end, projections of the cash flow of the borrower, rather than the nature of the particular transaction being financed or the collateral offered, would assure the self-liquidating character of the loan.

effectiveness, include the following:

- Controlling the availability and/or cost of foreign exchange
- Promoting exports of goods and services and, hence, foreign exchange revenues
- Introducing or stiffening restrictions on imports, thereby preserving foreign currencies
- Encouraging a net inflow of capital by promoting a favorable investment climate (through tax incentives, favorable repatriation provisions for profits and capital, and so forth)
- Drawing on its official reserves (gold, foreign exchange, and special drawing rights)
- Borrowing from other sources
- Obtaining foreign aid

As a result, in evaluating the debt servicing ability of a government, the lending officer should take into consideration such items as talent and quality of government officials, the efficiency of the government machinery, natural resources, industrial and scientific achievements, and all those related economic indicators that will allow for the country's evaluation over time. Analysts customarily distinguish these indicators into two clusters, the *dynamic* (denoting change in economic pattern) and *developmental* (identifying the stage or level of development). Examples of the former are such measures as growth in real GDP per capita in constant currency units (use of deflated monetary values enables a realistic gauge of the economy's ability to expand faster than population growth), export growth (sustained export growth to provide for the financing of imports), share of manufactured goods in total exports (stability of export revenues), and rate of inflation (changes in consumer prices) over time. Examples of developmental indicators include the GDP size and growth, and ratios of investment and savings to GDP (capital formation and extent of financing from domestic resources). Both groups of indicators are customarily reviewed in country risk analysis.

If the party requesting the loan is a government agency or other type of official entity, its debt servicing ability would depend, among other things, upon such considerations as sources through which this entity funds its activities--that is, the extent to which its operations are funded through annual allocations from a federal budget, its authority to borrow from the central bank or other government banks, and the right to issue its own obligations in the domestic credit markets; any tax benefits or duty-free import privileges that this entity enjoys and that may affect its operations favorably; its independent access to foreign exchange and its authority to effect payments abroad; and the pricing of its services in the domestic market (whether its services are underpriced for political reasons, in which case the users of the services are actually being subsidized).

Capital

A strongly capitalized company is a more acceptable credit risk than one that is highly leveraged. The utilization of this capital to purchase quality assets is an important factor in determining the financial strength of the company. A borrower's ability to obtain credit would thus be greatly affected by the amount and quality of the assets it owns. For example, a foreign manufacturer that owns modern machinery and equipment will be more certain of obtaining credit than will its counterpart with obsolete machinery and worn out equipment. Similarly, a foreign retailer with attractive buildings and fixtures, and adequate stock will be favored over his counterpart with rundown buildings and fixtures, and inadequate stock. The amount and quality of the assets owned thus serve as an indication of the prudence and resourcefulness of a company's management.

If the would-be borrower is an official entity, capital is important only to the extent that this entity is a joint-stock corporation, with private interests participating in the capital of the company. This has been the case, for example, of some public utilities, transportation enterprises, telephone and telecommunication networks, and specialized banks. If the government is a minority shareholder in such a corporation, the amount and quality of the assets owned by this corporation would be a decisive factor in determining the applicant's credit prospects. On the other hand, if the government is a majority shareholder, the borrowings of this corporation may enjoy the support of the government or a government entity (the ministry of finance or the central bank). Should that be the case, any analysis of this company in essence would be an analysis of the government itself.

Collateral

Though banks generally prefer to make short-term, self-liquidating or cash flow loans (that is, loans that would be collectible from the anticipated income or profits of the borrower), on various occasions they may request a would-be borrower to provide security. In some cases security is pledged because the maturity of the loan extends over a long period of time, which increases the risk factor for the bank; in other cases security is requested in order to increase the borrower's sense of responsibility. In most cases assets are pledged because they improve a lender's claim against a borrower. Broadly speaking, the proper function of collateral is to minimize the risk of loss to a bank if, for unforeseen reasons, the borrower's income or profits fail to materialize sufficiently for repayment of the loan. In other words, the purpose of the collateral is to provide a bank a second way out of a loan, and not to be the primary source of repayment. This view is exemplified by the axiom that collateral does not make a bad loan good but makes a good loan better.

The security pledged for collateral should be readily convertible into cash, and its market value should be greater than the value of the loan it secures. The assets pledged may consist of real property (land and improvements attached to land) or personal property (investment securities, accounts receivable, inventory, machinery and equipment). When accepting such assets as collateral, a bank seeks to establish a legally valid security interest in the country where the collateral is located. In many countries this is feasible because of legislation governing the rights of secured lenders. Such is the case, for example, in Mexico, which provides for the registration with the government of liens on fixed assets. The variety in the laws and regulations of different countries stresses the importance for banks to retain foreign counsel. A local law firm will have a thorough knowledge of local laws and procedures, and will be useful in structuring the transaction and preparing the necessary documentation.

Frequently a borrower may substitute the guarantee of payment by another party for collateral. For example, when the loan request comes from the foreign subsidiary (the production or marketing unit) of a domestic corporation (such as an automobile manufacturer), the latter may offer its guarantee in support of the loan. Parent support would ordinarily be justified on the ground that the operations of the subsidiary so supported are financially an integral part of the parent's. Assuming the explicit guarantee of the parent, the bank's risk is no different from that assumed in a direct loan to the parent itself. In recent years, however, parent guarantee has become increasingly rare because parent companies try to avoid additional contingent liabilities that must be noted in financial statements with consequent effects on leverage, capital adequacy, loan covenants or bond indentures. This has given rise to the parent practice of expressing support through a letter known variously as a comfort letter, letter of support, letter of awareness and in French *lettre de patronage*. Support letters are usually signed by the parent's most senior corporate officer although in Europe a second officer's signature has additional appeal. These expressions of moral support and are not legally enforceable guarantees.

Other instances where guarantees are sought and received by lenders are for support of loans to official borrowers. Bank emphasis on guarantees for such borrowers has increased so much in recent years that they have come to constitute a regular feature of loan agreements. Repayment guarantees may range from a pledge of full faith and credit by a national government to a guarantee by a government-owned enterprise (a commercial bank or a finance institution). This may lead to the question of how much more protection a lender receives from the repayment guarantee of a national government than from that of a government-owned enterprise. The record in recent years suggests that regardless of the level of the government guarantor, rarely have banks found it necessary to invoke a guarantee. Yet there has been an excessive reliance by banks on this concept. To some banks this concept is a substitute for independent analysis and judgment. To other banks it is simply a matter of emulating the lending practices of international organizations and foreign government banks, which have traditionally required such guarantees. For still other banks the merit of this concept is psychological--commitment by an additional official entity is a further evidence of the appropriateness of the transaction, not to mention the influence that the guarantor would have upon the borrower in ensuring repayment of the debt.

Conditions

Another factor to be considered by the lending officer in deciding on a loan request is the economic environment within which the borrower operates. Economic conditions are generally beyond the borrower's control. From a broader perspective, economic conditions reflect the political stability and the effectiveness of the government's fiscal and monetary policies for alleviating or counteracting business cycles. Therefore, evaluating the borrower's economic environment calls for appraising the effectiveness of the government's economic policy--assuming, of course, that the economy operates within a climate of political stability.

From a narrower perspective, evaluating the borrower's economic environment entails identifying the importance of the industry in the country's overall economy. To properly evaluate this factor, the loan officer must become familiar with the characteristics of the industry with which the firm is associated. This aspect of credit analysis has become increasingly difficult in recent years as more companies have grown into multiproduct and multinational concerns. Consequently, many banks have encouraged lending officers to acquire expertise in such industries as energy, shipping, airlines, and mining.

The kind of information that the lending officer should look for is the effect of economic conditions upon the industry, the industry's output relative to gross national product, the market structure of the industry, the applicant's position in the industry, the impact of technology (and technological changes) on the demand for the industry's product or its capital requirements, the industry's distribution methods, trends in industry profits, and the extent to which industry is regulated by the government. Answers to these and related questions will enable the lending officer to obtain a comprehensive understanding of the dynamics of the industry--a basic input for a more pragmatic appraisal of the firm's relative strengths and weaknesses. Clearly, the greater the importance of the industry to the smooth functioning of the economy, the more likely that the loan officer will act favorably on the company's credit application.

SOURCES OF CREDIT INFORMATION

Any evaluation of the applicant's creditworthiness must rely on available information. The bank will certainly need to accumulate information that will be used to evaluate the borrower's character, capacity, capital, collateral, and industry characteristics. Collecting information is the objective of credit investigation, the scope of which varies from case to case, depending upon the specifics of the loan request-- proposed size and maturity of loan, collateral offered, applicant's business record--and the existence of any prior relationship with the would-be borrower. Though a bank may draw upon several sources of credit information, some of the more important ones include an interview with the party requesting the loan, the bank's credit files, external sources, in-person visit to applicant's premises, and applicant's financial statements. These sources are applicable primarily to foreign private loan applicants rather than to public applicants. Each of these sources is briefly discussed below.

Loan Interview

It is customary for a loan officer to interview a would-be borrower for the purpose of developing credit information. During the interview the loan officer has the opportunity to inquire--or obtain additional information--about the history of the company, experience and background of the principal officers, the nature of the business, profitability of operations, extent of competition in the marketplace, availability of resources (labor, raw materials, and other essential services) for the smooth functioning of the business, and the objectives of the management as expressed in long-range plans. Other information that the loan officer can obtain from the interview pertains to the purpose for which the proceeds of the loan are to be used. Knowledge of the purpose of the loan is important not only because of risk considerations but also because it enables the loan officer to relate repayment to the nature of the transaction being considered for financing. For example, project loans (such as those to finance the development of raw materials, oil, mineral, and other resources) call for repayment provisions tailored to the cash flow of the project being financed.

The interview, moreover, provides the loan officer with an initial impression of the sincerity, integrity, and capability of the party requesting the loan.

Finally, the interview is an appropriate time for requesting the loan applicant to submit financial statements and any other additional information, and to arrange for a visit to the company.

Bank's Credit Files

A bank's credit files can be an important source of information for a loan officer. Banks establish for each borrower a credit file that contains detailed information on their credit relationship with that specific client. By studying these files, the loan officer can identify how well the customer complied with the terms and conditions of previous loans, and can thereby assess the bank's overall credit experience. The credit information contained in these files, though considered confidential, is customarily shared by banks when they consider extending credit to the same client.

Even if the borrower approaches the bank for the first time, a credit file may exist if the borrower is a sizable concern within the bank's location (a "prospect file").

External Sources

Besides the loan interview and the bank's own records, a loan officer may use external sources of credit information. One such source is other banks. Although banks compete vigorously among themselves, they usually share credit information regarding a mutual customer. This information is presented in a standardized format, as a result of certain well-established customs, and is confidential. The loan officer can find out, for example, the applicant's borrowing and payment record, balances carried in deposit accounts, and other pieces of information about the financial strengths or weaknesses of the applicant.

Other external sources of credit information are credit reporting agencies. One such agency, and one of the best-known, is Dun and Bradstreet. In addition to its coverage of companies in this country, this agency collects information on business activity in a great many countries around the world, mostly in European and other industrialized countries. The data collected enable the company to publish reference books containing concise information about and credit ratings of foreign businesses, on a firm-by-firm basis. Besides the rating services, Dun and Bradstreet issues written credit reports that provide more detailed information on individual firms. These reports contain a brief history of the company, and information on its principal officers, the nature of the business, the ownership, operating data, and other financial data.

Still another external source of credit information is the suppliers and customers of the prospective borrower. Suppliers can share with the lending bank information on the applicant's payment practices. Customers, on the other hand, can give information on the quality of the company's products or services, management's honesty and integrity in its dealings, and other factors.

Other external sources that may be tapped by the bank are public records, where reference is made, for example, to pending lawsuits, bankruptcy proceedings, and transfers of property; trade journals, which report developments and trends in the particular industries in which bank customers are engaged; public accounting firms; and newspapers, magazines, circulars, bulletins, and directories.

If the would-be borrower is an official entity, information about its activities customarily appears in diverse official publications--that is, in government documents or reports of national development banks and/or of the central bank. Often, write-ups on this type of borrower appear in international finance journals and periodicals (such as *Financial Times*, *The Wall Street Journal*, *Euromoney* and *The Economist).* Country statistics and other economic indicators are ordinarily available in the publications of international organizations and internationally oriented agencies of the U.S. government. For example, data on growth rates and on per capita gross national product (GNP) in constant dollar equivalents for a large number of countries are published by the U.S. Agency for International Development (AID) in its annual publication *Gross National Product;* balance-of-payments figures and foreign exchange reserves for member countries are reported in the monthly publication of the IMF *International Financial Statistics;* detailed data on the foreign trade activities of different countries and the composition of their exports are reported in the United

Nations' *Yearbook of International Trade Statistics* and periodically in the *Monthly Bulletin of Statistics;* information on the various countries' external public-debt service (including interest and amortization on all public and government-guaranteed debt) with original maturity in excess of one year is published by the World Bank in its *Annual Report, World Debt Tables,* and *World Debt Tables-Supplements;* and data on the capital flows to developing countries are published in the *Development Co-operation Review* of the Development Assistance Committee of the OECD. Relevant information may also be found in the publications of the BIS, the Board of Governors of the Federal Reserve System, private banks and organizations. An interested loan officer can also contact the commercial and economic section of the U.S. embassy in the relevant country. Staff members customarily monitor developments for congressional inquiries and special data calls.

On-site Visit

The financial status of a loan applicant and the quality of its management usually can be best determined by the loan officer through an on-the-scene visit to the applicant's business. Specifically, a visit to the borrower's business will offer the lending officer firsthand information on the condition and efficiency of its physical facilities; the extent of management sophistication in terms of nature and method of operation, and financial planning; and the local reputation and standing of the firm as perceived by local officials, indigenous bankers, other businessmen, and perhaps its competitors, though in the latter instance such information must be used with great discretion.

The information and impressions gained by the officer from the visit to the borrower's business are helpful not only in properly evaluating the business risk involved but also in offering the applicant sound financial advice. Capitalizing on the confidence and respect that may develop from such a visit, the loan officer can share with the would-be borrower financial expertise on such related issues as ideal capital structure, forecasting the amount and timing of future cash needs and ability to repay the loan, appropriateness of the type of credit requested, and other financial matters. The need for this type of financial counseling is especially apparent in the small and medium-size businesses of developing countries, which suffer from a lack of sophisticated financial planning and management, and the absence of a meaningful capital market.

If the would-be borrower is an official entity, an on-the-scene visit can be equally important. Depending upon the status of the official borrower, the loan officer can arrange for meetings with government officials at various levels, including officials in the ministries of finance, economy, and planning, and the central bank. These meetings may be expanded to the private sector and include discussions with local businessmen, bankers, and other individuals who customarily view the role and importance of official entities from a different perspective. Additional inputs may also be obtained from U.S. embassy officials in that country and specialists in such organizations as the IMF, the World Bank, and the Export-Import Bank.

The large number and diverse nature of the individuals contacted may eventually create a problem for the loan officer in having to cope with opposing views and conflicting statements on certain issues (e.g., the country's economic outlook and/or political prospects). This, of course, is to be expected, and is basically a matter of judgment--that is, a matter of weighing the value of the sources of contradictory information. Clearly, good judgment is a product of experience and intuitive grasp of what makes sense and what does not. It is judgments such as this that make lending an art rather than a mechanical process.

A country visit, beyond its importance in evaluating the creditworthiness of the borrower, enables the loan officer to obtain a realistic picture of the political, economic, and social conditions in the borrower's country. Comprehensive understanding of these conditions will be vital in assessing the country risk associated with the loan. In this respect a country visit offers vital on-the-spot knowledge for which there is no substitute.

Financial Statements

One of the most important sources of credit information is the applicant's financial statements. Because financial statements identify the expected ability of a would-be borrower to repay indebtedness, their submission is generally required.

A firm usually must provide balance sheets and income statements, covering the last three to five years, so that the lending officer can obtain a feeling of company direction. Clearly, when the loan applicant is a national government or a ministry thereof, the lending officer instead considers data reflecting the country's economic performance, its political stability, and its social background.

Though loan applicants are required to submit financial statements, the lending officer of a bank operating overseas is often confronted with the inadequacy of the financial information contained in them. Nowhere is this more true than in developing countries, where the inadequacy of financial information may extend to the industry level. Thus, the lending officer who has been trained to analyze historical financial statements, pro forma statements, and cash projections in evaluating a borrower's creditworthiness, is faced with the problem of having to draw conclusions on the basis of insufficient data. This is in striking contrast with his counterpart in an indigenous bank who has a thorough understanding of the local scene and may, therefore, be more favorably inclined to extend a loan on incomplete information or against a name rather than on an amortized cash flow basis. This situation is often encountered in emerging markets, where businesses may be owned by families with historical reputation or by individuals having strong political connections.

Similar are the experiences of the lending officer analyzing the financial statements of government-owned businesses and other official entities. The statements of these entities may be quite brief, or simply minimal, either because of a lack of data or because of a desire for secrecy.

Even if the financial statements of a prospective borrower--private or public--are available, the lending officer is confronted with the question of reliability. The validity of any conclusions drawn from such statements is no better than the information contained in them. Assuming, however, the availability and reliability of the financial statements of foreign borrowers, the loan officer needs to be aware of a set of issues that overlie the typical analytical approach associated with domestic loans. The next section is thus devoted to the identification of these issues because of their relevance to foreign financial statement analysis.

ISSUES UNIQUE TO FOREIGN CREDIT ANALYSIS

For any analysis of foreign financial statements to be reliable it must take into account the following critical issues. The applicant's financial statements are expressed in his national currency; prepared in accordance with accounting principles and reporting practices followed in his country; audited by an (often) unknown local firm governed by alien auditing standards; and reflective of a different legal tradition. Analysis of a prospective borrower's financial statements based on U.S. accounting and legal procedures will not do. The lending officer must have a good understanding of these issues in order to make a reasoned judgment on the credit transaction.

In addressing the first issue, the lending officer must always bear in mind that any translation into U.S. dollars of figures expressed in a foreign currency will misrepresent the applicant's operating results. For one thing, any dollar translation will be affected by the foreign exchange rate used. Specifically, given the strength of the dollar relative to emerging market currencies, any translation of historical financial data (e.g., the income statement) at today's exchange rate would understate the borrower's prior record. This understatement would make today's figures look better, thereby creating the illusion of a trend of growth and improvement in the borrower's performance. If, on the other hand, the translation of historical financial data is done on the basis of the going exchange rate for each corresponding year, the resulting data would be biased by the extent of currency depreciation or exchange rate fluctuations sustained in each individual year. Because of the distorting effect of exchange rates in currency translations, the lending officer is better off analyzing financial statements in the currency in which they are denominated.

The second issue calls for the lending officer to have an understanding of the important differences between U.S. accounting principles and practices and those of the country in which the financial statements originate. This is especially important in view of the prevailing variation in the principles and practices followed by different countries. Awareness, therefore, of prevailing differences in accounting practices enables the lending officer to better understand the basis on which the applicant's financial statements were prepared. Some of the better known examples of intercountry differences in accounting practices relate to the price-level accounting--adjustments in the value of fixed assets for inflation (revaluation); use of unconsolidated statements (statements that do not include the aggregate values of subsidiaries, affiliates, and investees of an entity); greater latitude in the establishment and use of contingency and other reserves; and income tax matters.

Information on the above and related items is ordinarily omitted from financial statements. Disclosure of such information may be requested from the would-be borrower, and is helpful in clarifying and/or adjusting specific items in the financial statements.

A related issue is the validity of the foreign auditors' report. The lending officer should use such a report with great discretion. Not only may the professional integrity of the auditing firm be unknown, but so may be the standards followed in the examination of the company's financial statements. In some countries auditors need not have any specific qualifications to examine financial statements, nor need they comply with any governing rules in the performance of such examinations. Even if the auditing firm is known and its integrity is respected, the statement that the would-be borrower has followed generally accepted accounting principles raises questions as to the degree of conservatism that this judgment may reflect. Thus, in the final analysis there is no substitute for knowing the borrower and trusting his honesty and integrity in the preparation of financial statements.

Another issue that the lending officer will have to bear in mind is the fact that the borrower's country of origin has a set of laws different from those of the lender's country. Indeed, differences in legal tradition have influenced the development of law in various countries differently. Specifically, Roman law and the Napoleonic Code have greatly influenced the development of law on the Continent and elsewhere (for instance, Latin America), as against Anglo-Saxon law, which is the basis of the legal systems of England, the United States, and most of the British Commonwealth. Even so, there is important variation in the laws of countries with the same legal tradition. Lack of awareness of such a variation by the lending officer could have an important bearing on financial analysis. For example, liabilities generally represent legal claims on assets. However, an intuitive assumption that the legal claims of various liabilities against assets enjoy the same status or priority as they do in the lending officer's country may lead to decisions that could prove expensive or even disastrous for the bank. This point may be illustrated by referring to the U.S. priority list of claims in the distribution of proceeds depicted in Exhibit 10.1.

Exhibit 10.1 U.S. Priority List of Claims in Liquidation
(Chapter 7 of the Federal Bankruptcy Reform Act of 1978)

1. Administrative expenses associated with the bankruptcy
2. Other expenses arising after the filing of an involuntary bankruptcy petition but before the appointment of a trustee
3. Wages, salaries, and commissions
4. Contributions to employee benefit plans
5. Consumer claims
6. Government tax claims
7. Payment to unsecured creditors*
8. Payment to preferred stockholders
9. Payment to common stockholders

*Secured creditors are entitled to the proceeds from the sale of security and are outside this ordering. However, if the secured property is liquidated and sale proceeds are insufficient to cover the amount owed, the secured creditors join with unsecured creditors in dividing the remaining liquidated value. On the other hand, if the sale proceeds are greater than the secured claim, the net proceeds are used to pay unsecured creditors and others.
Note: In many of the cited categories various limitations and qualifications apply which are omitted for brevity.
Source: 11 U.S. Code § 507.

ANALYSIS OF FINANCIAL STATEMENTS

Any analysis of a would-be borrower's financial condition calls for evaluating as accurately as possible current financial statements, examining historical financial statements, and studying pro forma financial statements and cash projections that show the borrower's future profitability and cash requirements. The lending officer should not rely too heavily on historical financial statements, because a prospective borrower's financial condition can change drastically if losses develop. Such caution about historical information is, moreover, justified on the ground that past profits often do not reflect future performance. On the other hand, borrower assumptions about future developments will affect the accuracy of cash forecasts and pro forma financial statements. Hence the importance to the lending officer of the soundness of such assumptions.

The current financial condition is a decisive indicator of the viability of the firm. Consequently, a good understanding of the borrower's financial condition calls for an in-depth evaluation of the significant items in his financial statements. Specifically, the lending officer will need to inquire about each important account and to determine whether the figure cited represents a fair and accurate statement of the values involved. Clearly, such evaluation may result in the trimming or adjustment of items from the figures originally reported by the foreign concern. This approach, however, provides a pragmatic picture of the prospective borrower's financial position. This section thus deals with the evaluation of items in the balance sheet and income statement, and some of the techniques widely used in analyzing financial statements. These techniques, borrowed from domestic practices, can be used in analyzing a foreign borrower's historical and current financial statements as well as his cash projections and pro forma statements.

Evaluation of Asset Items

In evaluating individual asset items, which are usually expressed in local currency, the lending officer will seek to determine their true worth and extent of liquidity. Cash holdings, though a small proportion of total assets, are essential to meeting a company's liquidity needs. The importance of this item in servicing the debt depends on the denomination of the loan and the existence of any foreign exchange restrictions in the borrower's country. For example, a prospective borrower's local cash holdings will be of limited value in servicing a foreign currency loan if the purchase of foreign exchange is prohibited by exchange controls. By contrast, cash holdings will be of significant value if exchange restrictions are nonexistent or if the loan is to be denominated in local currency.

Accounts receivable must be analyzed carefully because they constitute the principal source of repayment of a short-term loan. One of the first considerations is the currency of the receivables, because this may considerably affect the ability of this asset to repay debt. It is also important to determine the age of the receivables (aging schedule breaks up receivables into different time brackets) and the local repayment practices (that is, how many accounts are current or overdue by local standards, and, if overdue, for what period); the extent to which receivables are concentrated in a few large accounts, which would increase the inherent risk of nonpayment; the existence and/or adequacy of reserves for bad debts; and the bad debts record of the prospective borrower. The loan officer should also inquire whether the prospective borrower has sold any of its accounts receivable--and, if so, whether they were sold with or without recourse. If the accounts receivable are to be pledged to the lender, a system of control should be established.

Understanding the age, liquidity, and market value of inventory is vital to determining the prospective borrower's cash position. It is also important to know the extent to which inventory is exposed to obsolescence or deterioration, and the existence or adequacy of insurance coverage. The lending officer should arrange for a physical confirmation of the inventory as reported by the would-be borrower and determine the method of inventory accounting: LIFO (last in, first out), FIFO (first in, first out), or NIFO (next in, first out--that is, valuing inventory on the basis of the prices of goods on order). If the inventory is to be pledged to the lender, this pledge should be legally documented and, if possible, recorded at a public registry. In addition, a method of control over the movement of the inventory should be set up between the lender and the borrower.

Fixed assets, too, involve a number of considerations. As was stated earlier an important accounting question is whether fixed asset values are adjusted for inflation. For example, in countries like Chile, Argentina, Brazil, revaluation of fixed assets was based on government indices while in France and the United Kingdom on decree or custom. If the country of the would-be borrower provides for fixed asset revaluation, it is important for the credit analyst to know the basis for revaluation.

Another basic question, especially if the request is for intermediate or long-term credit, is the ability of fixed assets to produce income to service the debt. Other important questions relate to the adequacy of insurance coverage, marketability of these assets, and their liquidation value. In addition, the lending officer will be interested to determine if the borrower has made any commitment to acquire new fixed assets and what financial liability will arise from this acquisition. Since lenders are generally interested in tangible assets, limited consideration will be given to intangible assets such as goodwill, franchises, and leaseholds.

When the borrower has made substantial investments, the method of recording these investments should be determined (e.g., whether at cost or at market value). From the lending officer's perspective, the most conservative method should be used for financial analysis purposes. The lending officer should also determine if there is any intercompany relationship between the borrower and other firms. In some countries prevailing accounting practices do not call for preparation of consolidated financial statements, and hence no disclosure is made of the parent/subsidiary relationship except for the investment, which is carried at cost. Such a practice results in the understatement or overstatement of the value of the parent company depending upon the market value of the investment.

When the balance sheet shows loans to directors, officers, and their affiliated companies, the lending officer should carefully scrutinize those items. Loans of this type resulted in the demise of several financial subsidiaries in emerging markets.

Evaluation of Liabilities and Net Worth

Since liabilities represent legal claims on assets, thorough analysis of these items is of primary importance for a lending officer considering extension of credit. The first item of inquiry is notes and accounts payable. The lending officer will need to know the terms and to whom these obligations are owed. Also, if the past due amount of these debts is large relative to the prospective borrower's scale of operations, the borrower may need additional equity capital or borrowed funds. Slowness in payment of trade obligations is often encountered among the important family-group companies of developing countries, and stems either from inability to raise new capital or from unwillingness to accept the dilution of control that the infusion of new capital would entail.

If the notes payable are not trade-related, but are instead a result of amounts owed by the company to its shareholders or officers, the lending officer will investigate these notes and may ask their subordination to the bank loan, in which case they would serve, in effect, as additional capital. In many cases the lending officer will want to review the amounts accrued for salaries and wages. In several countries these social liabilities constitute claims senior to those of other creditors, and in the event of company liquidation they have preference over all other claims on assets by operation of law. Also, taxes owed to government bodies enjoy preferred creditor status.

Long-term liabilities represent debt due in more than one year. The lending officer will be interested in the type of these liabilities (mortgages, debentures, notes, term loans, and other), their proper reporting in financial statements, the maturity date of each of these liabilities, and the contractual provisions of each debt agreement. These provisions are of particular significance because in each case they reveal such information as the currency of the debt, terms of repayment, the existence of collateral, and the specific conditions under which the particular debt is immediately due and payable (default provisions). Clearly, the lending officer will be especially concerned with what constitutes an act or event of default in each loan agreement. The loan applicant's record of compliance with the provisions of the various loan agreements also will be of interest to the lending officer. Where long-term liabilities include debt due to affiliated companies, determination must be made as to whether this item is actual debt or quasi equity.

The size of the net worth, or equity, is of great significance for the lending officer. As indicated earlier in connection with the "five Cs," capital indicates ownership of assets, and therefore serves as security for a loan. Where a company is closely held by a few individuals (partners or shareholders), it is vital to know and evaluate the net worth of these individuals. It may be prudent in appropriate cases to request, as a condition of making the loan, that the partners or shareholders individually guarantee the loan.

Equity accounts include the original capital paid by the shareholders into the company. It is important for the lending officer to determine that this amount has been actually paid, and does not appear as accounts receivable from the shareholders. Other equity accounts to be reviewed are company earnings, surplus, and reserves. Of these accounts the lending officer will be especially concerned with reserves because of their varied characteristics. Specifically, existing differences in the accounting practices of various countries have contributed to the varied use of reserves, from being treated as a contingent liability to employment as a convenient account used for the smoothing out of annual fluctuations in income. For example, use of reserves as a contingent liability may result from the discounting of accounts or notes receivable with recourse, the endorsing or guaranteeing of the indebtedness of third parties, and the likelihood of additional tax payments. On the other hand, some countries permit companies to transfer income into reserves that later may be used to offset operating losses in any given accounting period. This practice thus enables companies to project to the public a record of continued profitability over the years. Since this practice is not ordinarily disclosed in financial statements, the lending officer will need to ascertain the size of real earnings in any given year. Because of the existing variation in the use of reserves--a potential liability, a means of controlling the earnings trend or something in between--this account will always be a matter of concern for the lending officer.

Evaluation of the Income Statement

The income statement identifies the sources of revenue of a prospective borrower, the expenses sustained to earn that revenue, and the net income realized in the accounting period involved. The revenue component of the income statement is of vital importance to the lending officer because it constitutes the principal source of cash generation for the repayment of loans. He therefore will be interested in such data as sales volume, composition of sales, selling prices, credit terms, sale returns, markets to which products are sold, size of foreign sales, and exposure to foreign exchange fluctuations.

In some instances the would-be borrower may be a subsidiary or an affiliate company with a scope of activities defined by the parent corporation. In such instances its scope and style of operation reflect its role in the organization. For example, the would-be borrower may operate as a manufacturing subsidiary producing a sizable portion of a global product line sold to sister subsidiaries and affiliates in other countries. This kind of relationship gives rise to different considerations than would otherwise be the case. Specifically, this company will have a higher proportion of its sales on credit than will other companies producing the same line of goods. This practice will have a bearing on the size of the company's accounts receivable and their aging. If these receivables are in different currencies, they add to the subsidiary's foreign exchange exposure, rendering credit analysis more complex. Clearly, the lending officer will have to review these and related questions in the context of the company's relationship to the corporate parent and its importance in the overall corporate picture. The same approach will be used if the would-be borrower functions as a marketing subsidiary selling a product manufactured by a foreign parent.

Another objective of the income statement analysis is to evaluate the costs of goods sold. Clearly, the method of inventory valuation will have an important effect upon costs, as will the consistency of the method used. For example, a change in the method of valuing inventory may be effected for the purpose of increasing profits, thus giving the impression that the would-be borrower has the ability to service the proposed loan. If the inventory is imported, the lending officer will consider, in addition, such information as the size of the overseas supplier, contract prices, the length of the shipment period, the cost effect of foreign exchange fluctuations, and the effect of local import tariffs upon costs. If the source of the imported goods or materials is a foreign subsidiary or affiliate, the lending officer will want to know the corresponding cost of these items, if they are acquired from independent sources. Another issue to be considered is whether local labor is unionized, and thereby increases pressure on costs. This is especially the case when union-imposed wage adjustments, combined with controlled prices, thin out profit margins.

Close scrutiny also will be given to administrative and other expenses. An item of importance in this respect is the amount of officers' salaries and the extent to which they may drain profits. Such concern exists mainly with family-owned or closely held companies, which frequently pay excessive salaries. Other items that may warrant investigation, or call for additional disclosures, include rent payments, the method used in the depreciation of facilities, and the actual size of uncollectible receivables.

A final item to be considered in arriving at net profit or loss is taxes. The lending officer should properly understand the country's tax practices. He will normally be interested not just in the amount of taxes but also in the timing of their payment, since their deferral can be an important source of cash. Reported profits may or may not reflect actual profitability. Closely held companies frequently use a number of devices to divert their earnings out of the country and into tax havens, thereby reducing their overall tax exposure. Awareness of this practice by the lending officer provides for a more realistic evaluation of the prospective borrower's level of income, and hence the ability to repay the proposed loan.

Techniques of Analysis

Though inquiring about the nature and determining the true worth of accounts in financial statements are essential to intelligent analysis of the prospective borrower's business, item-by-item evaluation does not identify any key relationships between accounts or groups of accounts, nor does it enable any judgment on the stability of the company's operations or the efficiency with which it is being managed. To address these and related questions, the lending officer must turn to such basic tools of financial analysis as cash flow; ratios; sources and uses of funds; and common-size analysis. Use of these tools helps the officer recognize exceptional situations quickly and distinctly, and encourages him to seek additional information, or clarification, from the would-be borrower on the reasons behind them. No single tool is by itself a complete method of analysis; instead, each sheds light on a different aspect of the prospective borrower's financial condition. Therefore, each of these tools should not be viewed as an end in itself, but as a means to reaching a reasoned decision.

Clearly, it is important to keep in mind that use of analytical tools in foreign financial statements assumes that the amount and quality of figures reported are satisfactory, and that any differences between domestic and foreign statement-account terminologies are completely understood. Another important assumption is that for any interpretation of the findings to be meaningful, it must take into account the underlying differences in legal, tax, accounting, and financing practices. Unless these assumptions are met, any effort to subject foreign financial statements to the standardized pattern of analysis used for domestic loans will produce only misleading results. For example, when reviewing financial leverage ratios of a Japanese corporation, it will be altogether misleading to evaluate them on standards other than those prevailing in that country. As is generally known, the close cooperation between government and business in Japan encouraged the extensive reliance of industry on debt financing. A U.S. corporation with similar reliance on debt financing would be viewed as an unacceptable credit risk. A brief description of some of the basic techniques used in the analysis of foreign financial statements is provided below.

One of the simpler methods used in analyzing foreign financial statements is the common-size analysis, which expresses all related items as a percentage of a basic magnitude. For the purpose of this analysis, the basic magnitude is given the rating of 100 percent. Thus, all items in the income statement are expressed as a percentage of net sales, and all balance sheet items are expressed as a percentage of total assets or liabilities and equity. Extended to the financial statements of preceding years, this method enables the lending officer to compare the relative importance of similar figures for previous periods and to identify any situations that appear to be out of line.

A related technique is the trend percentage method of comparison. This approach establishes as base year the earliest year for which financial statements were submitted by the would-be borrower, and gives each item appearing in that statement a rating of 100 percent. If the corresponding accounts in statements of subsequent years are related to the base year, the lending officer will be able to detect the extent of the increase of each statement account, or group of accounts, over the base year, and the revealed trend over the period under consideration. In some accounts the trend may be upward, and in others downward, while in still others no definite trend may be evidenced. In addition to the direction of the trend, the lending officer will be able to compare the trends of individual accounts, or of groups of accounts, over the period under consideration.

Another method of evaluating foreign financial statements is the sources-and-uses-of-funds statement. It is based on the computation of the net changes in the asset, liability, and net worth accounts from one balance sheet date to another. Specifically, the net change in each individual balance sheet item is listed under separate "source" and "use" columns, depending upon what such a change represents. Changes that reflect increases in assets and decreases in liabilities and in net worth are recorded under the "uses of funds" column; decreases in assets and increases in liabilities and in net worth, under the "sources of funds" column. The purpose of this method is ready identification of the sources tapped by the would-be borrower to meet his need for funds during the period under consideration.

Cash flow is still another technique of value to the lending officer in his credit analysis. Since borrowers are expected to repay loans out of income rather than from the sale of assets or refinancing from another lender, the lending officer must look to their future income for debt retirement. Made up of three segments--operating, investing and financing activities--a cash flow is based on information contained in projected income statements and balance sheets. Hence, the importance of always checking the reasonableness of the borrower's projected data against the economic and industry forecasts for the period that the loan will be outstanding. Since the accuracy of a cash flow depends heavily on the assumptions underlying pro forma financial statements, the lending officer may wish to develop cash flows under best, worst, and most likely assumptions in deciding on the borrower's ability to service the debt.

Cash flows are normally requested from would-be borrowers for each year that the loan will be outstanding. These cash flows, in addition to predicting loan repayment, provide important insights into management competence. In other words, a company's sources of cash and its cash needs, and the relative amounts involved, project a clearer picture of the degree of efficiency with which the company is being managed. If, for example, the company's net cash generation is poor because of a rapid growth pattern, this raises questions with respect to the soundness of credit practices, requirements for additional working capital, inventory policies, and payables policies.

Another widely used technique in financial statement analysis is ratios. The objective of ratios is to highlight the internal relationship between figures reported in financial statements. If discriminatingly calculated and wisely interpreted, ratios can be of considerable assistance in the analysis of these statements. In other words, ratio calculations are meaningful when the figures selected are reliable and come from accounts that bear a fundamental and important relevance to one another. Thus, though a large number of ratios can be computed, only a few are considered basic in analysis work. The lending officer customarily relies on these ratios to make interyear comparisons of borrower performance and to determine the general direction in which a company's financial condition is moving. To the extent that industry data are available, the lending officer may also use ratios to identify a company's relative strengths and weaknesses vis-a-vis other firms in the same industry and raise questions about the need for corrective action to improve future performance.

Because of the difficulty often encountered in the proper use and interpretation of ratios for analyzing foreign financial statements, every effort must be made to use relatively simple and basic analysis. Thus, of the various ratios, five are generally considered basic in foreign credit analysis: current ratio, receivables-to-sales ratio, sales-to-inventory ratio, debt-to-net worth ratio, and profits-to-net worth ratio.

Although analytical tools are important in evaluating the financial condition of a would-be borrower, it is necessary to supplement them with specific pertinent facts and direct contact with the borrower. After all, foreign credit analysis is not cut and dried. It is as unique as each individual borrower and each country. Every case involves a different number of variables, the most important of which is always the character of the specific borrower. If a borrower's character is poor, the probability of his respecting the terms of a loan agreement is low.

11 IMPORT FINANCING

Over the centuries international trade transactions have been characterized by limited or no knowledge of the financial strength and reputation of each party, as well as by uncertain delivery and payment. As a result, sellers usually have sought to retain legal control over their goods until receipt of payment, whereas buyers have been reluctant to pay before possessing the goods. Experience and necessity thus have contributed to the creation of instruments intended to reduce risk in international transactions by assuring the seller of payment and the buyer of receipt of the goods. During the last three centuries these instruments have evolved along with institutional financial specialization. Some of the larger European merchant houses eventually found it increasingly profitable to lend their good name to less well-known merchants by accepting these merchants' drafts. Out of this practice grew merchant banking, commercial letters of credit, and bankers' acceptances.

As specialization of functions progressed, banks began to assume an important role in international finance. By the twentieth century commercial banks dominated the financing of foreign trade. The major instruments developed to facilitate the financing of foreign trade transactions are the letter of credit, the draft, and the banker's acceptance. To discuss import financing, it is useful to review these instruments as they arise in the normal sequence of an import transaction. This approach will clarify the role of banks in this process, and place import financing arrangements in their proper perspective. The following sections review the major international financial instruments, identify the documents involved, and analyze the various types of import financing.

INTERNATIONAL FINANCIAL INSTRUMENTS

Letter of Credit

One of the safest and most common ways to finance a transaction between international trading parties is the commercial letter of credit, or simply letter of credit *(L/C).* This instrument, depending upon the party to which reference is being made, is also referred to as an import letter of credit or an export letter of credit. A letter of credit is a financial instrument issued by a bank at the request of a customer, whereby the bank undertakes to accept and/or pay drafts drawn upon it by a designated party, provided certain conditions are met by this party. In essence, the letter of credit provides for the substitution of a bank's strength for that of its customer, and assures the exporter payment against delivery of documents rather than of the actual merchandise. The exporter is also protected against government restrictions preventing payment by the importing firm. Experience shows that cases in which governments have prevented banks from honoring already issued letters of credit are limited (if there have been any). The importer is assured that the exporter will not be paid until the documents that transfer title to the merchandise are carefully examined by the bank and are found to be in order.

Issuance of a letter of credit by the importer's bank *(issuing* or *opening bank)* is the product of a process that usually begins with the exchange of correspondence between two parties located in different countries and interested in entering into a transaction. Once agreement is reached, a merchandise contract is concluded between the seller (exporter) and the buyer (importer). Two important features of this contract are the currency of payment and the means through which it is to be effected. If the invoice is to be expressed and hence be paid, in the exporter's currency, the importer will have to bear the foreign exchange risk of this transaction. On the other hand, if the invoice is to be stated in the importer's currency, the exporter will have to bear the foreign exchange risk. In either case this risk can be reduced by hedging in the foreign exchange market. The means of payment is another important aspect of this contract. If it is agreed that the transaction is to be paid by means of a letter of credit, the importer will contact his local bank and file a formal application for a letter of credit, which comes in a standardized printed form (see Exhibit 11.1). The importer's bank will want to know the amount of money involved, the terms of payment, the documents that the bank should receive to effect payment, the time period for which the credit will be valid, and other conditions.

Processing a letter of credit request is similar to processing a loan. The bank will seek to determine the ability and willingness of the importer to provide the funds necessary to honor the letter of credit and to pay the required fees. A well-established importer already has access to a substantial line of credit at the bank, in which case issuing a letter of credit entails no difficulty. The amount to be drawn under the letter of credit is charged against the total available under the credit line. Small and less-known importers, on the other hand, have to provide some type of security, such as a cash deposit (for part or all of the credit) or other collateral.

Once the bank is satisfied with the creditworthiness of the importer, it will proceed to open a letter of credit in favor of the exporter, guaranteeing its payment subject to the terms and conditions contained in the credit (see Exhibit 11.2). The letter of credit is then forwarded to a bank in the exporter's country (that is, to a correspondent bank or to the exporter's bank), which is instructed to advise the beneficiary of the establishment of a letter of credit in its name. This bank *(advising bank)* has no financial responsibility, nor does it receive fees. After receipt of the letter of credit, the exporter arranges for the shipment of the goods to the importer, to fulfill the conditions of the credit. Technological advances have expedited this process by replacing the traditional paper-based communication between banks with electronic letter-of-credit messaging.

Once the goods are shipped, the exporter draws a draft against the issuing bank and attaches it to the required documents, which are submitted to the exporter's bank along with the letter of credit. Assuming that the documents are found to be in order, the exporter's bank forwards them to the issuing bank for payment. If the draft and accompanying documents comply with the terms and conditions of the letter of credit, the issuing bank pays the exporter's bank, which then makes the funds available to its client, the exporter. The issuing bank, in turn, collects from the importer against release of documents that are essential for the latter's physical possession of the merchandise.

Exhibit 11.1 Commercial Letter of Credit Application and Security Agreement

MANUFACTURERS HANOVER BANK INTERNATIONAL (MIAMI)
INTEROFFICE LETTER

Gentlemen: **Date**.................. **L/C No**...............

Please issue an IRREVOCABLE letter of credit and transmit it by ☐ airmail ☐ cable ☐ airmail with brief preliminary advice by cable

ADVISING BANK	FOR ACCOUNT OF (APPLICANT)
IN FAVOR OF (BENEFICIARY)	AMOUNT

Available by drafts at sight or ....drawn, at your option, on you or your correspondent for ....% of the Invoice value.

When accompanied by the following documents, as checked:

CHECK REQUIRED DOCUMENTS

☐ Commercial Invoice

☐ Customs Invoice

☐ Marine

☐ War Insurance Policy and/or Certificate ....

☐ Air ....

☐ Other documents..

....

....

....

☐ Air Waybill consigned to Manufacturers Hanover Bank International (Miami).

☐ ON BOARD Bills of Lading (full set required if more than one original has been issued) to order of Manufacturers Hanover Bank International (Miami).

MARKED NOTIFY...................................AND MARKED FREIGHT: COLLECT/PAID.

COVERING: Merchandise described in the invoice as: (Mention commodity only in generic terms omitting details as to grade, quality, etc.) ....

....

Shipping Terms are: ☐ FAS ☐ FOB ☐ C&F ☐ C&I

Shipment From:

To:

Partial Shipments	☐ Permitted	☐ Prohibited
Trans-shipments	☐ Permitted	☐ Prohibited

☐ Documents must be presented to negotiating or paying bank within ..... days after the date of issuance of documents evidencing shipment or dispatch or taken in charge (shipping documents) but within validity of letter of credit.

☐ Insurance effected by ourselves. We agree to keep insurance coverage in force until this transaction is completed.

You may authorize Your Correspondent to Forward All Documents In One Airmail. ....

Special Instructions..

Source: Manufacturers Hanover International Banking Corporation.

Exhibit 11.2 Letter of Credit

EXCEPT SO FAR AS OTHERWISE EXPRESSLY STATED, THIS CREDIT IS SUBJECT TO THE UNIFORM CUSTOMS AND PRACTICE FOR DOCUMENTARY CREDITS*(1974 REVISION) INTERNATIONAL CHAMBER OF COMMERCE (PUBLICATION NO.290)

MANUFACTURERS HANOVER INTERNATIONAL BANKING CORPORATION
100 NORTH BISCAYNE BOULEVARD. MIAMI, FLORIDA 33132

DATE October 16, 2016

IRREVOCABLE COMMERCIAL LETTER OF CREDIT	OUR CREDIT NO. A-1001 / ADVISING BANK NO.
ADVISING BANK	**APPLICANT**
Banco Hispano Americano 38 y 40 Paseo de Gracia Barcelona, Spain	European Creations, Inc. P.O. Box 13221 South Miami, Florida 33133
BENEFICIARY	**AMOUNT**
Compania Proctora de Valencia Apartado de Coreos 341 Valencia, Spain	U.S. $90,000.00 (ninety thousand and 00/100) Dollars **EXPIRY DATE** November 16, 2016

GENTLEMEN:

YOU ARE AUTHORIZED TO VALUE ON Us,

BY DRAWING DRAFTS AT Sight, FOR FULL INVOICE VALUE WHEN ACCOMPANIED

BY THE FOLLOWING DOCUMENTS:

1. Commercial invoice, original and two copies
2. Customs invoice
3. Insurance policy, or certificate, covering marine and war risks
4. Certificate of origin
5. Clean on board ocean bills of lading (Full set required if more than one original has been issued) to the order of Manufacturers Hanover Bank International, Miami. These should be marked: notify European Creations, Inc.

COVERING Ladies wardrobe essentials
CIF Port of Miami

Advising Bank's Notification Advising Bank's Notification

SHIPMENT FROM Barcelona port TO Port of Miami	PARTIAL SHIPMENTS Permitted	TRANS-SHIPMENTS Prohibited

Documents must be presented to paying bank within 15 days after the date of issuance of documents evidencing shipment but within the validity of letter of credit

SPECIAL CONDITIONS :

The amount of any draft drawn under this credit must be endorsed on the reverse of the original credit. All drafts must be marked, "Drawn under manufacturers Hanover International Banking Corporation Letter of Credit Number A-1001 DATED October 16, 2016

We hereby engage with the drawers, endorsers and Bona Fide holders of drafts drawn under and in compliance with the terms of this credit that such draft will be duly honored on due presentation, if negotiated on or before the expriation date or presented to us together with this letter of credit on or before that date. Yours Very Truly AUTHORIZED SIGNATURE	Advising Bank's Notification

Source: Manufacturers Hanover International Banking Corporation.

The great majority of the letters of credit issued are *irrevocable*--that is, once the beneficiary is notified, the letter of credit cannot be cancelled prior to the expiration date or altered in any way without the prior consent of all parties to the transaction, including the beneficiary. If the letter of credit is *revocable* the credit is subject to cancellation or modification at any time before payment and without notice to the beneficiary. Not infrequently the exporter may request the advising or notifying bank to add its own liability to that of the opening bank. In such a case the letter of credit becomes *confirmed,* meaning that both the issuing and the confirming bank are obligated to honor drafts drawn in compliance with the credit. If both the irrevocable and the confirmed features are combined in the same letter of credit, such a letter is virtual guaranty of payment once the conditions of the credit are fulfilled, and is referred to as an *irrevocable and confirmed letter of credit.*

Over the years, because of particular needs of importers and/or exporters, there have been other important variations of the basic document to accommodate different conditions. Thus, a letter of credit may provide for advances to the exporter prior to shipment *(red clause letter of credit);* call for payments not at the time of shipment but later, in accordance with scheduled dates over the life of the credit *(deferred-payment letter of credit);* make possible the transfer of proceeds by the beneficiary (a trading intermediary) to another party (a supplier) in the transaction *(transferable letter of credit);* permit the exporter to seek the most favorable foreign exchange rate among those quoted by different banks or exercise its judgment as to the bank that would be most desirable to effect collection *(negotiable letter of credit);* or cover more than one transaction through successive reinstatements of the letter of credit, renewing the amount involved and extending the expiration date *(revolving letter of credit).*

Whatever the specific features of the letter of credit, the terms and conditions should be clear and simply stated. Reference to the quality or condition of the merchandise and other details are not customarily included in the letter of credit. No one would expect bank employees to open and examine the contents of boxes or crates-and even if they did, they would hardly be qualified to express an opinion on the state of these goods. If the exporter is dishonest, a letter of credit will not prevent shipment of inferior goods, or even rocks. Since banks deal only in documents, they cannot be held liable in such instances. However, the bank can withhold payment from the exporter if there is some irregularity in the necessary documents (those covering shipment and insurance of goods) or if some of the terms and conditions stated in the letter of credit have not been met.

Drafts and Acceptances

The final phase in the letter of credit financing process is the actual payment, which is effected by means of a *draft*. A draft is a written order to pay, signed by the drawer, requiring the party to which it is addressed to pay on demand, or at some future date, a stated sum of money. As follows from this definition, the *drawer* or maker is the exporter, who, after the goods are shipped, originates the draft and presents it--along with the required documents--to its bank for payment of what is due. The *drawee* is the party to which the draft is addressed--the importer's bank--and which is asked to pay the stipulated amount in accordance with the terms of the document. The *payee* is the beneficiary in favor of whom the draft is payable--that is, the drawer itself or some other party such as the drawer's bank. Drafts are usually drawn according to the terms of the letter of credit.

Another feature of the draft is the time of payment, often called a draft's tenor. Depending upon the prior agreement between importer and exporter, a letter of credit may call for a sight or a time draft. If the letter of credit provides for a sight draft, the issuing bank will make immediate payment once the draft and certifying documents are received and are found to be in accordance with the terms of the letter of credit. If provision is made for a time draft, payment by the importer's bank is due 30, 60, 90, or some other specified number of days after the date of the draft. As this implies, the main purpose of a time draft is to provide the importer with sufficient time to claim and dispose of the goods, and meet the maturity of the underlying draft.

Issuance of a time draft calls for an additional step in the financial transaction, its acceptance by the importer's bank and, hence, the creation of a *banker's acceptance*. The draft is changed into an acceptance by a stamp across the face of the draft that includes the words "accepted," the date, the signature of an authorized officer, the name of the bank, and other information exemplified in Exhibit 11.3. Clearly the accepting bank will charge its client a commission for creating this acceptance. Exhibit 11.4 identifies the alternate arrangements available to an exporter upon creation of a banker's acceptance. Depending upon its instructions, the banker's acceptance may be kept for safekeeping by the accepting bank or it may be returned to the exporter to hold (or borrow against it) until maturity when it is to be collected.

If the exporter wishes to receive payment immediately it will instruct the accepting bank to discount (sell) the draft at the prevailing rate. When the accepting bank is a U.S. bank, foreign exporters usually favor authorizing the U.S. bank to sell its dollar-denominated acceptance in the domestic money markets. This is because the U.S. money markets are gcnerally more liquid and have lower transaction costs than is true for markets in most other currencies. Such a request presents no problem, especially if the accepting bank has a strong reputation in international trading circles. The stature of the accepting bank makes it a prime asset--that is, a high-quality investment for banks and other institutional investors interested in holding liquid assets of this type. The selling of the acceptance will be at a discount from the face amount based on the going discount rate for bankers' acceptances. Since the importer may have agreed in advance to pay for this discount, the accepting bank will remit the exporter's bank the full amount of the draft for payment to the exporter. The investor, in turn, will hold the accepted draft until its maturity, then present it to the bank for payment. The accepting bank will then look to its customer for reimbursement.

In many cases, businesses well known to each other may find use of a letter of credit unnecessary, and instead agree on payment through a *bill of exchange* (a draft) to be collected via banking channels. In other words, the banks involved act only as agents performing a collection function, thereby earning a collection fee. Specifically, after shipment of the merchandise, the exporter draws a draft on the importer (rather than on its bank), in accordance with the terms agreed upon by the two parties, and submits it, along with the documents necessary for the transaction, to its bank for collection. The exporter's bank then forwards them to its correspondent in the importer's country which arranges for collection of the funds due the exporter. If the draft is a sight draft, the documents arc turned over to the importer upon payment

Exhibit 11.3 Banker's Acceptance Created Under a Letter of Credit

This acceptance arises out of a transaction involving exportation of TV sets from U.S.A. to Venezuela.

200-INT-6 (REV. 6/79) M 200-65-030

$ 100,000.00 Miami, Florida (City) March 17, (Date) 1982

At 180 days sight

PAY TO THE ORDER OF OURSELVES

One hundred thousand and no/100 DOLLARS

VALUE RECEIVED AND CHARGE THE SAME TO THE ACCOUNT OF U.S. Exporter, Inc.

TO: Southeast First National Bank of Miami

100 South Biscayne Banking Center

Miami, Florida 33131

Authorized Signer

Accepted
March 18, 1982
Southeast First
National Bank of Miami
by
Authorized Signer

Drawn under Southeast First National Bank of Miami Letter of Credit no. ELC-724

Source: Southeast Bank, N.A.

Exhibit 11.4 Exporter Options

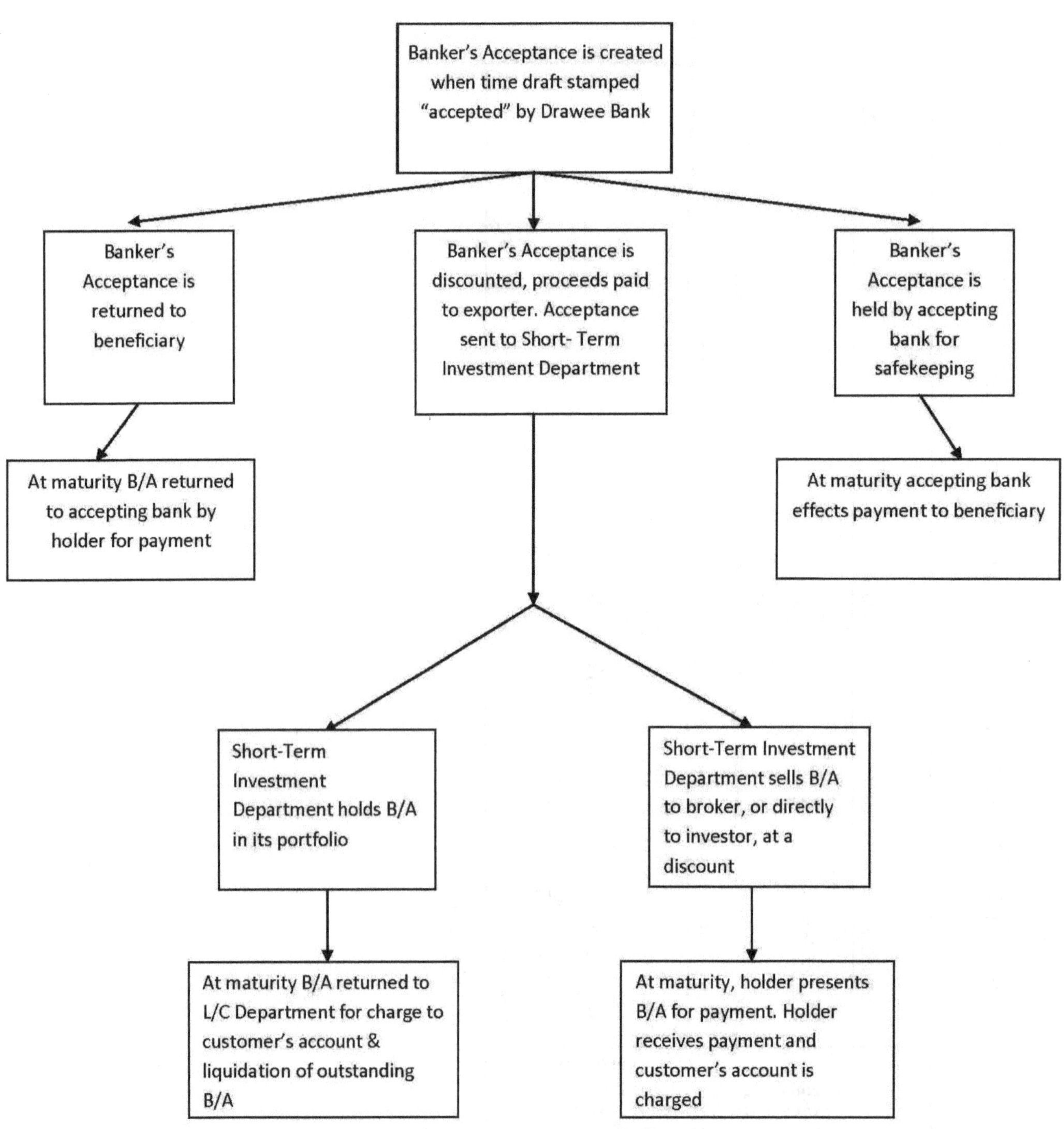

Source: Working paper.

of the draft. If the draft is a time draft, the documents are released to the importer when the latter accepts the draft liability, which is then known as a *trade acceptance.*

In either case the collecting bank may choose to time the presentation of the drafts to the importer--for payment or acceptance--when the merchandise arrives in the importer's designated port. On the basis of an exporter's letter of instruction to the collecting bank, the latter collects from the importer the stipulated amount (plus any fees) and remits it to the exporter's bank for payment. Clearly, should the importer fail to make any payment or go into bankruptcy after accepting the draft, the collecting bank has no obligation or commitment to pay. The risk of nonpayment is carried by the exporter.

DOCUMENTS

Whether drafts are part of a letter of credit transaction or merely items for collection, documents are an integral part of the transaction. These documents generally certify title to the goods and condition of shipment. With banks functioning as intermediaries between exporters and importers, it is only natural that they be concerned about these documents and make every effort to assure that they are in good order. Following is a list of the documents required in most international transactions.

Commercial Invoice

Once a merchandise contract is concluded, the exporter issues an invoice in the name of the buyer, describing the merchandise and its attributes, unit prices, the terms of sale and the total value of the transaction. The invoice includes information pertaining to shipping terms and charges, such as CF (cost of transportation and freight), CIF (cost, insurance, and freight), FOB (free on board), and FAS (free alongside ship). The data contained in the invoice should be consistent with the corresponding data on the letter of credit.

Bill of Lading

A key document in the financing of a foreign trade transaction is the bill of lading. This document, issued by steamship companies, airlines, railroads, and other common carriers, provides a description of the terms and conditions under which a shipment is accepted. It is a receipt from the carrier that it has accepted goods for transportation; a contract with the shipper for the transport and delivery of goods to a designated party or its order; and a transferable title to the goods, provided it is negotiable (made out "to order"). These attributes of the bill of lading render it the principal document supporting the exporter's draft and, hence, its claim for payment.

Insurance Certificate

Another important document stipulated in the letter of credit is insurance to protect the shipment from different types of risk. The question of insurance is a major one in a foreign transaction. The variety and magnitude of risks threatening the profitable conclusion of transactions have always been greater in foreign trade than in domestic. Distances are usually longer, and the number or handlings to which goods arc subjected is generally greater. As a result, the chance of financial loss is bigger. Hence the need for proper insurance coverage to protect not only the individual parties to the transaction but also the bank that is financing it.

Depending upon the terms of the merchandise contract, insurance may be placed by the exporter for his account or for the account of the importer; or it may be placed by the importer with his own underwriting firm. Active importers and exporters usually maintain open or floating policies on the basis of which they issue insurance certificates for individual shipments; these certificates accompany the required title documents. Marine insurance policies cover the normal hazards of voyage, usually referred to as *shipping risks.* These risks range from total loss of goods through sinking of the vessel to losses resulting from fire, collision, or fuel oil or freshwater damages.

In addition to sea perils, there are a number of other real risks that can interrupt the commencement and/or the completion of the voyage: strikes, riots, civil commotion, and war. Of these risks strikes are the most common peril faced by traders today. Strikes can prevent the transfer of the shipment from the dock to the vessel or vice versa. This can be especially disastrous for the importer when the shipment consists of perishables. The same is true for seasonal items--for example, Christmas ornaments are landed in time for the season but are delayed by a longshoremen's strike. If insurance is desired to cover against strikes or any of the other risks, it can be included in the marine insurance policy by endorsement. The exception is war risk which requires a separate contract.

Upon arrival of the vessel at the port of import, and after the shipment is unloaded at the docks, it is exposed to the added risks that include theft and pilferage, which are usually referred to as *dockside risks.* These are also subject to marine insurance coverage.

The vast variety of risks against which insurance coverage can be obtained makes it all the more important for the importer's bank to review thoroughly the insurance arrangements associated with the import transaction and to make sure that the policy is adequate, transferable, and written by a reliable firm.

Other Documents

Other documents that may be required by a letter of credit are the *certificate of origin,* which certifies the country where the goods are grown or manufactured; a *weight list,* which itemizes the weight of each package or bale; a *packing list,* which identifies the contents of individual packages, especially when these are numerous (e.g., spare parts); an *inspection certificate,* which is usually issued by a third or independent party to verify the contents or quality of the shipment. Since banks deal only in documents, this certificate assures the importer that it is receiving what it ordered.

Occasionally the shipment arrives in the importer's designated port in advance of the title documents, or the latter may be received incomplete (for instance, one of the original bills of lading issued by the shipping company may be missing). In such instances the importer may request its bank to issue a letter, known as a *steamship guaranty,* on the basis of which the merchandise can be moved off the docks in order to avoid costly charges and other risks. Since this letter functions as a third-party guaranty, its issuance is conditional upon prior indemnification of the bank by its customer.

FINANCING IMPORTS

Issuance of a letter of credit by a bank may or may not entail extensions of credit.

As indicated earlier, when the importer makes a cash deposit or maintains adequate balances in its bank account, issuance of a 1etter of credit entails no bank financing. The bank issuing the letter of credit will be paid in cash by charging the customer's account. By contrast, if the importer does not have all or part of the funds for the transaction, it will have to negotiate a loan from the bank. If the importer has sufficient creditworthiness, the bank will extend it an unsecured loan. Otherwise, the bank will extend it credit only through a security agreement that enables the bank to perfect a lien on a particular asset or assets of the importer. Both unsecured and secured financing, and the alternate ways of structuring a secured credit facility, are depicted in Exhibit 11.5 and discussed below.

Unsecured Financing

Unsecured bank credit or working capital loans are the most conventional source of short-term accommodation for U.S. business firms. The importer that can obtain its cash requirements through properly priced unsecured bank borrowing has adequate capital and net worth, competent management, stable earnings, a record of prompt payment of obligations, and a bright business future. An importing firm that meets these criteria will have little trouble obtaining a short-term unsecured loan through the signing of a promissory note.

Importers that qualify to borrow on an unsecured basis arc generally few in number. A typical firm in the import trade is relatively small, and its capital investment is almost entirely in trading assets--that is, in working capital. To a banker accustomed to traditional liquidity levels (a current ratio of 2:1) or leverage ratios (debt/equity ratios of 1:1), a typical importing firm constitutes a major deviation from such standards. For example, it is not unusual for importing firms to have less than acceptable liquidity (such as 1.25:1) and/or quite excessive leverage (for instance, 5:1 or even higher).

Another decisive factor weighing heavily against unsecured financing is the vulnerability of the import business. An importing firm usually has as its outlets businesses that are far larger than itself. For example, import companies include among their clients large tire companies, coffee roasting companies, chain stores, and

Exhibit 11.5 Financing the Importer

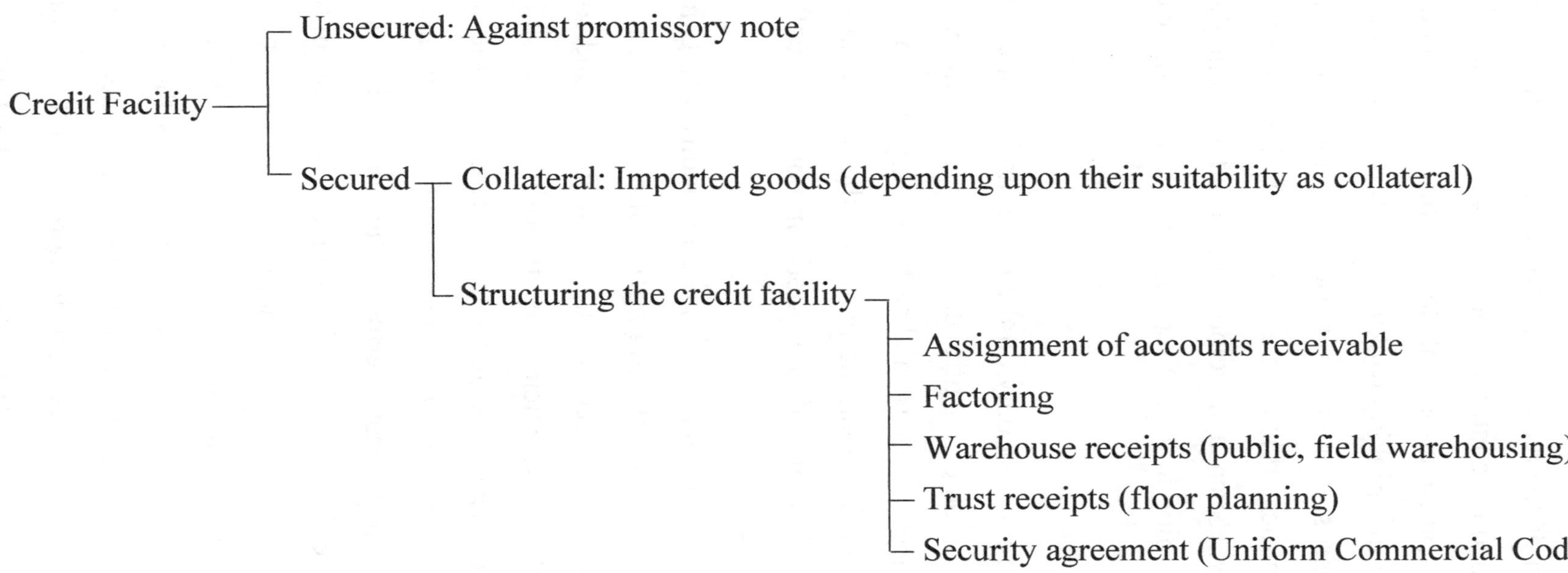

Source: Developed by the author.

department stores. This inequality in size increases the dependency of the importing firms upon their customers, and tends to create problems when business conditions are slack. Specifically, when the economy contracts, importing firms are faced with requests for delayed deliveries, cancellations of letters of intent, and difficulty in obtaining new orders--all resulting in shrinking backlogs and business. Importing firms are also vulnerable vis-a-vis their suppliers. In periods of increased tightness in foreign suppliers' markets, contract prices are reopened for negotiation, and deliveries are delayed or rationed. Such a development could prevent the importer from honoring customer orders, leading to loss of reputation and, in turn, income.

Secured Financing

In secured financing a bank relies not only on the moral and financial integrity of the importer but also on the possession of, or title to, an asset as additional protection for its repayment. In many instances the merchandise being imported may qualify as collateral for bank financing, depending upon the nature of the merchandise and how much margin is required. The suitability of the goods imported as collateral will significantly influence lending terms.

A bank will be more liberal in its terms if the commodity being imported is readily salable and standard in nature, and if hedging facilities exist on a recognized commodity exchange. Products such as coffee, sugar, cocoa, cotton, and some metals are all examples of commodities that trade extensively in world markets and constitute excellent collateral for bank loans. This type of commodities allows the importer to command greater bank credit, thus leveraging its own capital to a greater extent. A bank will be less inclined to extend generous terms if the commodity is subject to spoilage (e.g., fresh produce), style factors (e.g., shoes or textiles), or, in the opinion of the bank, to a decreasing demand because of oversupply or a change in buying habits.

As indicated in Exhibit 11.5, extension of a secured loan may be structured in a number of ways. One of the oldest forms of import financing is the assignment of accounts receivable arising from the sale of the merchandise. Other forms include factoring, warehouse receipts, trust receipts, and security agreement. Used widely in the extension of short term loans to local businesses, each of these forms of financing entails a different type of arrangement as discussed below.

Assignment of Accounts Receivable

Borrowing secured by the assignment of accounts receivable normally provides enough cash flow for the importer to meet his current obligations. Accounts receivable frequently make up the largest portion of an importer's current assets, assuming his inventory is turning over at a normal rate, and represent the primary collateral for secured short-term borrowing. Importers usually have little in the form of fixed assets that can be used as collateral. To assure proper cash flow and to be able to fund the drafts when they are presented, as well as to meet normal operating expenses, the importer must be able to pledge, and borrow against, his accounts receivable.

The receivable loan may be short-term or on a revolving basis, and the amount of credit available tends to increase as the need for credit grows. The importer may use his accounts receivable line to fund a large shipment, and then, since receivables are collateral, the line will be reduced. Or the line may be on a revolving basis, depending on the borrower's needs.

Usually the financing is done on a nonnotification basis, with the customers of the importer not being notified that their accounts are being pledged as collateral for a loan. The importer collects all payments, and forwards the collections to the lender. In notification financing the lender advises all account debtors to send their checks directly to the lender, who credits the loan account on receipt. The lender usually makes the decision as to notification or nonnotification. Notification may help in the collection of accounts by virtue of the borrower's customers' desire not to become delinquent with a large lending institution. Another theory is that the lender shows more confidence by nonnotification financing.

The lender looks not only to the integrity and creditworthiness of the borrower but also to the collateral itself. The type and quality of the merchandise sold is an important factor, as is the demand for it. The amount of returns in relation to sales is one of the determining factors in arriving at the percentage of advance. The lender also must review carefully the aging of accounts receivable to determine the paying habits of the debtors of the importer. Depending on the custom in the trade, accounts delinquent beyond a certain period are ineligible for advance. Accounts that also may be considered ineligible are those to affiliated companies or those in which there is a high degree of concentration to anyone customer, usually 25 percent of the total receivables. When 50 percent of the total receivables is delinquent, the balance, or the current portion, may be considered ineligible.

A prudent lender, depending on the collateral, will take means to ascertain that the receivables actually do exist by confirming with the debtor that the merchandise was received and that there is a valid trade debt that conforms to the collateral. Internal controls dictate that the lender conduct field examinations of the books and records of the client and, each month, reconcile agings with the past month after taking into account sales represented by assigned accounts and collections.

The percentage of advance is determined by an analysis of the foregoing factors, and usually ranges from 75 to 80 percent of the total receivables pledged, less those considered ineligible or not worthy of advance.

An accounts receivable security agreement is entered into, and constitutes a contract between the lender and the importer imposing obligations on both. As long as the importer meets all the requirements called for in the contract, the lender has the obligation to lend. Since the document is a loan agreement, certain covenants protect the lender:

- Requirements for timely financing information
- Submission of aging schedule on a monthly basis
- Responsibility to forward all payments received directly to the lender
- Availability of books and records for inspection by the lender
- Right of the lender to determine the eligibility of collateral
- Dollar amount of line of credit
- Duration of contract
- Percentage of advance

The prudent lender will build credit files on the larger customers of the importer and be prepared to cut back on the percentage of advance, thus warning the importer of "danger ahead." Slow accounts receivable constitute a "red flag" to the credit grantor.

Factoring

A factor (from the Latin "he who does things") was originally a business, not a financier. It originally referred to an agent for a property owner, following the Roman practice of entrusting property management to others. It was in connection with the growth of the wool industry in England, beginning in the late fourteenth century, that the commercial factor was developed as an institution. The factor served as a commission merchant or selling agent for the mill. Because of the slowness of transportation and communication in those days, geographical distances were cumbersome obstacles to business transactions. The factor would, therefore, advise the mill of the styles and merchandise most popular in the local market. The mills would ship merchandise in bulk to the factor who would sell it in his area and assume the responsibility for the creditworthiness of his customers.

Typically the factor buys the accounts of his clients on a nonrecourse basis and provides credit analysis, bookkeeping, the collection of accounts, and the assumption of the credit risk. The importer submits a list of his current, or prospective, customers to the factor, who establishes credit limits in advance. The customers of the importer are notified that the invoice has been purchased by the factor, and are instructed to remit directly to him. Upon receipt of the invoice value the factor calculates, usually at the end of each month, his fees and makes any excess funds available to the importer (*maturity factoring*). Prior to the maturity date of the invoice or prior to the agreed-upon date that the factor will remit to the importer, the latter may request an advance (*advance factoring*), which the factor may make, up to 90 percent of the invoice value. A reserve is maintained to cover shortages in goods shipped, returns, and disputes.

The factors charge a commission, based on the invoice value that covers the assumption of the credit risk, bookkeeping, and collection of the accounts. Commission charges usually run from 1 to 2 percent of the gross amount of the accounts factored. Interest charges, ranging usually from 2 to 3 percent over prime, run from the date of the advance to the due date of the receivables.

Factoring was ruled a legitimate U.S. banking activity in the early 1960s contributing to the entrance of many banks into this line of business. Some banks entered the market through acquisitions, others through joint ventures with factoring companies. Confined initially to the textile and furniture industries factoring spread quickly into other areas of business activity. Factoring operations may develop into a continuous process instead of a single cycle transaction. Once the factoring agreement is in force it lends itself to repeat transactions. For the borrower, it turns into a spontaneous source of funds in the sense than an increase in sales will automatically generate an increase in credit.

Warehouse Receipts

The underlying or primary collateral for the importer is the merchandise being imported. To protect the lender and to control the collateral, the services of a warehouse company are enlisted and warehouse receipts are issued as collateral for the loan. These warehouse receipts may be either negotiable or nonnegotiable, with the latter the more desirable because the former are transferable and must be presented to the warehouse company each time a release is made. Nonnegotiable warehouse receipts are issued in the name of the lender, and describe in detail the merchandise being stored.

As the importer makes sales and notifies the lender, the latter, either by telephone followed by a letter of confirmation, or with a prior letter authorizing partial releases up to a specific dollar amount, gives instructions to the warehouse for partial releases of merchandise. The lender may require the importer to pay a percentage of the loan when releasing inventory, or may depend on the cash flow from the accounts receivable being generated to replace the collateral. The lender, therefore, is a partner in the transaction from the opening of the letter of credit to the collection of the accounts receivable generated from the sale of the imported merchandise. It therefore behooves a prudent lender to know the merchandise being imported and its salability, the market conditions, the reliability of the shipper, the character of the importer, and the ability of the importer to market and the ability of the credit department to collect.

Since it is difficult to chart the peaks and valleys of an importer's cash flow, secured financing lends itself to import financing rather than to working capital loans.

In cases where a public warehouse is not conducive to the normal conduct of a business, or is too costly for the importer, the goods may be stored on the importer's premises. The storage facility can be a separate building, part of a building, an oil tank, or any kind of area on the borrower's premises where commodities such as lumber, coal, and iron bars may be stacked or stored and kept under control. This type of warehousing is called a *field warehouse* and is under the control of a person bonded and employed by the warehouse company. Actually, the individual may be an employee of the borrower who, while continuing his normal duties, goes on the payroll of the warehouse company and reports the "ins and outs" as the goods are moved.

When a loan is made on the security of field warehouse receipts, great reliance is placed on the integrity and the competence of the warehouse company. Signs are posted around the collateral area to show that the goods, although on the premises of the importer, are under the control of the warehouse company. The lender is furnished inventory certificates that state the present inventory value at a specific date below the dollar amounts received and shipped. In order to preserve the proper collateral balance and loan amount, the field warehousing company is given a "hold" figure beyond which they must not release goods. The amount of advance is negotiated between the lender and the importer, and will usually be about 50 percent of the cost.

This type of financing requires a little more of the "C" represented by character than do nonnegotiable warehouse receipts because there is little to separate the importer from the goods except, in most cases, a flimsy participation. Also, the warehouse receipt is only as good as the issuing company. How long has the warehousing company been around? What is its reputation? Its net worth? (A lender should not be afraid to ask for a financial statement.) Remember the salad oil scandal of the early 1960s when "Tino" De Angelis cost the most sophisticated banks in New York City well over $100 million, bankrupted two brokerage companies, and sent reeling American Express Field Warehousing Company, a subsidiary of American Express Company, because field warehouse receipts had been issued against salad oil that existed only in Tino's fertile mind. Loans were based on a reasonable percentage of the market value of the salad oil, as shown in the warehouse receipts, that proved to be stored in tanks in New

Jersey that were as hard to locate as the salad oil.

The prudent lender visits the premises, locates the tanks and peers into them, opens the boxes where the goods are stored, and, if the collateral is perishable, sees that it is stored under proper conditions.

Trust Receipts

Providing the importer is a retailer or wholesaler who must have the goods in his possession to sell, trust receipts or floor planning is appropriate where the importer holds the goods in trust for the lender. The lender holds legal title to each item being financed until it is sold, at which time the borrower is obligated to remit the amount owing and represented by the item. Trust receipts are used extensively in financing the inventories of automobile dealers, heavy equipment dealers, and retailers of major appliances. This type of inventory can be identified by serial numbers as well as by physical descriptions, both of which are outlined in the financing agreement. The prudent lender will make spot checks on his importer to be sure items are not sold "out of trust"--that is, without the funds being remitted to the lender. Trust receipts imply "trust" in the importer, and are close to being unsecured financing because the lender does not have physical control of his collateral.

Security Agreement

The adoption of the Uniform Commercial Code by all of the states except Louisiana, which still clings to the Napoleonic Code, gives a lender a security interest by the execution of a security agreement and by complying with the statutes of the state as to proper filing.

The security agreement gives the lender a security interest in the borrower's changing assets, for a specified period of time, whatever the value of such assets may be at the time the loan is made and afterward (floating or blanket lien). By proper filing in the county seat or the state capital, the lender gives public notice of the lien, the type of collateral, and the parties involved. The floating lien may provide security for future advances of funds and may cover the inventory itself, and/or the proceeds from the sale of such inventory--that is, the borrower's present and future accounts receivable. In order to monitor the accounts receivable at any particular time, schedules of all credit sales are prepared and presented to the lender. Once a month a complete aging of accounts receivable is given to the lender for the purpose of reconciling collections and new receivables.

Since the underlying collateral is the inventory and the consignment thereof, the importer presents, on a regular basis, a computation of inventory. Such a computation includes the inventory carryover from the previous period, purchases identified by particular consignments, sales after giving consideration to gross profit, and inventory at date of computation. Using the dollar value and the rate of advance, the lender and borrower can readily see if the loan is in balance.

There are various ways a lender can obtain a security interest in at least a portion of the borrower's assets if another creditor has interest in them by means of a security agreement. If the first lender has a security interest in the inventory and proceeds thereof, he can be asked to subordinate his interest in the accounts receivable so the second lender can base a loan on accounts receivable. If the lender wants to obtain a security interest in goods coming into the possession of the borrower through a letter of credit or new items, the lender can perfect a security interest in new items before they are delivered to the borrower. The floating-lien holder must be notified by registered mail that these particular purchases are being financed by the lender.

A floating lien does not provide the same protection as a warehouse receipt or trust receipt, and requires diligence by the lender and the expertise expected of a commercial finance company.

12 SYNDICATION

WHAT IS SYNDICATION?

Syndication is the most important form of a loan to a government or a corporation with sizeable funding needs. The cost of processing a number of allowable, smaller loans from several banks is usually too great for most borrowers to justify. On the other hand, for a government or corporate borrower to receive a single, very large loan, only the biggest banks would be willing, or legally permitted, to grant. In the United States statutory provisions prohibit banks from lending more than 15 percent of capital and surplus to one borrower. Other countries have similar statutory and regulatory prohibitions. Syndication solves this problem by making it possible for borrowers to secure funding from a group of lenders each contributing a part of the large loan. They all sign the same loan agreement and have equal standing with regard to the right of repayment. The importance of this form of financing in the world today may be sensed from the information presented in Exhibit 12.1. As seen in this Exhibit global syndicated loans during full year 2015, amounted to $4.7 trillion. The top ten arrangers alone accounted for $1.85 trillion or 39.7 percent of the total syndicated lending activity, suggesting their dominance of the industry. Bank of America Merrill Lynch was the lead arranger in terms of loan proceeds, deals completed, and fees earned.

Syndicated loans usually extend from three to ten years and their pricing is based on LIBOR, the most commonly used benchmark for floating-rate loans to large borrowers. The spread over LIBOR is reset each successive three- or six-month period over the life of the loan. Syndicated lending typically takes place in Eurodollars, but

Exhibit 12.1 Global Syndicated Loans by Top Ten Arrangers, 2015

(in billions of dollars)

Mandated Arrangers	Proceeds	Market Share (%)	Deals per Arranger		Imputed Fees	
			Number	Market Share (%)	Amount	Market Share (%)
Bank of America Merrill Lynch	$300.8	6.5	1,497	14.2	$1,277	6.7
J.P. Morgan	259.3	5.6	1,224	11.6	.985	5.2
Citigroup	229.1	4.9	859	8.1	.746	3.9
Mitsubishi UFJ Financial Group	201.8	4.3	1,500	14.2	.589	3.1
Wells Fargo & Co	176.1	3.8	1,119	10.6	.616	3.3
Mizuho Financial Group	159.2	3.4	1,016	9.6	.383	2.0
Barclays	140.2	3.0	689	6.5	.695	3.7
HSBC Holdings PLC	139.8	3.0	974	9.2	.495	2.6
Deutsche Bank	123.3	2.6	607	5.7	.747	3.9
Sumitomo Mitsui Financial Group	123.1	2.6	1,091	10.3	.358	1.9
Top 10 Total	**1,852.7**	**39.7**			**6,891.1**	**36.3**
Industry Total	**$4,662.5**	**100.0**	**10,561**		**$18,953.0**	**100.0**

Source: *Global Syndicated Loans Review*, Thomson Reuters, 2015. http://share.thomsonreuters.com/general/PR/Loan-4Q15-(E).pdf

other Eurocurrencies are also used. Syndicated loans can be made to both sovereign states and businesses. Sovereign states have used syndicated loans to fund such diverse needs as debt rescheduling, infrastructure projects, balance-of-payments deficits, and budgetary shortfalls. In recent years plunging oil prices have produced budgetary deficits for many of the crude oil exporting countries, some of them already suffering from fiscal problems. With oil accounting for the majority of a country's exports and gross domestic product, collapsing oil prices caused dramatic declines in government revenue undermining spending commitments and the maintenance of social stability. Qatar and Oman are examples of sovereign states that secured syndicated loans to address their fiscal problems in 2015 and 2016 respectively. Qatar obtained a $5.5 billion five-year loan from six banks, priced at 90 basis points over LIBOR. In the case of Oman, eleven banks took part in the $1 billion five-year loan that was priced 120 basis points over LIBOR.

Corporate borrowers may use loan proceeds for such purposes as financing a company acquisition, purchasing fixed assets, and satisfying working capital needs. Companies with heavy fixed capital requirements (e.g., refineries, public utilities, and mining facilities) make frequent use of such financing. Exhibit 12.2 shows the single largest global syndicated loans made during 2015. As seen in this Exhibit, Anheuser-Busch InBev secured a record-breaking $75.0 billion loan package to fund its $107.0 billion acquisition of SABMiller, topping the list of all-time syndicated loans. Other notable acquisition-related loans include a $31.5 billion loan for Teva Pharmaceuticals and a $30.5 billion facility to Charter Communications to fund its $78.4 billion acquisition of Time Warner Cable.

SYNDICATION AND PARTICIPATION

The most typical kind of syndication used in the Euromarkets is the "true syndication" in which a manager (syndicate manager or lead bank) assembles a syndicate of banks that simultaneously make several loans to the same borrower pursuant to the terms of the same agreement. Usually they will be treated as equals,

Exhibit 12.2 Top Ten Global Syndicated Loans, 2015
(in billions of dollars)

Closing Date	Borrower	Target Market	Package Amount	Primary Use of Proceeds
10/28/2015	Anheuser-Busch Inbev	Belgium	$75.0	Acquisition financing
11/19/2015	Teva Pharmaceutical Industries	Israel	31.5	Acquisition financing
08/7/2015	Charter Communications, Inc.	United States	30.5	Acquisition financing
8/25/2015	Anthem P&C Holdings, Inc.	United States	30.0	Acquisition financing
12/2/2015	Volkswagen AG	Germany	21.2	General corporate purposes
3/19/2015	AbbVie, Inc.	United States	18.0	Acquisition financing
6/3/2015	Wal-Mart Stores, Inc.	United States	17.0	General corporate purposes
10/12/2015	Dell International LLC	United States	16.0	Acquisition financing
5/28/2015	Glencore PLC	Switzerland	15.2	General corporate purposes
5/1/2015	Royal Dutch Shell PLC	Netherlands	15.2	Acquisition financing

Source: *Global Syndicated Loans Review*, Thomson Reuters, 2015.
http://share.thomsonreuters.com/general/PR/Loan-4Q15-(E).pdf

and each maintains a direct contractual relationship with the borrower. Consequently, any individual bank may sue the borrower if he is in default.

Members of a syndicate are often called "participants." If a participant determines that his exposure to the borrower is too great, it may decide to sell part of its exposure to another bank. Although lenders may assign all or part of their interest in the loan to a purchaser--in which case the purchaser will stand in the same relationship to the borrower as that of the selling bank--this course is frequently not employed, often because the borrower may wish to avoid the administrative technicalities involved in registering another lender, or, more importantly, the selling bank may wish to preserve the appearance of being a direct lender to the borrower.

In these circumstances the selling bank may instead grant a subparticipation to the purchasing bank. This is essentially a subloan between bank and participant that is governed by many of the terms of the main loan between bank and borrower. For the selling bank subloans have the virtue of preserving its relationship with the borrower; however, for the purchasing bank there are several disadvantages. A subparticipant has no direct contractual relationship with a borrower, and consequently may not exercise a right of offset. It will not normally benefit from, or be protected by, indemnities or yield protection clauses in the main agreement between the borrower and the lender. Moreover, all repayments of principal or interest on the loan are due to the original lender, who has a duty to pass on these sums to the purchaser. But if the original lender goes into liquidation, the liquidator would be entitled to the repayments, and the purchaser would become a mere creditor of the original lender. Some participation agreements are structured to constitute a sale of a right to receive payment. This is essentially an assignment, but one where the selling bank acts as a collecting agent or trustee for the purchasing bank. Although this arrangement appears to provide a way to protect the subparticipant, if the selling bank adopts the common practice of mixing the funds it receives in respect to the loan, then the purchasing bank will simply have the status of a creditor in the liquidation, and the advantage of having a subparticipant agreement would be lost.

Occasionally a syndicated credit may be structured as a loan by the lead bank, subparticipated to members of a syndicate. This may enable the banks to take advantage of favorable withholding tax arrangements--or to avoid a penalizing one--between the country of the borrower and that of the lead bank. This arrangement may be desirable if one bank is to hold collateral security in instances where it would be impracticable for all members of the syndicate to do so. In such cases the subparticipant banks should ensure that the documentation is structured to avoid the problems mentioned above.

PARTIES TO A SYNDICATED LOAN

The parties to a syndicated loan will appear in the tombstone (public announcement) of a Eurocredit and will include the borrower, the guarantor when a third party is primarily liable under the loan, the participating banks, and the syndicate manager or lead bank. The syndicate manager, or a participating bank, may also function as the agent bank.

The Borrower

The borrower is trying to raise a large amount of money efficiently and inexpensively. It therefore prefers to deal with only one bank. But at the same time it wants to develop relationships with other banks, perhaps in disparate regions of the world, in order to enhance its credit reputation.

The Guarantor

Some agreements rely upon the credit of a guarantor. For instance, if the borrower is an offshore financing subsidiary with a nominal capital structure, the guarantor of the loan may be a parent company. In these cases the guarantor is included in the main loan agreement, and the guarantor is primarily liable under the loan.

Participating Banks

Each member of the syndicate becomes a direct lender to the borrower. Consequently, each member must verify and analyze the credit independently. Typically, some members will be large banks in the same marketplace as the lead bank; others may be relatively small regional and/or correspondent banks. These latter banks, in particular, need to be cautious and to ensure that they are in fact able to accurately judge loan credits that may be proposed.

The Agent

Typically the syndicate manager serves as the agent, but sometimes an affiliate of the manager or another member of the syndicate may assume this responsibility. The agent services the loan throughout its entire duration. The agent's responsibilities, which are established in the loan agreement, include collecting interest and principal on the loan and disbursing those funds to the syndicate members, distributing information to the syndicate members, and generally representing their interests. This is a fiduciary relationship.

The Syndicate Manager

The syndicate manager or lead bank originates the transaction, structures it, assembles the syndicate, supervises the documentation, and, in most cases, services the loan after signing. Its position is the most crucial and the most exposed legally. It has a duty to the borrower to arrange the syndicate and a duty to the other banks not to mislead or misrepresent any aspect of the credit. It will also be a lender. (These problems are considered in more detail under "Legal Problems" below.) It is possible for several banks to perform the duties of the syndicate manager; in such cases marketing, publicity, organizing the signing ceremony, and other functions will be divided as agreed upon among the members of the managing group.

The four major functions of the syndicate manager, frequently referred to as the 4Ss, are described below.

SOURCING THE LOAN

Simply stated, a lead bank seeks to find a creditworthy borrower and a group of banks willing to lend, and to structure a loan among those parties. For loans in the Euromarket, the lead bank must first ensure that the borrower really requires a syndicated Eurocurrency loan and not, for example, domestic finance or the issue of bonds or commercial paper. Second, it must assess the creditworthiness of the borrower. Third, it must establish terms with the borrower that a syndicate will find acceptable. The lead bank must know the types of risks and the spreads over LIBOR; its reputation will become tarnished if it obtains a mandate from a borrower that it cannot syndicate. Prospective borrowers are large corporations, governments, or governmental agencies, and a prospective lead manager must have the marketing capabilities to attract such borrowers. A bank that has already successfully managed a number of Euromarket credits will find it relatively easy to attract prospective borrowers.

STRUCTURING THE LOAN

Before it begins to assemble a syndicate, the prospective manager must develop with the borrower a clear idea of the purpose of the loan and structure it accordingly. The purpose must be clearly stated and should be balanced against the capacity of the borrower to meet its obligations in a timely fashion. In the case of private sector borrowers, the borrower must prepare and the manager must approve detailed cash flow projections and other documents concerning any extraneous factors that may affect the fortunes of the borrower during the term of the loan. Public sector borrowers such as governments typically do not go into liquidation, but several key issues must be addressed beforehand including questions of sovereign immunity, future political stability of the country in question, the likelihood of its government keeping control over the balance of payments, and the size of its current and future debt in proportion to its gross national product.

Reference to these and related issues (e.g., borrower background and financial data, purpose of the loan and cash flow projections) are customarily presented in the *information memorandum* circulated among prospective banks. Initiated by the borrower, the information memorandum includes a waiver of responsibility by the syndicate manager(s). Prospective syndicate members must carefully consider this information along with such matters as term of the loan, spread (or price), fees, and other pertinent aspects of the credit.

Term

The acceptable tenor for each particular loan varies according to an array of considerations, such as what the market is currently accepting, whether the loan poses a public sector risk, how the country of the borrower is viewed in political and economic terms, and the financial strength of the borrower. For example, after the Asian financial crisis of 1997, medium term maturities shrank as the market for syndicated lending tightened up.

Spread

Loans are normally made at a margin or spread over LIBOR in the Euromarket or at the rate offered in another appropriate market, such as Singapore or Hong Kong. This spread depends upon the nature of the risk and how the market assesses the country where the loan is being sought. Historically these spreads have varied between, for 0.25 and 3.0 percent and remained fixed over the life of the syndicated credit. However, after the Asian financial crisis, syndicated lenders sought to protect themselves by altering the pricing or structure of the loan as market conditions fluctuated. Initially introduced by Chase, *Market-flex* clauses adjust the spreads of syndicated loans to borrowers in emerging markets (e.g., a Chilean electric company that had borrowed at LIBOR plus 0.25 percentage points in early 1998, had its spread reset to 2.25 percentage points by year-end).

Fees

Due to the costs of maintaining credit and syndication departments, most banks require a spread of at least 1 percent in order to make a profit, although there is some fluctuation in this among banks. In order to ensure profitability, a structure of fees is imposed at the time of signing or drawdown of the loan. The borrower must pay management fees of up to 2 percent to the syndicate manager, who in turn pays participation fees of lesser amounts to members of the syndicate. These participation fees are calculated so that in any event the syndicate manager will be adequately rewarded for its work in assembling the syndicate and managing the transaction.

Other fees may include commitment fees and agency fees. Commitment fees compensate the banks for any unused portion of the credit, e.g., in the event that the borrower does not drawdown all the funds requested until it needs to use them. So the banks do not suffer by committing a portion of their lending limit without reaping any profit. Agency fees are specific amounts paid annually by the borrower to compensate the manager or agent for administering the loan.

Documentation

The basic documentation for Eurocurrency loans are loan agreements, which are usually governed by the law of England or the state of New York, even though the participants may not reside in either jurisdiction. Historically these two legal systems have been chosen in part because they are familiar, a large pool of legal talent is present in London and New York, and because they have developed a more extensive body of case law on these financial topics than most other jurisdictions. In addition to utilizing loan agreements many transactions require promissory notes, guarantees, and security documents. The loan agreement will normally contain, *inter alia,* the following:

1. *Amount and term of loan.* Loan amount, tenor, interest, drawdown, and repayment.
2. *Prepayment clauses.* These specify when early repayment is required or permitted. Prepayment will normally be required in some instances of default if funding becomes impossible, if political or other risks adversely affect the market, or if withholding taxes that make the continuation of the loan uneconomic for the borrower are imposed. It may be also permitted upon due notice or upon payment of a fee.
3. *Representations and warranties*. These are statements in which the borrower makes claims about its condition, such as its ability to carry on a business, about its possession of title to its assets, and about the absence of material litigation or default under other debt arrangements. Typically they are required only at the time of signing and/or drawdown, but the contract may require them to be reissued at intervals throughout the term of the loan. Breach of any warranties or representations constitute an event of default that allow the lenders to call the loan if they so choose.
4. *Conditions precedent.* Before any drawdown may be made the lenders will need to see the borrower's constitutional documents, copies of necessary

exchange control and other government consents, registrations, opinions on the legal ability of the borrower to perform under the agreement, documents pertaining to the enforceability of the agreement, any supporting documentation, and any other necessary documents.

5. *Covenants*. Unlike representations and warranties, covenants are promises the borrower makes about its future condition during the term of the loan. They extend to such matters as obeying laws and regulations, maintaining government approvals, and paying taxes. In financial covenants the borrower may promise not to exceed a prescribed debt-to-equity ratio (*affirmative covenants*). Covenants may also include negative pledges or prohibitions on liens, mortgages, or encumbrances (*negative covenants*). Care should be taken to anticipate exceptions to the covenant that may arise without deliberate action by the borrower. Breaches of covenants constitute an event of default that enables lenders to call the loan.
6. *Withholding tax clause*. A key principle of the Euromarkets is that interest payments on loans or bonds should be free from withholding taxation. Withholding tax clauses appeal to lending banks because they ensure that the lending banks will receive the full amount of interest they expect to receive, even if this means that the borrower will have to gross up the net payment and submit some withholding tax on the payment to a taxing authority. In some instances some or all of the paying banks can obtain a credit against their own domestic tax payments depending upon the terms of relevant double taxation treaties.
7. *Governing law and jurisdiction*. These clauses pertain to issues discussed earlier on the governing law and country of jurisdiction for the settlement of disputes.
8. *Increased costs and availability of funds*. These clauses ensure that the borrower is responsible for any increased costs, such as reserve requirements or risk of underlying funds being available. Under such clauses it becomes possible that a borrower who believes that its loan has a term of several years might discover that the loan is due at the end of the current funding period.
9. *Events of default*. The clause usually referred to as an "events of default clause" lists events that can enable the banks to accelerate the payment date of the loan and thereby transform it into a demand facility. The clause enables all the lending banks to terminate the loan and to declare all amounts immediately due if a default event takes place. Typically this clause requires the agent to call the loan if the banks holding the majority of the outstanding debt so direct. This will also thwart any minority of banks that may wish to accelerate the loan, and these banks will normally be able to proceed only for past-due interest and principal. They cannot unilaterally accelerate the debt.

10. *Agency clause*. This clause attempts to absolve the agent from breach of any duty to the borrower or, more importantly, to the other banks. It also sets out the duties of the agent in servicing the loan and may permit the agent to have other financial dealings with the borrower without prejudice to the loan in question.

SELLING THE LOAN: ASSEMBLING THE SYNDICATE

First, the prospective syndicate manager must decide which banks to invite into a syndicate. There will be some who may offer participation in their loans if the prospective manager makes similar offers to them. There will be some correspondent banks and other banks with whom the prospective manager maintains a close relationship. Sometimes invitations are made on the basis of personal relationships: a syndications officer in Bank A has previously worked well with his counterpart in Bank B and therefore feels comfortable in asking Bank B to participate. Likewise, the borrower may also suggest including some banks, often in different regional markets, with whom the borrower already maintains a good relationship.

The syndicate manager typically approaches prospective partners by sending an offering telex to those banks it wishes to invite. If some of the manager's "first choices" decline the offer, then it may approach a wider circle of banks. The offering telex should request a reply by a specified date and should contain enough information for banks to decide whether they are interested even in making this type of loan. This information should include the amount of the loan, its maturity, interest rate, purpose, fees, a very brief description of the principal terms of the documentation, the identity of the lawyers who will prepare the loan document, and any other relevant information.

If an invited bank expresses an interest in joining the syndicate, the next step is for the syndicate manager to supply any supplementary information that the invited bank may require for its credit decision. This will initially include an information memorandum describing the borrower, its financial history and prospects, and other helpful information. Sometimes the manager may supply a draft loan agreement as well, although comments on the drafting are not normally dealt with until banks have committed more firmly to participate.

Depending upon the terms of the mandate document the manager has secured from the borrower, the syndicate manager may already be committed. If it has made a **firm commitment** the manager will be obliged to proceed with the loan, even if it has been unable to find any syndicate banks and must take the entire transaction on its own account. On the other hand, if the manager's commitment is made on a **best efforts** basis it will be obliged only to attempt to put together a syndicate. If it fails, the loan is not made. **Club syndicate** are deals put together by a limited group of banks.

SERVICING THE LOAN

Once the loan agreement has been signed, the agent bank takes over from the syndicate manager. In many cases these are one and the same institution, but now it performs a different function. The agent's responsibilities include collecting funds from the banks at draw down and distributing interest and principal to the banks when these payments are due. These are the simple mechanical duties. It also enforces the loan, distributes information about the borrower to the other banks, and generally acts in accordance with the wishes of the banks holding a majority of the outstanding loan. These duties are normally spelled out in the loan agreement or in a separate interbank agreement. In any event, an agent must act strictly in accordance with this document and with the duties of a fiduciary. In practice an agent must have first-class legal advice, since the most difficult situations tend to arise when a borrower is about to default or has just done so. Then the agent must promptly ensure that all banks have all the information available.

LEGAL ISSUES

If the syndication of a loan falls within the purview of the U.S. Securities Act of 1933, and if syndication takes place within the United States or if the Securities Act of 1933 is considered to have jurisdiction over a transaction outside the United States, the syndicate manager may be liable to the syndicate members under the act's anti-fraud provision that asserts, "It shall be unlawful to make any untrue statements of a material fact or to omit to state a material fact necessary in order to make the statements made in the light of the circumstances under which they were made not misleading." Under this standard anything stated or omitted, whether orally or in writing, could constitute a liability. This extends to matters that the syndicate manager knows or, with the exercise of due diligence, should know.

The courts have not ruled definitively as to whether participation in a syndicated loan constitutes a security, which requires an especially high standard of care. A liberal reading of the act indicates that it is a security, but courts have ruled both ways. The Colocotronis suit brought against a syndicate manager in 1976 highlights the latter's exposure under the antifraud provisions of the U.S. Securities Act. However, the suit was settled and the courts did not rule on it.

Nonetheless the Colocotronis suit influenced the syndication process in a number of ways. First, it led to the practice of including a strong waiver of responsibility by the managers at the front of the borrower's information memorandum. And it established the practice of requiring the borrower to confirm that the information memorandum is true, correct, and complete, and that the borrower authorizes the distribution of the document. Second, the suit showed that prudent syndicate managers must be careful to send the memorandum only to banks that are considered to have the experience and expertise to make a good credit judgment and that its own syndication department is aware of all the information that the bank has, including that which other branches or departments possess. Prudent managers should also advise all syndicate members of any conflicts of interest that it may have as a lead bank, such as enjoying security under another loan or being an agent under another Eurocurrency credit agreement.

Some of the most pertinent legal considerations for a manager are as follows:

1. Misrepresentation. Managers can avoid liability by taking the precautions they would use to avoid securities legislation liability.
2. Negligent misstatement. Managers can avoid by taking the precautions used to minimize liability under the securities legislation. If a syndicate member relies on a statement the manager has made negligently and thereby suffers a loss, then a breach of duty will have taken place, and in some jurisdictions damages will be awarded.
3. Common law fraud. This involves an intention to deceive. In practice, banks prefer to deal with other banks they know, and in such cases the chances of

participating in a fraudulently-induced credit are small.

Since many syndicates exist outside the borders of the United States, U.S. securities acts will not apply in every case. When they do not apply, the potential sources of liability for a syndicate manager are also misrepresentation, common law fraud, and negligent misstatement, together with any other locally effective sources of liability. However, if a syndicate manager takes the precautions listed above to minimize liability under the securities acts and any local requirements, it should be protected from legal actions against it.

Since agents must act in accordance with their mandates as set out in the loan agreements, they should ensure that the agency clause and any other clauses affecting their function are as explicit as possible. Once the loan has been signed, the agent will be the conduit between the borrower and the banks and will be liable for any breach of the terms of that agency. It will owe a duty of care and diligence, and in order to perform this the agent must, at all times, make available to the banks all information that it has about the borrower. This applies even if the information has been deliberately or inadvertently made available to a department of the agent bank other than the syndication or agency department.

Some of the agent's duties appear to be straightforward, but if disclosure of information will involve the agent in a conflict of interest, the agent will have to tread very carefully. For example, the disclosure of some information about the borrower may be harmful to the borrower. In this case the agent should persuade the borrower to make the disclosure. The agent may have lent to the borrower under other facilities or may be an agent under other facilities, and it may therefore have a conflict when it comes to recovery of money from a borrower who has insufficient funds. This type of conflict should always be provided for in the agency clause.

In the event of a default, the agent may need to act very quickly, and should always have first-class legal counsel available. Any delay may involve the risk of liability.

The best protection available to an agent is to insist on an explicit agency clause in the syndication documentation, to obtain in the loan agreement an indemnity from the other banks for all operations it may perform or omit, other than cases of gross negligence or willful default. Agents also protect themselves by acting promptly, and retaining first-class legal counsel.

13 LOANS AND PLACEMENTS TO FOREIGN BANKS

Extension of credit between banks in different countries is not significantly different from credit extended between banks in the United States. In either case a credit risk must be assumed, although it is always more difficult to analyze offshore credits because of differences in legal and regulatory provisions, not to understate differences in accounting principles as well as in other foreign practices. International extension of credit takes place in many forms: notable loans, interbank deposits, purchase of negotiable Eurodollar CDs and Yankee CDs, foreign exchange, acceptances, letters of credit, and overdraft facilities.

Traditionally most credit extensions in international banking have been directed in the financing of international trade. Regardless of the form that credit extension has taken, once it has been determined that the repayment ability of the borrower is in jeopardy, it is generally too late for the lending institution to take steps to secure its credit. In the modern world of international banking, a lending institution may not fully recognize the exposure it may have with other institutions at any one time. The ability of even the best banks to fully recognize their exposure in various credits at any one time is limited. While an institution may extend a firm lending line, the various areas of the organization may also be extending credits that in the aggregate exceed the confirmed line. The possibility that the foreign exchange area, CD trading, interbank placements, in addition to the loan extension, all combined at any one time, may exceed the credit line should not be dismissed. More than one bank discovered such overextensions when it became known that a credit was in difficulty and it was too late for recovery.

Bank-to-bank international business takes two basic forms: deposits and loans. In both instances extension of credit is involved. In recent years the growth of the Eurodollar interbank market for deposits (both negotiable CDs and nonnegotiable) and loans has been substantial.

The sheer size of individual transactions in both categories clearly indicates the need for credit review and market knowledge of the reputation of the borrowing banks. Knowledge of domestic banks, while helpful, cannot alone be relied upon to measure international credit risks. The participants are a rapidly growing list domiciled in a number of countries, each possessing its own economic, financial, and political considerations.

While the credit record with respect to international bank depositing and lending has been good, risks are still inherent, particularly as the number of participants increases and international credit conditions begin, possibly, to experience strain. The volatility in interest rates and foreign exchange alone can create great uncertainty for individual banks with respect to their creditworthiness.

USE OF CREDIT FACILITIES

As seen in Exhibit 13.1, interbank credit facilities are of different types--placements, lines of credit and special facilities. The maturity and terms for these facilities vary almost as much as the underlying reasons for the credit requests. Placements involve the trading of Eurocurrency time deposits in the interbank market for maturities ranging from call money and overnight funds to longer periods. Traders usually handle the placing of interbank deposits with institutions in an approved list of eligible banks, within prescribed limits for each bank. Banks that bid for time deposits usually relend the funds to their clients for the financing of imports and exports or working capital requirements. There have been instances where the purpose for bidding for interbank deposits has been to redeposit the funds with other banks in the interbank market. While the business is marginal on a matched book basis, on a mismatched book it can be very profitable, although funding risks for the deposit-taking bank are real. In

Exhibit 13.1 Credit Facilities Extended to Foreign Banks

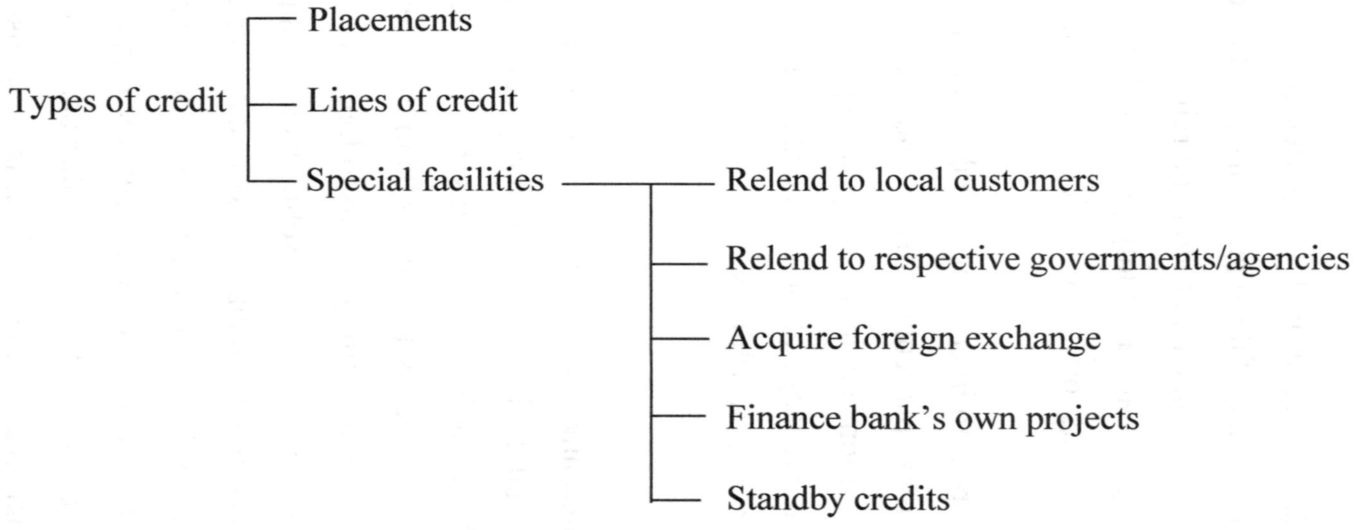

Source: Developed by the author.

the early 1980s, for example, several banks, both domestically and in their international operations, had mismatches that resulted in sizable interest losses completely unrelated to any credit risk. It is difficult (until too late) to discover if the borrowing bank has a mismatched book, even if it is known that the purpose of the borrowing is for interbank placements. The credit risk in this activity is the redepositing in a poorer credit risk bank for an increase in spread, even where the bank is engaged in matched book redepositing. The volatility of interest rates and foreign exchange has caused some concern among banks lending interbank deposits where the proceeds are being used for "interbank trading."

Lines of credit account for the bulk of bank-to-bank loans and draw their origin to the earliest days of commercial banking. Typically provided from correspondent banks, they are used to finance customary international department transactions. It is a common practice among banks that are active internationally to extend each other this kind of facility. The transactions covered by these credit lines include advising and confirming letters of credit opened by the issuing bank, accepting drafts under these letters of credit, effecting payments prior to receipt of cover, extending advances against collection of checks and drafts, and covering any overdrafts in the correspondent bank's account. As the credit lines relate to underlying trade transactions they are self-liquidating, and hence regarded as of highly safe nature.

The third type of bank-to-bank loans are special credit facilities often of medium term maturity. Exhibit 13.2 exemplifies this type of credit. Special credit facilities may be granted for a great variety of purposes as identified below.

1. To relend to clients. The loan proceeds may be reloaned to clients to support pre-export financing. The borrower usually requests this funding in order to produce and supply the goods against confirmed orders from qualified foreign buyers.
2. Loans to government-owned banks, government agencies, or the government. While the loan is made to the bank, if the latter is government-owned or controlled, the lending institution must basically look to the government in measuring credit risk. This does not mean the individual bank should not be

Exhibit 13.2 Syndicated Bank-to-Bank Credit Facility

Zagrebačka banka

€ 270,000,000

Syndicated Term Loan Facility

Joint Mandated Lead Arrangers

Deutsche Bank AG London   JPMorgan

Arrangers

Alpha Bank A.E.   Bank Austria Creditanstalt
Bayern LB   Commerzbank Aktiengesellschaft
Erste Bank   HSH Nordbank AG
ING Bank N.V.   KBC Bank N.V.
Wachovia Bank, NA

Co-Arranger

WGZ - Bank Westdeutsche Genossenschafts - Zentralbank eG

Lead Managers

Baden Württembergische Bank AG   Bank of Montreal

Managers

American Express Bank GmbH   Banca Nazionale del Lavoro S.p.A.
Commercial Bank of Greece S.A.   Israel Discount Bank of New York
Kommunalkredit Austria AG   Magyar Kulkereskedelmi Bank Rt.

Participant

Adria Bank Aktiengesellschaft   Bank of Valletta plc
LHB Internationale Handelsbank AG   National Savings and Commercial Bank Ltd
Raiffeisen Zentralbank Österreich Aktiengesellschaft   Živnostenská banka, a.s.
Zürcher Kantonalbank

Agent

Deutsche Bank AG London

Deutsche Bank

Source: Reprinted by permission of Euromoney

reviewed from a credit point of view. In these instances the banks are the conduit through which the borrowings are channeled.

3. To acquire foreign exchange. The special facility is used for the purpose of acquiring foreign exchange to finance general imports to the country through importing clients. This type of loan may be seasonal, short-term, or long-term. In any case, the general credit of the bank must be relied upon for repayment, since it is all but impossible to obtain specific collateral for this type of borrowing.
4. To address bank's own needs. Loans for the bank's own purposes may take the form of short-to-intermediate-term notes. Loan proceeds may be used for a variety of bank projects, such as enhance liquidity, increase loanable funds, finance an acquisition, expand premises, or an IT upgrade.
5. Standby facility loans. Such loans are rare because they will most likely be activated when conditions in the marketplace are unsettled, with the result that the granting institution may also be facing difficulties. These facilities can take the form of either a deposit or a loan, and usually are paid for through a fee arrangement. These standby credits are generally sought by smaller banks that from time to time may find their name unacceptable in the marketplace because of uncertain or abnormal conditions. This "back-up" facility is also used by banks entering the international money markets as a source of funding until their name is established. These credit agreements also specify a rate usually based at some spread over LIBOR.

LINES OF CREDIT AND SPECIAL FACILITIES

Booking of a foreign loan request, whether under a line of credit or a special facility, rests at the discretion of the lending institution. The actual funds may come from the lending bank's head office or a foreign branch. Special facilities, in spite of variation as to form, are usually structured as Eurocurrency credits from London, or from Nassau, Grand Cayman, or another offshore branch. However, regardless of the funding source and booking location of the loan request, a credit exposure exists that requires proper credit review and approval. The fact that the loan is made from a U.S.

branch to a foreign bank in the same country adds little to its collectability should the borrower default.

Occasionally, less well-known foreign banks may obtain guarantees from larger banks (for loans rather than interbank deposits) for a fee. The value of the guarantee must, therefore, be measured by the credit standing of the guaranteeing bank, although to some extent the lender has "two-named paper." In case of default, many types of legal complications should be expected as a result of local laws and regulations.

Generally in the event of default a depositor ranks ahead of a lender. However, different countries have different laws, with the result that it may be possible that the two parties are equal. Should a bank that has outstanding foreign exchange contracts, loans, deposits, acceptances, guarantees, and other liabilities default, the "lineup" of creditors in a foreign country may be very difficult to assess without substantial legal research and cost. These hazards are nevertheless real. It is very possible for one bank to be holding all of the latter liabilities if the failing bank was a close international correspondent.

INTERBANK DEPOSITS

The placement of interbank deposits, both negotiable and nonnegotiable, cannot be ignored as a credit risk. The amounts are enormous, with the minimum transactions approaching $5.0 million. While the maturity in most instances is shorter than that of the interbank loan, the credit risk nevertheless is present. In view of the fact that the negotiable Eurodollar CD gives the depositor greater flexibility (at some concession in rate), by possibly allowing a sale should the credit of the bank come under suspicion, the market may already have recognized the deteriorating credit situation, with the result that no bids may exist.

Most interbank time deposit placements have maturities of 90 days or less, although maturities of up to 5 years are not uncommon. Floating-rate, longer-term negotiable Eurodollar CDs have also increased substantially, with the result that credit extension periods have been lengthened. Interbank commitments pose a new type of credit extension heretofore not witnessed. Under the latter arrangement, the placing bank under contract must rollover a CD every three months for a given period, which may extend up to three years, at the prevailing LIBOR rate plus some prefixed spread. Should the accepting bank encounter financial stress at the time of a rollover, the depositing institution may attempt to refuse to refund. The major credit problem in this situation continues to be the period between the refundings when no market may exist and the depositing bank is holding the CD of the failed, or failing, institution.

The interbank market, while very sizable and broad-based, nevertheless is very sensitive to credit conditions that affect the name of an individual bank operating in the market. Generally, well before a particular bank's name is tarnished in the market, the dealer fraternity and participants have already recognized the problem. While it is not the purpose of this chapter to examine the complexities of interbank trading, traders are keenly aware of increasing premiums paid by deposit-seeking banks because of individual financial difficulties or of higher rates due to increases in paper outstanding.

The fact that the interbank deposit market is largely one in which contracts are arranged through brokers rather than directly tends to make most of the transactions impersonal. Those operating the individual trading (placement) desks are, therefore, largely guided by internal lines established by various credit committees. When a particular credit has begun to deteriorate in the interbank market, the traders, because of their daily contact with the market, are generally the first to recognize the problem. Deposits with various branches besides head offices must also be considered in any overall exposure assessment.

The ability of a bank to fund or refund liabilities under various market conditions in most maturity sectors is the supreme test of strength. In times of financial stress, such as was experienced during Germany's Bankhaus Herstatt collapse, a rush to quality becomes evident , with the less-than-prime names either unable to fund themselves comfortably or forced to pay substantial premiums.

The fact that in the interbank dealing function, interbank deposits between two organizations may exist concurrently should not cause relaxation of credit qualifications. Differences in maturities may exist in addition to the question of "right of offset" and the problems associated with explaining a position to the market.

RISK EXPOSURE

All international lending and depositing entails risk. In lending to and depositing with foreign banks, there is an omnipresent risk of bank failure in addition to country risk. The overall risk range extends from complete loss to partial loss or a long delay in repayment. Repayment, but at a reduced interest rate, is also a reality. Rescheduling of credits in many instances means longer terms and further credit problems.

Bank Failures

Complete bank failures, both domestic and international, are few and far between. While stockholders may eventually receive nothing, bondholders and other lenders may end up having partial recovery, depending on the seriousness of the failure. Because banks are examined and are involved with the public's funds, governments tend to work closely with institutions in difficulty, in order to prevent their failure. The spillover or secondary negative impact on a country's internal and external financial stability, and the confidence it may undermine, are too great to be treated lightly.

Before a bank is allowed to fail, with possible losses to depositors, government, central bank, or other bank, support (through merger or guarantees) is generally arranged. While these arrangements may secure depositors, others, such as noteholders and foreign exchange and acceptance beneficiaries, may not be as fortunate.

Because international bank failures are rare, there is no general statement of how, or in what order, creditors are paid. Each case is different, for many reasons. Two identical conditions may be handled differently, depending on the nation in which the failed institution is incorporated. While it is difficult to generalize in an area where failures are few and far between, it would appear that deposit obligations (particularly short-term) are paid first, so as to maintain some form of financial confidence in the marketplace. Restructuring of longer obligations, particularly loans at reduced interest rates or reduced amounts, generally are sought concurrently, as part of a stabilization or reorganization plan.

The longer the term of the obligation, the greater the potential risk. The ability of the borrowing institution to service and repay long-term debt is always difficult to predict, regardless of the original purpose of the loan. Because it is virtually impossible to trace the flow of funds through the bank, the original purpose of a note issue generally is lost quickly, with the result that lenders must have confidence in the overall ability of the institution to generate earnings to repay all deposits and debts as they mature. In any case, depositing or lending to foreign banks should not be done on the theory that some form of government or other official aid will be forthcoming, should the borrowing institution fall into difficult times.

Country Risk

Overshadowing individual bank credit analysis is the question of country risk. Regardless of the quality of an individual foreign bank, the government of the country in question ultimately will determine the fate of all payments should an economic or financial crisis occur. Therefore, the risk a bank assumes in lending to foreign banks--or, for that matter, to any foreign concern--constitutes its foreign risk exposure.

The risk exposure assumed by a bank in dealing with foreign banks is a product of a wide spectrum of activities, and is defined by the extent of the institution's involvement. The principal areas of "hidden" exposure are the following:

- Acceptances owned
- Letters of credit purchased or confirmed
- Foreign exchange contracts
- Federal funds sold
- Interbank deposits or negotiable CDs owned
- Clearing payments (direct or through Edge Act corporations)
- Commercial paper or notes issued by bank, subsidiaries, and affiliates
- Current accounts (working balances)

It is substantially easier for a bank to capture the various exposures from the home office than for banks with a worldwide network of international operations and various time zones. Not only is total exposure important to recognize, but information about the maturity distribution of such exposure should be immediately available. Offsetting balances and safekeeping items should be noted and recorded.

In addition, the role of the central bank and its relationship to the government must be considered. In the long run, both economic and political stability must be present for the banking system to function effectively and for the country's foreign exchange rates to maintain a reasonable parity with those of other countries. Anyone not believing country risk is real in recent times need only consider the collapse of communism in the Soviet Union (1991), the Syrian crisis and the Arab spring that led to the overthrows of the presidents of Tunisia, Egypt, and Libya (2011).

The role of the central bank and regulatory authorities should not be underestimated. While it is no guarantee that official aid will be provided in times of stress, countries with well-developed internal banking systems generally have reasonably good examination procedures and strong central banks that aid in the early detection of banking problems.

TYPES OF FOREIGN BANKS

Credit risk assessment of foreign banks may be aided if addressed in the context of country risk. This approach calls for a two-step classification of banks--first by type of ownership and then by size. The resulting categories would consist of the following groups of banks:

1. Government banks which service most of the government's financial needs
2. Government agency banks (state and local institutions) that are government-owned and service particular areas of the country or sectors of the economy, such as agriculture or export
3. Privately-owned commercial banks of national status and importance
4. Privately-owned commercial banks operating within the country
5. Privately-owned specialized banks, such as development banks, investment banks, merchant banks and discount houses.

Exhibit 13.3 identifies the main groups and subgroups in this classification.

Government Banks

Lending government banks (whether federal/national or state and local) is tantamount to lending a country and entail consequently the same degree of risk. It is safe to say that a government-owned bank is probably a better credit risk than a privately owned bank in the same country, although it is possible that both could fail or may

Exhibit 13.3 Classification of Foreign Banks

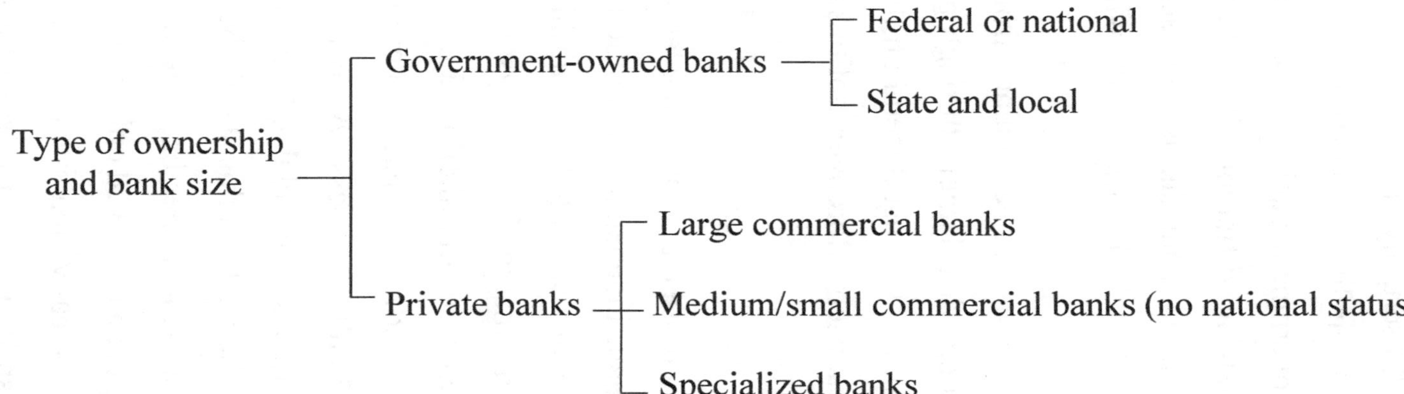

Source: Developed by the author.

experience temporary inability to meet their internal and external obligations. Government-owned banks are basically only as good as the government itself. This is not to say that a new government will accept the liabilities of the prior administration. On the other hand, a stable government does not "turn over." Government-owned banks created by "new" governments need careful scrutiny. Their ability to repay is based on factors well beyond financial analysis. Their livelihood depends on politics and the health of the local economy. Because government banks perform many tasks for the government, their statements are somewhat different from those of the normal commercial bank. The problem in such an analysis is the lack of comparison. Attempting to compare government-owned banks in one country with those in another country is less than fruitful.

Information on government-owned banks can be obtained from the IMF and the World Bank, since both of these institutions deal largely through government-owned banks. The real ability to service and repay debt must depend on the government, the economy, and the management of the bank itself. Moreover, politics cannot be ignored.

Nongovernment Commercial Banks

These banks may range in size from those that rank as the largest in a country (or possibly the world) to those that are small, independent operations. The factors that should be analyzed for this category of banks are noted later in this chapter. In some instances nongovernment banks are so large that the banking system of a country could not operate without their survival. In such cases the likelihood of official government intervention to assure their continuance is extremely high. Where the cutoff between major and nonmajor banks lies is difficult to assess. At what level or size the government or other banks would step in to offer financial aid cannot be easily defined. Needless to say, however, somewhere in the analysis this should be noted.

For obvious reasons the medium-size-to-smaller bank needs greater screening. Problems associated with such institutions can be solved only by the banks themselves. They have limited resources both domestically and internationally. Their funding ability under adversity is rapidly diminished. This is true even for those banks which under normal conditions are active participants in global funding.

In the medium-to-smaller institution, management's reputation becomes increasingly important in the analysis. Their limited resources mean that management's skills must make up for the lack of capital or for smaller size. As will be described later, a full analysis of the financial statements must be completed in order to properly evaluate the ability of the bank to meet its liabilities and to withstand reasonably negative news.

Specialized Banks

In the case of specialized banks, such as development banks, merchant banks or discount houses, the same problems exist as in the case of medium-to-smaller banks, except that they are greater. Each firm's business is slightly different from that of others. By most standards they are highly leveraged. Their earnings tend to fluctuate more than those of a commercial bank. Turnover in personnel is somewhat higher. Earnings projections are more difficult to make. Both contingent liabilities and inner reserves are more difficult to establish. Obtaining new capital in times of stress is more difficult for them. Their earnings and financial reporting are more complicated, making analysis more challenging. Their businesses are less understood. Their earnings in some cases are based on factors beyond their control, such as interest rates or foreign exchange movements. One bad decision, because of the impact it may have on the business, can severely affect earnings.

BANK CREDIT REVIEW

Because of foreign accounting and other customs, foreign bank balance sheets and income statements tend to be somewhat difficult for the inexperienced credit analyst to analyze. Banks active in the international markets generally use their senior credit analysts to research foreign bank statements. Because foreign bank credits are less well understood than those of domestic banks, a somewhat more conservative posture toward the foreign credit should be taken. In many instances supplementary information will be required to establish a bank's financial ability to service its debts in the foreseeable future. To this end, additional inquiries may be required and directed to such parties as the bank management, competitor banks, as well as to correspondent institutions. The major areas of investigation, not listed in order of importance, include the following

- •Earnings record and reason for any major deviations
- •Capital adequacy compared to domestic and international requirements
- •Growth in assets, deposits, borrowings, and reason for any unusual deviation
- •Quality of income
- •Loan losses and/or other major losses
- •Reputation of bank in both local market and international money markets
- •Level at which bank's obligations trade in local and international markets
- •Type of general banking the institution is engaged in, including major areas of loan and investment concentration
- •Ownership of institution
- •Major subsidiaries and their earnings contribution and risks
- •Lines or back-up credits, both domestic and international
- •Trends in foreign exchange earnings
- •Management changes
- •Liquidity position
- •Contingent liabilities
- •Balance sheet compared with those of other local banks
- •Funding sources, including foreign network
- •Unrealized gains or losses not shown on balance sheet
- •Gap analysis (sensitivity ratio), particularly if bank is active in interbank market
- •Nature of hidden reserves
- •Expansion plans of bank

Some of the items identified above are components of a rating system commonly referred to by the acronym CAMELS. The system draws its designation from its focus on the six distinct areas of bank operation and conditions for evaluation: Capital adequacy, Asset quality, Management and administration, Earnings quantity and quality, Liquidity level, and Sensitivity to market risk. Although developed in the United States to classify a bank's overall condition the system is also implemented abroad by various bank supervisory regulators. Clearly when reviewing a foreign bank's CAMELS evaluation it will be altogether misleading to rely on standards other than those prevailing in that country.

Ownership and Management

Both ownership and management are important in the analysis of foreign banks. From time to time, in both the domestic and the international markets, individual names or families become associated with particular banks. Depending on the name(s), the reputation may range from unacceptable to first-class. Most lenders do not basically desire to deal with another bank if there is questionable ownership, even if the earnings or financial conditions appear adequate. It is difficult to describe the "financial uneasiness" that exists when the latter situation is present.

In any analysis of ownership, careful checking with local competition and well-regarded individuals will generally give the first clues of undesirables taking a position directly or indirectly in the institution.

The ability to measure management is difficult by itself. Management's success or failure must ultimately be the financial result over a reasonable period of time. A consistent upward earning pattern, coupled with reasonable ratios and small turnover in management, is basically a good sign. In most cases it is impossible to know management in the interbank deposit market unless the depositing bank restricts itself to a very small list. One must depend on the financial numbers and information gathered from all other sources regarding the owners and the management. While knowledge of the board of directors is helpful, it should not be relied on alone. Even the best boards are not made up entirely of individuals who remain informed about current practices and events. Some boards still have members who are figureheads. A large turnover of directors or key officers should be carefully screened. A bank cannot have high turnover without some deterioration in its basic fabric.

Banks that show large swings in foreign exchange or securities trading profits should be carefully analyzed. Managements that allow nontraditional, nonrecurring types of income to become significant may not be completely acceptable, viewed in terms of conservative management.

Early Signs of Problems

In many cases the early signs of problems are reflected in the marketplace, the borrowing institution paying over the market to attract deposit or loan funds. Traders and participants in the market are quick to observe growing rate differentials between institutions that result from market knowledge that a particular institution may be facing difficult times. Banks' financial conditions do not deteriorate overnight. Bank creditworthiness is judged by both the price of a bank's stock (if publicly owned) and the rate the bank pays for overnight or term funds. The collective judgment of the marketplace is difficult to escape in terms of the cost of money reflecting the credit-worthiness of individual banks.

Capital and Ultimate Strength

Of the various functions performed by bank capital, of paramount importance is the protection of creditors. This, in fact, is the absolute test of a bank's financial responsibility. The adequacy of capital in protecting creditors has been the focal point of bank regulation both in this country and abroad. In an effort to converge measurement and standards of capital adequacy, U.S. regulators, and their counterparts in other member countries of the Bank for International Settlements, have jointly implemented (January 1, 1993) risk-based capital ratios formally known as the Basel Agreement (now denoted as *Basel I*). As these measures addressed the different credit risks of assets, successive revisions expanded capital adequacy rules to include market risk (1998) and operational risk (2006). A new agreement, *Basel II,* allowed banks a range of measurement options in determining exposure to these risks. The financial crisis of 2008 revealed the need to strengthen further the risk coverage of the capital framework. The immediate result of this assertion was the adoption of *Basel III* (2010) which will become fully effective in 2019 by updating capital requirements against market risk from banks' trading operations. As this update applies only to the largest U.S. banking organizations (e.g., consolidated assets in excess of $250 billion or foreign exposures over $10 billion), all other banks are subject to the standardized approach of capital adequacy requirements.

International convergence in the measurement and standards of capital adequacy enable regulators to identify well capitalized banks and enforce corrective action on those that fall short of the minimum capital requirements--e.g., undercapitalized, significantly undercapitalized and critically undercapitalized institutions. International convergence in measurement and standards is also helpful to the loan officer or analyst who evaluates the adequacy of a foreign bank's capitalization. To the extent that the foreign bank may be owned by other major institutions it can also mean that additional capital may be available should the bank's own capital be impaired. The degree of "back-up" capital is difficult to assess unless it is clearly defined. While support may be forthcoming from other owner-banks in times of difficulty, the degree of financial support should be viewed on a conservative basis.

The question of capital should not be viewed lightly. Once it becomes known that an institution is in difficulty, the drain of deposits that generally occurs is swift and the question of capital becomes paramount.

Evaluating a Bank's Financial Condition

Ultimately, the analyst must focus at the bank statements and inquire about loans and deposits. Regardless of the bank's size or reputation, the periodic review must be performed. The major problem in this analysis, of course, is the differences in the reporting between U.S. banks and those in foreign countries. Compounding this problem is the fact that each country has its own accounting practices and tax regulations, which make comparable analysis quite demanding. With foreign banks' accounting and reporting practices subject to change, updated information is essential.

To some extent the financial condition of individual banks depends on the central bank, its method of operation, and the role it plays in the banking system. Central bank policies pertaining to the ease or difficulty in rediscounting, government-guaranteed loans, and reserve requirements are some of the aspects that directly or indirectly influence the statement of the bank, and consequently its compliance to prudent management over a period of time.

Individual bank analysis should take into consideration earning trends, deposit growth, capital, losses, return on assets, leverage, and other ratios or percentages that appear reasonable. The ratios or percentages should, however, be measured against banks operating in their own country, rather than against banks in the United States. Any bank that stands out from others in a comparison year after year should be further analyzed for specific reasons. What may at first appear to be an asset could quickly become a liability or negative factor. What is acceptable in a foreign country may not be acceptable in the United States.

Directly influencing individual banks in a foreign country is the government's role in the financial market through subsidiaries, grants, guarantees, or partial ownership positions. Other areas of investigation are government deposit guarantees, foreign exchange profits, government or government agency deposits, types of deposit growth (or no growth), and types of business in which the bank is directly or indirectly engaged.

Equally important in any analysis is the country risk exposure that individual banks have in their loan portfolios. Country exposures overshadow any and all other factors concerning bank finances.

The volatility of both interest and foreign exchange rates has brought to the surface another dimension in bank analysis: gap analysis or interest sensitivity. Basically this analysis attempts to measure the profile of the bank's interest-sensitive liabilities versus its interest-sensitive assets. The balance of the sensitivity becomes pronounced when interest rates rise or decline sharply over the interest cycle and quickly impair the earnings of the bank. During such periods, banks find themselves either liability-sensitive or asset-sensitive at the wrong time, or find substantial maturity mismatches of assets and liabilities. In some instances both conditions prevail, resulting in a severe earnings squeeze. The latter conditions are completely separate from any loan and credit problems. In those instances where substantial swings in earnings result from the various mismatches, bank management reaction is to adhere to a firm position on interest rates. Absolute, firm views on interest rates should be avoided by bank managements. The more conservative approach is to have a more balanced book or one that is moderately unbalanced in either direction.

The major problem in attempting to measure the sensitivity is obtaining sufficient and accurate data. U.S. banks report information that can aid in this type of analysis. In the case of foreign banks, this information probably can be obtained only through conversations with bank management.

Lending banks are interested in relationships that shed light on the direction in which a foreign bank appears to be moving. In identifying relationships and analyzing trends, a lending bank will make use of ratio analysis. While a detailed analysis of individual bank ratios should be kept and updated, only a certain number of them need be closely monitored, with the other ratios used as supporting data. The data should be viewed over a period of time and, as noted elsewhere, should be compared with those of other banks operating in the same country.

Ratios that should be noted, analyzed, and considered as major financial indicators include:

- Deposits to capital
- Loans to deposit
- Liquid assets to deposits
- Inner reserves (if obtainable) to total capital
- Growth of published capital
- Deposit growth
- Contingent liability growth
- Trend in foreign exchange profits
- Trend in reported earnings
- Loan or asset concentration to one country, borrower, or industry.

An analyst should look for balanced growth in earnings as well as total asset growth. At the same time the sources of earnings and their vulnerability to various influences should be noted. Over time the major ratios noted above should promote sufficient insight into any bank's financial condition. No one ratio is more important than another; hence, each must be reviewed in the context of the total. Significant alterations should be noted and explained.

14 LOANS TO FOREIGN GOVERNMENTS

LEVELS OF GOVERNMENT AND SOURCES OF FINANCING

Following the dramatic rise in oil prices in the 1970s an increasing number of foreign governments entered the credit markets to finance their needs. Although lending a foreign government seems straightforward, American bankers distinguish, from a legal perspective, five different levels of government borrowers. This approach enables closer scrutiny when analyzing risk and pricing a credit request. The specific levels are as follows:

1. Government at the national (federal), provincial (state), and local level
2. Ministries of the national (federal) government and central bank
3. Statutory authorities and agencies at all government levels
4. Statutory or chartered corporations wholly or majority-owned by the government
5. Statutory or chartered corporations in which the central government is a minority owner and may or may not exercise full control

This classification recognizes the different gradations of risk among the alternate levels of government. When considering making loans to any of these entities banks should determine the degree to which the central government assumes responsibility under law or by policy for repayment of the loan. The banks should also be clear about who, specifically, within the government is in charge of making payments, and the responsibilities of the central government should be well defined under law, charter and/or regulation. Any ambiguity may undermine the quality of the loan and pose significant problems for the lender in the future. To control against credit and country risks, U.S. law requires certain key conditions to be satisfied when lending foreign borrowers in which the national government has a direct or indirect ownership interest. The foreign borrower must possess sufficient *autonomy* that sets it apart from the central government. Further it must demonstrate that the *purpose* of the loan is consistent with the borrower's mandate.

While industrialized countries with access to their domestic markets have established strong credit credentials and raised funds internationally, less developed countries (LDCs) have relied heavily on official and other noncommercial bank flows. The Development Assistance Committee (DAC) of the OECD has traditionally favored lower interest rates and longer-term loans to LDCs. Comprised of the major industrialized Western European countries, DAC makes official development assistance (ODA) grants or concessional loans containing a grant element. DAC and ODA loans are channeled through United Nations agencies, the World Bank, and regional development banks.

In the course of the 1960s and 1970s the amount of loans issued by DAC to LDCs grew nearly tenfold, from $8.4 billion to $78.4 billion. Although initially there was some private-sector lending, the vast majority was governmental. However, the share of private lending grew steadily over time. In the early 1960s, for example, nearly 71 percent of the net capital flows originated from governmental sources, while by the late 1970s, private lending accounted for about 64 percent of capital flows. The shift from official to private sources of financing gained momentum partly because legislative support for governmental foreign aid diminished within many industrialized countries (e.g., the United States and Japan), and partly because commercial banks increasingly demonstrated their ability to meet the demand for credit by foreign governments. Exhibit 14.1 shows the alternate sources of funds for foreign governments in the postwar decades.

As seen in this Exhibit, government borrowing in international financial markets takes place through either medium or long-term syndicated bank credits or issue of international bonds (foreign bonds or Eurobonds). One major advantage of syndicated lending is that it helps develop a permanent relationship between the borrower and lender. On the other hand, when a bond is issued, the transaction is a one-time affair--investors do not anticipate a continuous or permanent relationship with the issuer. In fact investors may sell their bonds prior to their maturity and in the case where these bonds are of the bearer type their names may not even be known to the issuer.

Exhibit 14.1 Sources of Government Borrowing

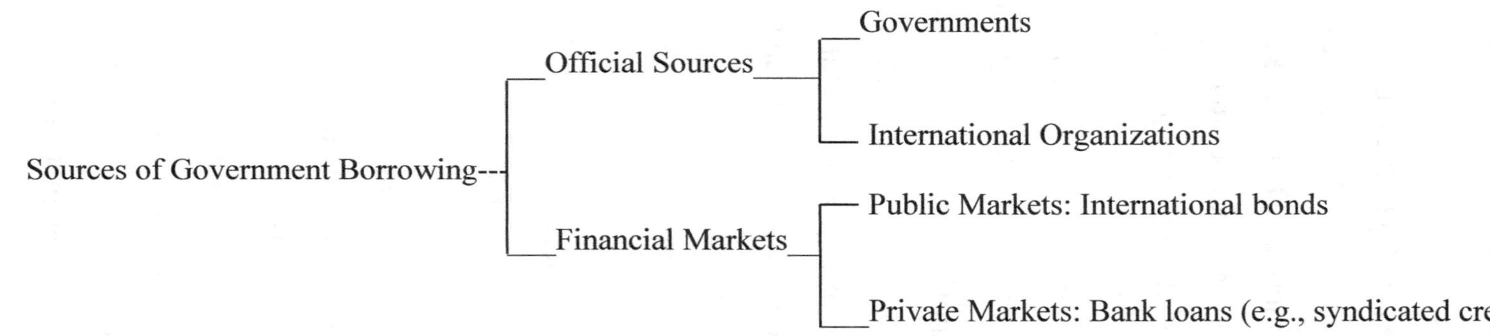

Source: Developed by the author.

Another advantage of syndicated lending is that loan maturity and repayment schedule is tailored to the borrower's needs. Further, syndicated lending offers greater flexibility compared to dealing with a large number of bondholders. Most bonds and notes contain provisions in which a change in the agreement can be negotiated through a trustee who represents the bondholders after they have met and agreed unanimously to changes in any of the provisions. In syndicated loans nonmaterial loan provisions can be altered by a designated majority of the participating banks; therefore, commercial bank lenders enjoy an advantage over bondholders and noteholders in this respect. However a rescheduling of a loan normally requires the unanimous consent of all the lenders.

Although syndicated credits to governments have experienced significant growth, no less important has been government reliance on international bond issues. Since the mid-1980s floating-rate notes issued by sovereign governments have become common in international markets. Because of their large size, these issues became known as *jumbos*. Following the precedent set in 1993, when the World Bank made a "global" bond issue, Italy floated a $5.5 billion two-part offering structured as global bonds, tradable in major markets and registered in countries that required it. U.S. investors accounted for about 40 percent of the total demand, with the balance sold to Euromarket and Asian investors. The success of this offering encouraged issues by other sovereign European and Latin American governments that targeted different markets. These global, jumbo offerings were in some cases below investment grade, and were well received by U.S. institutional investors under SEC rule 144A which provides for the private placement of securities among QIBs.

PURPOSES OF FOREIGN LOANS

There are several reasons why a nation may wish to borrow, and each reason entails a different degree of risk and raises its own unique set of considerations. Loans for financial, social, and developmental programs are usually handled by ministries, the central bank, public service entities of the central government or their political subsidivisions. Examples of such loans are as follows:

1. Economic infrastructure loans. These loans finance construction, expansion, and modernization of infrastructure facilities, including airports, railways, subways, port facilities, and telecommunications, atomic energy, and other high-tech projects.
2. Economic and social infrastructure loans. These loans fund infrastructure projects that are closely connected to social needs, such as sewage treatment plants, highways, bridges, multipurpose dams, and water supply systems.
3. General welfare social loans. These loans finance the building of schools, health facilities, low-cost housing, and other projects closely tied to the well being of the citizenry.
4. General budget support to the central government. These are usually short term loans made in expectation of forthcoming budgetary receipts from sources related to normal public sector activities including the export of traditional products (e.g., sale of petroleum, minerals, or commodities).
5. Loans to build foreign exchange reserves to finance seasonal export/import variations. Although these loans were mostly of short-term nature and made against foreign exchange export receipts, they are now issued as bank lines of credit to accommodate fluctuations in seasonal foreign exchange. Reviewed annually, they are made on the basis of the borrowing country's overall foreign trade cycle. However, given the nature of such financing, the very need for the loan raises concerns about the level of net exchange reserves or about the conditions that could undermine the supply of reserves and increase the credit risk.
6. Reconstruction and development loans. These loans, whose interest rates and terms are related to the borrower's needs and general creditworthiness, are intended to finance economic growth and/or help nations rebuild after natural and human-made disasters, such as earthquakes, floods, drought, and war. The loans can be either project or program types, and they are made by both private and public sector entities. They may or may not be made for specific projects, and they may

finance a group of projects that advance the overall goals of a particular program. Loans for "general economic purposes" may be made to finance the construction of new facilities that are specified only in very general terms.

7. Economic and financial stabilization financing. These loans are often comprised of packages of grants and new loans from international, governmental, and private institutions, and they are often used for general balance-of-payments deficit financing.

Although some of the government loans described above are occasionally cited in public media, two deserve special mention: General Budget Support to the central government (item 4 above) and the Infrastructure and Social welfare loans (items 1-3). With respect to General Budget Support loans the experience of the OECD governments is highly pertinent. In 2007, the sovereign debt of OECD governments amounted to $23 trillion. The subsequent financial crisis of 2008 prompted an explosive growth of borrowing needs. The key policy issue was how to smoothly raise new funds at low cost while also managing a rapidly growing debt stock. The funds were needed to finance bailout operations and other crisis-related expenditures and to address the shortfall in tax revenues (budget deficits). The immediate effect of the need for this funding was a $13 trillion increase in government debt over the next five years, rising to $36 trillion by year-end 2012. For many OECD countries, government debt levels increased close to historical highs unseen since the 1940s. The deterioration of fiscal accounts was so sharp as to cause the downgrade of the sovereign debts of Greece, Ireland, Italy, Portugal and Spain. Exhibit 14.2 identifies the crisis-induced budgetary deficits in 2009 and 2010 for the United States and select European OECD member countries. As seen in this Exhibit the budgetary deficits as a percent of the respective GDPs for Eurozone member countries were well in excess of the 3 percent benchmark rate. By 2015 they had dropped to pre-crisis levels or were moderately higher of the Eurozone's prescribed maximum.

Exhibit 14.2 Budgetary Deficits as a Percent of GDP for the United States and Select European OECD Member Countries

OECD Countries	2005	2009	2010	2015
Members of Eurozone:				
France	-3.2	-7.2	-6.8	-3.5
Greece	-6.2	-15.1	-11.2	-7.5
Ireland	1.6	-13.8	-32.1	-1.9
Italy	-4.2	-5.3	-4.2	-2.6
Netherlands	-0.3	-5.4	-5.0	-1.9
Portugal	-6.2	-9.8	-11.2	-4.4
Spain	1.2	-11.0	-9.4	-5.1
Nonmember countries:				
Iceland	4.5	-9.7	-9.8	-0.8
Romania	-0.7	-9.1	-6.9	-0.7
United Kingdom	-3.3	-10.2	-9.6	-4.4
United States	-4.1	-12.7	-12.0	-4.2

Source: *General Government Deficit*, Organization for Economic Cooperation and Development (OECD), 2015. https://data.oecd.org/gga/general-government-deficit.htm.
For Romania see http://www.tradingeconomics.com/romania/government-budget.

Infrastructure and social welfare loans (items 1-3) represent capital intensive investments. With tax increases politically inexpedient, cash strapped governments have began to pursue different arrangements to finance their infrastructure projects. Exhibit 14.3 identifies the alternate models: co-financing, establishing vehicle company, and build operate transfer (BOT). Each of these is described in the sections that follow.

Exhibit 14.3 Government Infrastructure Financing Models

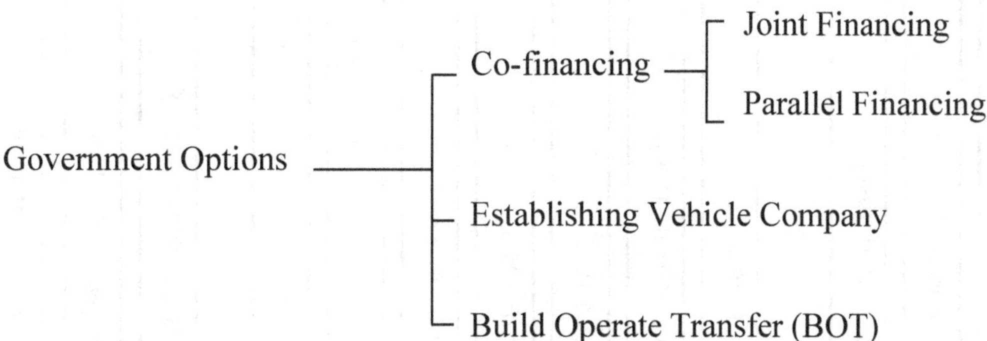

OPTIONS FOR FINANCING

Co-financing

Exhibit 14.4 identifies some of the organizations commissioned to provide financial support for infrastructure projects. The World Bank, the IFC, regional development banks and other intergovernmental institutions have historically been among the most prominent sources of such support. Administered largely through co-financing agreements, official aid requires the direct participation of host country governments. Official-source aid has been especially instrumental for sizable infrastructure projects in developing countries that exceed conventional financing capabilities. In this hemisphere the largest source of development financing for the Caribbean and Latin America is the Inter-American Development Bank (IDB). Exhibit 14.5 shows the co-financing projects undertaken by IDB in 2015. The Exhibit identifies the beneficiary country, the nature of the project, and the amount of investment in each case. Since its inception (1959), IDB is credited for having completed 18,043 projects.

Other participants in co-financing projects, in addition to development organizations, include export credit agencies (which offer export assistance to domestic firms) and commercial banks. Participation of the latter is sought to fill any funding gaps that do not qualify for World Bank assistance (e.g., start-up costs, or working capital needs). Exhibit 14.6 portrays the different types of co-financing partners in infrastructure projects.

Exhibit 14.4 Select Development Banks and Institutions

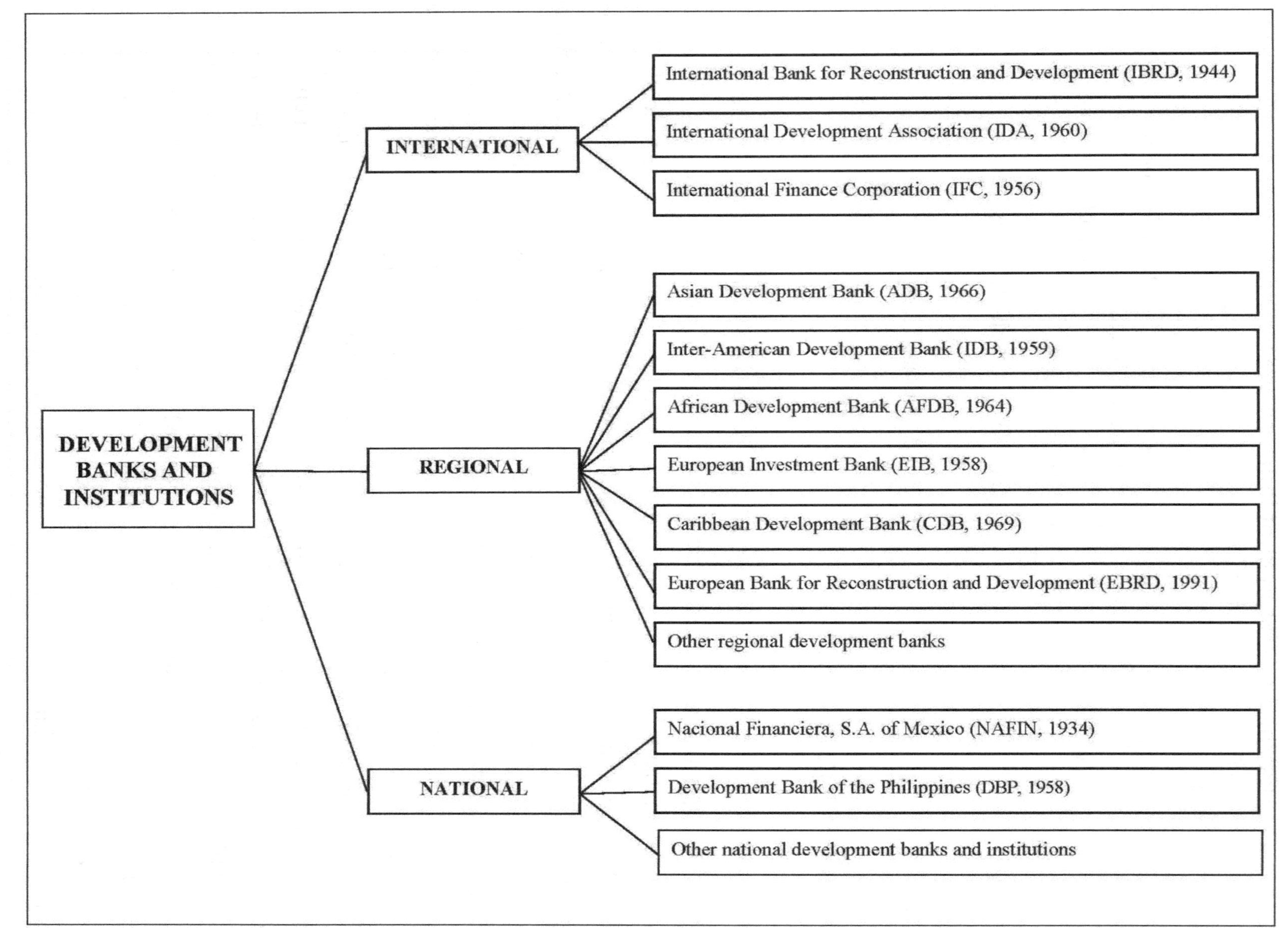

Source: Developed by the author.

Exhibit 14.5 Select Inter-American Development Bank Co-Financing Projects

Country	Sector	Project Title	Amount (in millions of dollars)	Status
Argentina	Water and Sanitation	Water and Sanitation Program for Metropolitan Areas	200	Approved
Argentina	Water and Sanitation	Reconquista River Basin Environmental Sanitation Program	230	Approved
Bolivia	Transport	Road Infrastructure Development	179	Approved
Brazil	Financial Markets	Banco Sicredi—Partnership for Rural Loans	50	Preparation
Brazil	Urban Development and Housing	Urban Development and Municipal Public Investment	150	Approved
Brazil	Agriculture and Rural Development	Farming Credit Program	35	Approved
Central America	Energy	Central America Electric Interconnection	431	Approved
Chile	Education	Early Childhood Education	75	Approved

Chile	Energy	Crucero Solar Photovoltaic Power Project	66	Approved
Colombia	Transport	Support Public Private Partnerships in Infrastructure	25	Approved
Costa Rica	Transport	Infrastructure Transport Program	450	Approved
Ecuador	Reform/Modernization of State	Improve Internal Revenue Service	30	Approved
Guatemala	Regional Integration	Integration border Guatemala Mexico	200	Preparation
Haiti	Agriculture and Rural Development	Artisanal Fisheries	15	Approved
Honduras	Social Investment	Social Safety Net Support Program II	100	Approved
Jamaica	Private Firms and SME Development	Competitiveness Enhancement Program III	60	Approved
Venezuela	Health	Strength, Modernization of Health Sector	150	Approved
Venezuela	Transport	Rehabilitation and Maintenance Highways and Bridges	200	Approved

Source: Inter-American Development Bank, 2015, http://www.iadb.org/en/projects/projects,1229.html

Exhibit 14.6 Co-financing Categories of Institutional Partners

1. DEVELOPMENT ORGANIZATIONS
   - International (global)
   - Regional
   - National
2. EXPORT CREDIT AGENCIES
   - Export-Import (Exim) Bank of the United States
   - Export-Import (Exim) Bank of China
   - Compañía Española de Seguros de Crédito a la Exportación
   - Compagnie Française d'Assurance pour le Commerce Extérieur (COFACE)
   - Other countries' Export Promotion Agencies
3. PRIVATE LENDERS

   Commercial Banks

Source: Developed by the author.

In infrastructure projects where the World Bank and IFC are involved, they work closely with co-lenders to prepare and appraise these projects and negotiate and even administer loans. Co-financing arrangements are of two types: joint and parallel financing. Joint financing involves a common list of goods and services whose financing is shared by the participating lenders; in parallel financing, on the other hand, each lender finances a different part of the project.

In joint financing the World Bank assumes the primary responsibility for day-to-day supervision. Co-lenders and the World Bank consult regularly with one another during the period of the loan's implementation. One advantage of joint financing is that it avoids duplication of effort in loan administration and related functions.

Parallel financing has become a more common choice in cases where each co-lender administers its own part of the project. Under parallel financing, agreements and memoranda of understanding set the terms for consultation and joint action during the loan's implementation.

To date the World Bank has entered into numerous co-financing arrangements, mostly to the industrial and utility sectors. In Brazil, for example, it helped assemble a group of 16 private banks to finance a steel plant. In this project, the private banks' medium-term Eurocurrency loan was $55 million, while the World Bank provided $95 million, the Inter-American Development Bank supplied $63 million, and other lenders provided $490 million in export credits. In this and similar loans private lending institutions negotiated and entered into separate loan contracts with the borrower.

Co-financing arrangements have several advantages for commercial banks. Because the World Bank is better able to conduct a comprehensive credit analysis than a private borrower, it provides the private lenders with credit information on the borrowing country and the project. Moreover, the World Bank assumes the administrative responsibilities of the private loan, including the disbursement of funds and receipt of debt service payments. Cross-default clauses in the loan agreement allow the World Bank to suspend disbursement or accelerate repayment of the loan if the borrower fails to meet scheduled payments.

Co-financed loans can be structured to give participants maximum protection and selection of risk and return. Moreover, the presence of the World Bank and other official lenders adds prestige to a loan, and the host-country governments make repayment and servicing of World Bank loans a top priority because they want to establish a favorable credit rating.

Establishing Vehicle Company

Project finance techniques, basically a U.S. invention, are often used to facilitate exploitation of natural resources, as well as infrastructure projects and other long-term investments. The major challenge in such undertakings is financing the capital requirements of the project, such as the extraction of mineral and oil resources in the mining, oil and natural gas industries. The cash flow generated by the project, such as the sale of oil and minerals in those industries, is expected to provide the necessary revenues for the servicing of the loan. Banks often have difficulty evaluating the risk inherent in financing such projects because they must assess the amount of resources in the ground (resource risk) and the future prices they are likely to command in the marketplace (market risk). Additional risks include completion delays (completion risk), change in the cost or availability of critical elements (operating risk), natural disasters (force majeure risk), adverse political conditions (political risk) or change in government rules pertaining to the industry (government risk). Therefore, project finance depends not only on the country's credit status, but, more importantly, on the type of project being financed.

A common approach used in the corporate world to develop a project is through the establishment, by the sponsoring firm(s), of a vehicle company that will undertake, and eventually operate the project. This approach has been followed by governments in the financing of infrastructure projects. A corporate example, is the case of Alyeska Pipeline Company (known as Trans-Alaska Pipeline), which was established in 1970 as a joint venture among Standard Oil of Ohio, Atlantic Richfield, Exxon, British Petroleum, Mobil Oil, Philips Petroleum, Union Oil, and Amerada Hess. The company's objective was to design, construct, operate and maintain a pipeline to transport oil from the North Slope of Alaska, where oil was discovered in 1968, to an ice-free deep-water port in Valdez. The company's initial project cost of $900 million rose to $8 billion by the time the project was completed in 1977. The project's funding came from private and public sources with 50 banks participating in the financing.

This model was also used by two government-owned public utilities Electrobras of Brazil and Administracion Nacional d'Electricidad of Paraguay. These entities established in 1974 a vehicle company, Itaipu Binacional, with a $100 million capitalization contributed equally by each of the parent firms. The venture firm was to secure funding for the construction of the largest hydroelectric facility that would provide for 80% of the electrical needs of Paraguay and 20% of Brazil. Guaranties by the parent companies enabled the funding, and the project was completed in 1991 at a cost of $17 billion.

The BOT Model

Governments sometimes allow private firms to assume responsibility for the development and operation of an infrastructure project. Such arrangements rely on a BOT model: Build, Operate, and Transfer. In these cases a private firm may assume the responsibility for a project (e.g., develop a mine, build an airport), or maintain a physical facility (e.g., a bridge or a toll road). In exchange the firm is granted a concession to manage the project for a period of time at the end of which ownership reverts to the government. The government fulfills its economic policy goals (e.g., creates employment opportunities and promotes growth) while the investor earns an acceptable return. Compañía Minera Antamina (Peru), Rio Antirio bridge (Greece) and the Eurotunnel (British/French venture) are examples of projects developed through the BTO model.

COUNTRY RISK

All cross-border loans and investments, involve country risk, the likelihood that the borrower's willingness and/or ability to repay the debt may be affected by negative political and economic developments. Banks can reduce their overall exposure to country risk by building a portfolio of diversified exposures, but the possibility of adverse occurrences means that lenders will always face a form of systematic risk that falls into the larger category of country risk. Significant forms of country risk are *transfer risk, foreign exchange risk* and *sovereign risk.* A blocked fund-restriction to the transfer of funds into and out of the country is known as transfer risk. Foreign exchange risk occurs when forces that impact a country's condition affect its foreign exchange rates and thereby undermine the borrower's creditworthiness in servicing foreign debts. Sovereign risk refers to government inability or unwillingness to service its foreign obligations.

Sovereign Risk

Sovereign risk exists not only when loans are made to governments but also to non-governmental agencies if those loans are guaranteed by the central government. Banks may reduce their overall sovereign risk by diversifying their portfolios, but uncertainties always remain as changes in the price of oil or minerals, condition of international financial markets, business cycles, protectionism, and global or regional events can increase the level of risk inherent in a particular loan. For instance, although Brazil and South Korea have independent economies, both are vulnerable to changes in global interest rates or financial crises in other nations such as Russia.

Contagion risks are a special kind of sovereign risk, as they are associated with contingencies beyond the local borders of the borrower's home country. In the 1990s, contagion risks were often associated with short-term capital flows. Although contagion risk can be reduced by moving into asset classes that historically have been less vulnerable to international disruptions, such as gold or real estate, some country risk and contagion risk will always remain in loans to foreign governments and their agencies.

Methods of Assessing Country Risk

In recent decades banks have increasingly relied on analytical methods to assess country risk. Although advances in computer technology have made possible the use of more quantitative systems than in the past, jolts in the international community such as the 1979 Islamic revolution in Iran and the civil war in Lebanon (1975-1990) have heightened the importance of factoring political risk into the assessment of a country's risk. Accordingly, there is now greater emphasis on quantification and modeling in the analysis of country risk. The need for more sophisticated methodologies for assessing country risk has given rise to a number of evaluation systems that may be classified into the following four categories: fully qualitative, structured qualitative, checklist, and other models.

Fully qualitative approach consists of the Delphi and the Scenario techniques. The former calls for assembling a group of experts to present their views on the likely future of a country's relevant economic and political conditions and to debate until they reach a consensus opinion. The Scenario technique provides three future scenarios based on *the best*, *the most likely* and *the worst* set of assumptions. The probability of each scenario is then debated until a consensus is reached. Both of these techniques focus on a country's attributes and current problems without reference to a standardized format that would allow for cross-country comparisons. Updating can be relatively difficult because of the nature of qualitative analysis.

Structured qualitative provides for the evaluation of specific criteria in a standardized format of analysis that facilitates cross-country comparisons.

Checklist method establishes formal criteria for the evaluation of a country's performance and generates their rating by means of numeric scores on a common scale of risk that is consistent across countries and ensures comparability.

Other models range from letter or numeric ratings to statistical indicators and multiple discriminant analysis.

While dependence on modeling has increased, many banks still perform structured qualitative analyses, coupled with a weighted checklist for purposes of comparison. Most banks have centralized their country assessment system at the head office to ensure that their global portfolio as a whole is consistent with institutional risk constraints. Country evaluations are updated at least annually, with more frequent reviews for high-exposure countries. The responsibility for such reviews typically rests with the bank's line personnel or staff specialists, if they are not one and the same. In addition to banks, multinational enterprises and consulting services, such rating agencies as Moody's and Standard & Poor's, perform country risk analyses. They view sovereigns with higher credit ratings as safer investments than those with lower credit ratings. Other organizations with widely used country-risk ratings include *Euromoney* magazine (*Euromoney Index*), *Institutional Investor* magazine (*Institutional Investor Index*) and the *International Country Risk Guide*.

Although rating agencies employ different methods to develop their country risk ratings, their inputs are derived from the same data bases that synthesize a country's fundamental aspects. All assessment models for determining risk in a particular country take into account political, economic, and financial factors, and the interactions among those factors. Some of the key determinants in each subcategory are identified below:

1. *Political factors*. The crux of the political analysis is to gauge government willingness to fulfill foreign debt service by focusing on whether the government is firm and has the political will to carry out necessary but often unpopular programs. This may be determined by evaluating such

variables as the

- political system
- power base
- efficiency and flexibility of government bureaucracy
- domestic insurgency, political conflict
- links with major trading partners

2. *Economic factors*. Economic performance projections are helpful in determining the relative capacity and willingness of a country to honor its existing and future financial obligations in a timely manner. Economic analysis must take into account such macroeconomic issues as
    - fiscal state of the government stance (deficit or surplus)
    - monetary policy
    - government intervention in the economy
    - natural resource base
    - technology, entrepreneurship, labor force
    - rate of inflation
    - growth in real per capita GDP

3. *Financial factors*. Ability to service current and future foreign debts may be established through such indicators as
    - international reserve position (foreign exchange reserves and other assets held by the central bank)
    - size and structure of external indebtedness
    - debt service ratio (debt service payments relative to earnings from exports)
    - import coverage ratio (international reserves relative to imports)
    - capital inflows and outflows
    - current account balance
    - stability of the foreign exchange rate

The 2012 Greek debt exchange illustrates the dangers of country risk, as the debt write-down, also known as a "haircut," hit private investors hard. It was the largest debt restructuring in the history of sovereign defaults, and the first within the Eurozone. Although it achieved historically unprecedented debt relief that amounted to 66% of Greece's GDP--its historical significance lies not only in its unprecedented size, but also in its timing and size of creditor losses against the background of the Eurozone crisis. Private investors such as banks, insurance companies and investment funds, as well as ordinary savers holding Greek bonds, were issued a public offer. As part of the deal (haircut) they were asked to trade in their Greek bonds for new ones offering lower interest rates and longer maturities. Greek government debt holders ended sustaining a nominal loss of 53.5 percent of their $265 billion investment (alternate valuation models place the real loss to investors at 65 percent or at 73 to 74 percent).

Banks can address country risk by taking an integrated approach to analysis that combines both quantitative and qualitative considerations for assessing such basic indicators as domestic instability, foreign conflicts, and the economic and political climate of a country. But country risks are unlike all other types of risk, as even macroeconomic data are often not timely or accurate, and major countries regularly revise their data in ways that can have profound effects on a risk analysis. Changes to methods of reporting and inaccurate or missing data also introduce uncertainty into the analysis. Moreover, many of the factors that can influence the well-being of a country's political and economic future simply do not lend themselves to quantification, thereby making the assessment process inherently subjective to a greater or lesser extent. So lenders should be alert to this problem and remain aware that any effort to quantify the unquantifiable entails significant uncertainty.

But even if there was no issue with the data used in modeling, the fact remains that the task is to forecast a country's politico-economic prospects and track a bank's exposure to risk. Here lies another limitation of modeling: Risk, by its nature, arises from future events while the statistical data used to assess it are historical.

Essentially, country assessment tries to identify future trends and anticipate risk by analyzing historical data. Evidence indicates that the prediction track record of country risk analysis has been spotty at best. No models predicted the collapse of communism in the Soviet Union (1991) and the independence of Eastern Europe, or the Arab spring that led to the overthrow of the presidents of Tunisia, Egypt, and Libya (2011). The same argument holds true about the crisis in Ukraine (2013), or the Syrian civil war which resulted in the emergence of the Islamic State of Iraq and the Levant (2014). The recent political turmoil underlines the need to revamp the old country risk systems to fit the new environment. Greater emphasis on potential linkages for contagion (e.g., geographical proximity, similar economies) and a global system of money and capital markets highly sensitized to developments anywhere in the world are only some of the added considerations that need to be addressed by risk analysts.

REFERENCES

Ehlers, Torsten. "Understanding the Challenges for Infrastructure Finance." BIS Working Paper No. 454, 2014.

Blommenstein, Hans J., and A. Gok. "OECD Sovereign Borrowing Outlook 2009," *OECD Journal: Financial Market Trends*, Vol. 1, 2009, pp 187-195.

Demirguc-Kunt, A., et al. "Measuring Financial Inclusion around the World: The Global Findex Database." World Bank Group Policy Research Working Paper 7255, 2014.

Federal Deposit Insurance Corporation, *Risk Management Manual of Examination Policies*, September 2016.

Hughes, Jane E., and Scott B. MacDonald. *International Banking: Text and Cases* (Boston: Pearson Education, Inc., 2002).

International Monetary Fund, "World Economic Outlook Update: Uncertainty in the Aftermath of the U.K. Referendum," July 2016.

Kosmidou, K., et al., eds. *Country Risk Evaluation* (New York: Springer, 2008).

Liaw, K. Thomas. *The Business of investment Banking*, 2nd ed. (Hoboken: John Wiley & Sons, 2006).

Magerle, Jurg, and David Maurer. "The Continuous Linked Settlement Foreign Exchange Settlement System (CLS)," *Swiss National Bank*, November 2009, pp. 1-9.

Murphy, Edward V. *Who Regulates Whom and How? An Overview of U.S. Financial Regulatory Policy for Banking and Securities Markets* (Washington, D.C.: Congressional Research Service, 2015).

Organization for Economic Cooperation and Development. "Tax Co-operation 2010: Towards a Level Playing Field, OECD, 2010.

Roussakis, E.N., ed. *International Banking: Principles and Practices* (New York: Praeger, 1983).

Saunders, A., and M. M. Cornett. Financial Markets and Institutions, 6th ed. (New York: McGraw-Hill Education, 2015).

Smith, Roy C., Ingo Walter and Gay DeLong. *Global Banking*, 3rd ed. (New York: Oxford University Press, 2012).

The Boston Consulting Group. *Global Retail Banking 2016: Banking on Digital Simplicity* (Boston: BCG Publications, 2016).

The Boston Consulting Group. *Global Wealth 2016: Navigating the New Client Landscape* (Boston: BCG Publications, 2016).

Turner, Charles F. "Internal Organization and Personnel." *The International Banking Handbook,* W.H. Baun and D.R. Mandich, eds. (Homewood: Dow Jones-Irwin, 1983), pp. 615-623.

INDEX